The Ultimate Guide to SAT Grammar

3rd Edition

Erica L. Meltzer

ISBN-13: 978-1511944137
ISBN-10: 1511944137

DEDICATION

To Emma and Joey, for whom these exercises were first written. I know you never asked to have a *grammar* book dedicated to you, but I hope you'll accept the gesture. And to Jane, Joe, Lily, and Frisco, for food, company, inspiration, and hilarity.

Table of Contents

Introduction: How to Use This Book

This book has two purposes. The first purpose is to teach you a number of fundamental grammar concepts that you will undoubtedly use in your own writing, both in high school and beyond. The second purpose, of course, is to teach you to take the SAT. More specifically, it is to teach you to apply the concepts covered throughout this book to the specific ways in which they are tested on the SAT. To that end, this book is intended to complement official College Board material. Instead of simply providing lots of practice questions for you to blaze through, it is designed to teach you to quickly identify just what each question type is really testing, to reduce seemingly complicated questions down to the simplest terms possible, and to provide ample practice for you to practice each concept. Moreover, this book is designed to allow you to target your areas of weakness in the most efficient way possible. Core concepts – those guaranteed to be tested on every exam – are presented first, while less frequently tested concepts are presented later.

If you have a limited amount of time to prepare for the SAT, you should work as follows: take a College Board practice test as a diagnostic. Mark your errors, and compare them to the list of questions by test on p. 240. Note the category of each error you make. Then, read the explanations in the appropriate chapter, and do the corresponding exercises. (You can also consult the "Questions by Category" list on p. 237 for College Board examples.) When you feel you have a good grasp of those concepts, take another test and repeat the process. Keep working this way until you are consistently scoring in your target range on full-length, timed exams.

The four College Board practice tests, released in conjunction with Khan Academy, can be downloaded from the following links:

Test 1:   https://collegereadiness.collegeboard.org/pdf/sat-practice-test-1.pdf
Answers: https://collegereadiness.collegeboard.org/pdf/sat-practice-test-1-answers.pdf

Test 2:   https://collegereadiness.collegeboard.org/pdf/sat-practice-test-2.pdf
Answers: https://collegereadiness.collegeboard.org/pdf/sat-practice-test-2-answers.pdf

Test 3:   https://collegereadiness.collegeboard.org/pdf/sat-practice-test-3.pdf
Answers: https://collegereadiness.collegeboard.org/pdf/sat-practice-test-3-answers.pdf

Test 4:   https://collegereadiness.collegeboard.org/pdf/sat-practice-test-4.pdf
Answers: https://collegereadiness.collegeboard.org/pdf/sat-practice-test-4-answers.pdf

If you are starting six months to a year before you plan to sit for your first exam, however, you may simply want to work through this book in order. While that approach will require a substantial time commitment, it will also allow you to acquire a very solid foundation. Knowing why you are answering questions correctly – rather than simply relying on your ear – will improve both your speed and your confidence. Otherwise, you risk second-guessing yourself if a concept is tested from an unfamiliar angle.

While the passaged-based format of the redesigned SAT Writing section obviously looks very different from the primarily sentence-based format of the old exam, the reality is that many of the same concepts will continue to be tested. The new test will likely include a few unpredictable questions, but in general, the vast majority of the material tested can be safely anticipated. The goal of this book remains to teach you how to anticipate it.

Erica Meltzer
New York City
June 2015

SAT Writing Cheat Sheet

1. Shorter is better.

2. Being = WRONG.

3. Period = Semicolon = Comma + and/but.

4. 2 commas/dashes = non-essential clause. If the information between the commas or dashes is crossed out, the sentence will still make sense.

5. Its, their = possessive; it's = it is; they're = they are; there = a place.

6. Colon = list or explanation. A complete, standalone sentence is required before but not after.

7. All items in a list must match (noun, noun, noun; verb, verb, verb, etc.).

8. Comma before preposition = WRONG.

9. Comma + *it, this, he, she, they* usually = comma splice = WRONG.

10. Than = comparison; then = next.

11. Singular verbs end in –*s*; plural verbs do not end in –*s* (e.g. *she reads, they read*).

12. *This, that, these,* and *those* should be followed by a noun.

13. Keep pronouns consistent: one = one; you = you; a person = he or she; people = they.

14. Transition questions: cross out the transition and determine the relationship (continue, contradict, cause-and-effect) between the two sentences/parts of a sentence BEFORE you look at the answer choices.

15. Insert/Delete: reread the surrounding sentences and state the topic **in your own words** before checking the answers. If the sentence is directly relevant to that topic, it belongs. If not, it doesn't belong.

Remember: before you choose an answer, plug it back into the passage to make sure that it works. An answer that makes perfect grammatical sense on its own may create a serious error when considered in context of the passage.

Parts of Speech

There are eight parts of speech in the English language, seven of which are relevant to the SAT. If you are not comfortable identifying them, it is suggested that you begin by reviewing this section. Although portions of these definitions are repeated throughout the guide, familiarizing yourself with these terms before you begin will help you move through the explanations and exercises more easily.

The seven parts of speech tested on the SAT are as follows:

1. Verb

Verbs indicate **actions** or **states of being**.

    Examples: To be
                      To have
                      To seem
                      To go
                      To speak
                      To believe

The "to" form of a verb is known as the **infinitive**. All of the verbs listed above are infinitives. If you are uncertain whether a word can be used as a verb, try placing *to* in front of it to form an infinitive.

Verbs are not always used as infinitives, however. In order to indicate who is performing an action, we must **conjugate** the verb and provide its **subject**.

To be and *to have* are the most common verbs. Because they are **irregular**, their conjugated forms are different from their infinitives; you must therefore be comfortable distinguishing between their singular and plural forms. *To be* is also unique in that it is conjugated in both the present and past.

Conjugation of the verb *to be*:

Singular (pres.)	Plural (pres.)	Singular (past)	Plural (past)
I am	We are	I was	We were
You are	You are	You were	You were
He, she, it, one is	They are	We were	They were

Conjugation of the verb *to have:*

Singular	Plural
I have	We have
You have	You (pl.) have
He, She, It, One has	They have

The **number** of a verb indicates whether is singular or plural. **Singular** verbs end in –*s*. **Plural** verbs do not end in –*s*.

I, you, he, she, it, one speaks = Singular

We, you, they speak = Plural

The **tense** of a verb tells us when an action occurred.

She speaks = Present	She would speak = Conditional
She has spoken = Present Perfect	She would have spoken = Past Conditional
She spoke = Simple Past	She will speak = Future
She had spoken = Past Perfect	She will have spoken = Future Perfect

2. Noun

Nouns indicate people, places, objects, and ideas, and can always be preceded by *a(n)* or *the*. **Proper nouns** indicate specific people and places.

Examples: house, bicycle, supervisor, idea, Julia Child, Chicago

The **girl** rode her **bicycle** down the **street** to her **house**.

In the **theater**, the **dancer** moved across the **stage** with her **arms** held above her **head**.

3. Pronoun

Pronouns replace nouns.

Examples: she, you, one, we, him, it(s), their, this, that, these, those, which, both, some, few, many, (n)either

Samantha loves basketball. **She** plays **it** every day after school.

Marco walks to school with Sherri and Ann. **He** meets **them** at the corner.

Personal Pronouns are often referred to in the following manner:

1st Person Singular = I	1st Person Plural = We
2nd Person Singular = You	2nd Person Plural = You
3rd Person Singular = He, She, It, One	3rd Person Plural = They

4. Preposition

Prepositions indicate where someone/something is, or when something happened.

> **Example:** The dog ran **under** the fence and jumped **into** the neighboring yard **in** only a matter **of** seconds.

Common prepositions include:

Of	To	Within/out	Over	Beside	Next to	Against
From	At	Between	Above	About	Toward(s)	Upon
In	For	Under	Along	Among	Before	Around
On	By	Beneath	Beyond	Near	After	Outside
Off	With	Below	Behind	Across	During	Through(out)

5. Adjective

Adjectives modify nouns and pronouns.

> **Examples:** large, pretty, interesting, solid, wide, exceptional, smart, dull, caring, simple

> The class was so **boring** that I thought I would fall asleep.

> The **stunning** view left him at a loss for words.

6. Adverb

Adverbs modify verbs, adjectives, and other adverbs. They frequently end in –ly.

> **Examples:** rapidly, calmly, mildly, boldly, sharply, well, fast, very

> She smiled **brightly** at him when he entered the room.

> He received an **exceedingly** good grade on the test.

7. Conjunction

Conjunctions indicate relationships between words, phrases, and clauses.

> **Examples:** and, but, however, therefore, so, although, yet, when, because, since

> Alice went to the dentist, **but** first she went to the candy store.

> **Because** it rained yesterday, the ceremony was held indoors.

Preliminary Exercise: Identifying Parts of Speech (answers p. 224)

Directions: identify and write the part of speech (e.g. noun, verb, adverb) for each underlined word.

Although igloos are usually associated with

Alaskan Eskimos (Inuits), <u>they</u> have mostly been

1

constructed by people who lived in the central

Arctic and Greenland's Thule region. Other Inuit

peoples <u>tended</u> to use snow to insulate their

2

houses, which were constructed <u>from</u> whalebone

3

and hides.

Traditionally, three types of igloos <u>were</u>

4

constructed. Small igloos were constructed as

temporary shelters <u>and</u> used only for one or two

5

nights. These were built and <u>used</u> during hunting

6

trips, often on open sea ice. Medium-sized igloos

were <u>usually</u> single-room family dwellings that

7

housed one or two families. Often, several of these

igloos <u>were</u> located in a small area, forming an Inuit

8

village. The largest igloos were normally built in

pairs: one of the buildings was a <u>temporary</u>

9

structure for community feasts and dances, while

the other was <u>intended</u> for living. These igloos

10

could be constructed from several smaller igloos

attached <u>by</u> tunnels.

11

1. _____

2. _____

3. _____

4. _____

5. _____

6. _____

7. _____

8. _____

9. _____

10. _____

11. _____

Today, igloos are used mostly for <u>brief</u> camping
                                    12
trips; however, the principles behind their

construction <u>remain</u> the same. The snow used to
            13
build an igloo must have enough strength to be cut

and stacked correctly. The best snow to use for this

<u>purpose</u> is snow blown by wind because <u>it</u>
  14   15
contains interlocking ice crystals, which increase

the amount <u>of</u> weight the ice can support.
          16
      Because of snow's excellent insulation

properties, inhabited igloos are <u>surprisingly</u>
                                      17
comfortable and warm inside. Sometimes, a short

tunnel is constructed at the entrance <u>to reduce</u>
                                          18
heat loss when the door <u>is</u> opened. Animal skins
                        19
can also be used as door flaps to keep warm air in.

      Architecturally, the igloo is unique <u>because</u> it
                                                20
is a dome that can be constructed without an

<u>additional</u> supporting structure. Independent
  21
blocks of ice lean on one another and are polished

to fit. <u>In</u> the traditional Inuit igloo, the <u>heat</u> from
        22   23
the *kudlik*, or stone lamp, causes the interior to

melt slightly, creating a layer of ice that

<u>contributes</u> to the igloo's strength. In fact, a
  24
correctly-built igloo will support the weight of a

person standing <u>on</u> the roof.
                25

12. _____

13. _____

14. _____

15. _____

16. _____

17. _____

18. _____

19. _____

20. _____

21. _____

22. _____

23. _____

24. _____

25. _____

13

Maria Tallchief: All-American Ballerina

– 1 –

"A ballerina takes steps given to her and makes them her own. Each individual brings something different to the same role," the great ballerina Maria Tallchief once said. Tallchief combined great individualism and extraordinary talent, creating a remarkable and vital chapter in American dance.

– 2 –

Maria Tallchief was born Elizabeth Marie Tall Chief on an Indian reservation in Fairfax, Oklahoma on January 24, 1925. A member of the Osage tribe, she became a trailblazer for Native Americans in the world of ballet. The Osage language is similar to the language spoken by members of the Sioux tribe. When Maria was five years old, she began music lessons and soon discovered that she had perfect pitch. It was dance that captured the young girl's heart, though. After five years of study, she joined the Ballet Russe de Monte Carlo, where she quickly became a soloist. It was during her time with the Ballet Russe that she became known professionally as Maria Tallchief, combining the two parts of her Indian name.

– 3 –

[1] Balanchine then brought Tallchief home to his Ballet Society, the company that would become New York City Ballet. [2] Her immense popularity with the American public grew in part from the demands the company made on its phenomenally gifted principal dancer. [3] Tallchief was called upon to dance as many as eight performances a week.

[4] In fact, many audience members did not realize how technically difficult the part was until much later, when they saw other great ballerinas attempt to perform it. [5] Audiences were awed by her dedication to her art. [6] When she danced the lead role in *Pas de Dix* (1955), for example, she dazzled audiences with her radiance and impeccable technique.

– 4 –

In the 1950s, Tallchief became one of the first ballet dancers to make regular appearances on television. They first worked together in Paris in 1947 – the same year Tallchief became the first prima ballerina of the New York City Ballet – and Tallchief learned to keep her back straight, her head high, and her feet arched. These included *Orpheus*, *Night Shadow*, and *The Four Temperaments*. In 1954, Balanchine choreographed Tallchief in what would become her most famous role: the Sugar Plum Fairy in *The Nutcracker*. Although it was an obscure ballet at the time, Tallchief's extraordinary performance helped make it an instant classic.

– 5 –

In 1965, Maria Tallchief surprised the world by announcing her retirement. She had no intention of dancing past her prime and wanted to pass her love for her art to younger dancers. She was a revolutionary performer who broke many barriers for Native American women.

1. Is it Relevant?
Adding, Deleting, & Revising Information

In keeping with the redesigned SAT's focus on supporting evidence, questions that ask you to add, delete, or revise information will make up the largest component of the Writing test. You can expect around 12 add/delete/replace questions per test, or three per passage. These can be phrased in a variety of ways, but **they all test essentially the same thing**: whether information is **relevant** or **irrelevant** to the topic of a paragraph or passage, or whether it is consistent with a particular emphasis indicated in the question.

Most questions will require that you consider the context of the surrounding sentences and/or paragraphs. These questions can be broken into the following steps:

1) Reread the paragraph

2) Briefly restate the topic in your own words

3) Check each answer choice against that topic

When a question asks you to take the entire passage into account, you should not spend time rereading the entire passage. Instead, focus on couple of key places: the beginning of the passage, where the main idea or theme is most likely to be presented, and the surrounding sentences (usually the preceding sentence), among which the sentence in question must fit logically.

It is important that you go through these steps on your own before you look at the answer choices. Otherwise, you are more likely to be distracted by plausible-sounding choices that don't actually answer the question.

To be clear, you do not need to answer the questions in great detail. You should simply take a few moments to get a general idea of the paragraph's focus and determine what sort of information the correct answer should contain. If you keep those things in mind, you'll generally get to the answer pretty quickly. If you don't, however, then relatively straightforward questions can become unnecessarily confusing and time-consuming.

Some insert/delete/change questions will ask you to identify the information that best **begins** or **concludes** a given paragraph. Although these questions ask about different parts of the paragraph, they are both essentially testing whether you understand the topic and main idea of the paragraph or passage, and they should be approached the same way.

The general purpose of both the topic sentence and the concluding sentence is to present or reinforce the main idea of the paragraph/passage. The fact that one is at the beginning while the other is at the end is incidental; **the information in the middle is what you actually need to focus on**.

Remember also that topic sentences and concluding sentences tend to contain main ideas; as a result, **answers that include specific details are less likely to be correct**.

Let's start by looking at a "topic sentence" question, using the fourth paragraph from the passage on p. 14.

1 In the 1950s, Tallchief became one of the first ballet dancers to make regular appearances on television. They first worked together in Paris in 1947 – the same year Tallchief became the first prima ballerina of the New York City Ballet. Eventually, Tallchief inspired a number of Balanchine's ballets. These included *Orpheus*, *Night Shadow*, and *The Four Temperaments*. In 1954, Balanchine choreographed Tallchief in what would become her most famous role: the Sugar Plum fairy in *The Nutcracker*. Although it was an obscure ballet at the time, Tallchief's extraordinary performance helped make it an instant classic.

1

Which choice provides the most effective introduction to the paragraph?

A) NO CHANGE
B) Throughout her career, Maria Tallchief was known for her collaborations with choreographer George Balanchine.
C) The people of Oklahoma honored Tallchief with statues and a day in her honor.
D) The New York City Ballet was founded by George Balanchine and Lincoln Kirstein in 1946.

Although this question asks about the introduction – i.e. the topic sentence – you cannot answer it until you know what the rest of the paragraph is about. **That means you need to read the rest of the paragraph, or at least the next few sentences.** You can even cross out the first sentence (in pencil) if it is likely to distract you.

If we had to sum up the paragraph, minus the first sentence, we might say something like "Maria Tallchief worked with George Balanchine," or even just "Maria Tallchief and George Balanchine." B) is the only answer that mentions both Tallchief and Balanchine, and it's almost exactly what our summary says. So it's correct.

Now we're going to look at a "conclusion" question:

In 1965, Maria Tallchief surprised the world by announcing her retirement. She had no intention of dancing past her prime and wanted to pass her love for her art to younger dancers. **1** Throughout her life, she broke many barriers for Native American women.

1

The writer wants a concluding sentence that restates the main idea of the passage. Which choice best accomplishes this goal?

A) NO CHANGE
B) She eventually became the artistic director of the Chicago City Ballet.
C) Her remarkable grace and stunning technique continue to inspire dancers around the world.
D) Some people have criticized her dancing for being too athletic and modern.

When a lot of people encounter a question like this, they aren't quite sure what to do. Because they've been focusing on the details as they read, they don't have a particularly strong sense of the passage as a whole, and they don't particularly want to go back and read the whole thing. At that point, they usually guess. Needless to say (I hope), that's usually not a very good idea.

The bad news is that if you're not totally sure what the passage was about, you do have to go back and do some rereading. The good news, however, is that you won't usually have to reread very much – often only a few sentences.

To reiterate: **"Big picture" information will virtually always be presented right at the beginning of the passage**. Because passages are so short, main ideas tend to come first by necessity; there isn't room to take time getting to the point. **Rereading the title can also help focus you; after all, its purpose is to tell you what the passage is going to be about.**

For "conclusion" questions, you can also **focus on the sentence right before the last sentence**. Even though these questions ask you to think about the big picture, the concluding sentence must still follow logically from the sentence before it. Any answer that is unrelated to the information in that sentence must be incorrect.

In this particular case, you don't get a whole lot of information from the title. *Maria Tallchief: All-American Ballerina* just doesn't provide that much to go on. If you skim through the first paragraph, however, you get everything you need: *Tallchief combined great individualism and extraordinary talent, creating a remarkable and vital chapter in American dance.* That's the main idea right there.

Based on that information, you can eliminate D) immediately. The main idea is very positive, so the conclusion should be positive as well. The word *criticized* indicates that D) is negative.

You can also be suspicious of B) because it mentions a specific event, and concluding sentences are usually much more general.

Be careful with A). The second paragraph does mention that Tallchief was Native American, but there's nothing about that in either the title or the introduction, suggesting it's actually not the main focus of the passage. If you skim through the rest of the passage, you'll also see that it isn't mentioned anywhere else, and by definition, **an idea that only shows up in one part of the passage can't be a main idea.**

So that leaves C), which is positive, a broad statement, and consistent with the main idea.

Other "main idea" questions will be presented in a less direct manner. In fact, they may involve sentences that appear in the middle of a paragraph. In such cases, you will be asked to identify the answer that correctly "sets up" or "transitions" to the information/examples that follow. Although these questions may not include the phrase "main idea," they are in fact asking you to identify the general claim or idea that the information afterward would support.

For example:

In the 1950s, Tallchief became one of the first ballet dancers to make regular appearances on television. They first worked together in Paris in 1947 – the same year Tallchief became the first prima ballerina of the New York City Ballet – and Tallchief **1** learned to keep her back straight, her head high, and her feet arched. These included *Orpheus*, *Night Shadow*, and *The Four Temperaments*. In 1954, Balanchine choreographed Tallchief in what would become her most famous role: the Sugar Plum fairy in *The Nutcracker*. Although it was an obscure ballet at the time, Tallchief's extraordinary performance helped make it an instant classic.

1

Which choice provides the best transition to the information that follows?

OR:

Which choice most effectively sets up the examples that follows?

A) NO CHANGE
B) became well known outside the United States.
C) eventually inspired a number of Balanchine's ballets.
D) grew very fond of Balanchine.

Don't be fooled if a question asks about a "transition," which implies a relationship to the information that comes before and after. Unless you are specifically directed to look at the information before, these question are really asking which choice is most relevant to the information that **follows**. It doesn't matter whether an option makes sense on its own, or even in context of what comes before. **What counts is what comes after.**

What comes after here? A list of ballets. So we're looking for something that's going to set up that list – presumably it's a list of ballets that Maria Tallchief danced in.

The original version doesn't make sense. There's no relationship between Tallchief improving her technical skills and the list of ballets. B) and D) don't fit either: Tallchief's reputation outside the United States and her relationship with Balanchine have nothing to do with a list of ballets either.

The only answer that makes sense is C): logically, the list that follows is the list of ballets that Tallchief inspired.

"Topic sentence" and "conclusion" questions test your ability to determine main points from supporting ideas and pieces of evidence; **"supporting evidence" questions** do the opposite – that is, they test your ability to determine what type of information or examples support a larger idea.

Let's look at how some "support" questions might be phrased:

[1] Balanchine then brought Tallchief home to his Ballet Society, the company that would become New York City Ballet. [2] Her immense popularity with the American public grew in part from the intense demands the company made on its phenomenally gifted principal dancer. [3] Tallchief was called upon to dance as many as eight performances a week and **1** learned roles in more than 30 different ballets. [5] Balanchine made use of her artistry to great effect. In fact, audience members did not realize how challenging the part was until much later, when they saw other great ballerinas attempt to perform it. [6] When she danced the lead role in *Pas de Dix* (1955), for example, she dazzled audiences with her radiance and impeccable technique.

1

Which choice gives a second supporting example that is most similar to the example already in the sentence?

OR:

Which choice provides the most relevant detail?

A) NO CHANGE
B) remained with the company until 1956.
C) became known for her exceptional musicality.
D) earned worldwide recognition.

The first version of the question gives us more information, but it does not tell us everything. While it directs us to the first example, it does not tell us to read the *previous* sentence – which is where the point is located. It is possible to answer the question without that information, but it is a lot easier to answer the question with it.

The second question is phrased even more vaguely, but it requires us to do exactly the same thing: back up to the previous sentence and determine the point. We can't determine which answer is relevant to the point without knowing what the point is.

What is the point that we must support? The Ballet Society made intense demands on Tallchief.

A) **learned roles in more than 30 different ballets** – That's a pretty good example supporting the idea of intense demands. 30 ballets is a whole lot. So we're going to keep it.

B) **remained with the company until 1956** – No, this has nothing to do with intense demands.

C) **became known for her exceptional musicality** – Again, completely off topic.

D) **earned worldwide recognition** – This is consistent with the passage but not the sentence. So no.

That leaves us with A), which is the answer.

Let's look at another example:

Maria Tallchief was born Elizabeth Marie Tall Chief on an Indian reservation in Fairfax, Oklahoma on January 24, 1925. A member of the Osage tribe, she became a trailblazer for Native Americans in the world of ballet. **[1]** <u>The Osage language is similar to the language spoken by members of the Sioux tribe.</u> When Maria was five years old, she began music lessons and soon discovered that she had perfect pitch. It was dance that captured the young girl's heart, though. After five years of study, she joined the Ballet Russe de Monte Carlo, where she quickly became a soloist. It was during her time with the Ballet Russe that she became known professionally as Maria Tallchief, combining the two parts of her Indian name.

1

The writer is considering deleting the underlined sentence. Should it be kept or deleted?

A) Kept, because it provides additional background information about Maria Tallchief's heritage.
B) Kept, because it explains why Maria Tallchief developed an early interest in music.
C) Deleted, because it does not provide specific examples of other Native American dancers.
D) Deleted, because it detracts from the paragraph's focus on Maria Tallchief's early life and career.

Although the question only asks directly about one sentence, it's really asking us to look at the entire paragraph. The sentence itself is only important insofar as it is relevant – or not – to the surrounding information.

Because we have two "keep" options and two "delete" options, we're going to tackle the question in two steps.

1) Determine **whether** the sentence should be kept.
2) Determine **why** the sentence should or should not be kept.

The first thing we're going to do is therefore to forget the underlined sentence (preferably crossing it out – lightly, and in pencil, so that the line can be erased if necessary) and look only at the rest of the paragraph.

If we had to sum up the topic of the paragraph in a few words, we might say something like "Maria Tallchief's childhood," or "how Maria Tallchief started dancing." Even if you said something slightly different, chances are it would have something to do with Maria Tallchief.

Let's come back to the sentence:

The Osage language is similar to the language spoken by members of the Sioux tribe.

Is this sentence about Maria Tallchief? No, it's about the Osage *language*. It has nothing to do with Maria Tallchief. So it doesn't belong. We can eliminate A) and B) right there.

Now for the "why:" simply put, it's off-topic. The fact that the Osage language is related to the Sioux language has nothing to do with the rest of the paragraph. C) makes no sense: the passage indicates that Tallchief was a "trailblazer," implying that she was the first Native American dancer to become highly accomplished. There is thus no reason to provide other examples of Native American dancers.

D) fits perfectly – *detracts from the paragraph's focus* is simply a fancy way of saying that the sentence is off-topic. So that is the answer.

The question could also be asked this way:

Maria Tallchief was born Elizabeth Marie Tall Chief on an Indian reservation in Fairfax, Oklahoma on January 24, 1925. A member of the Osage tribe, she became a trailblazer for Native Americans in the world of ballet. **1** When Maria was five years old, she began music lessons and soon discovered that she had perfect pitch. It was dance that captured the young girl's heart, though. After five years of study, she joined the Ballet Russe de Monte Carlo, where she quickly became a soloist. It was during her time with the Ballet Russe that she became known professionally as Maria Tallchief, combining the two parts of her Indian name.

1

At this point, the writer is considering adding the following sentence.

The Osage language is similar to the language spoken by members of the Sioux tribe.

Should the writer make this addition here?

A) Yes, because it provides additional background information about Maria Tallchief's heritage.
B) Yes, because it explains why Maria Tallchief developed an early interest in music.
C) No, because it does not provide specific examples of other Native American dancers.
D) No, because it detracts from the paragraph's focus on Maria Tallchief's early life and career.

Even though the question is phrased differently, the same logic still applies: the sentence in question is off-topic and should not be added, again making D) the correct answer.

Specific Emphasis or Example

Sometimes, a question might also ask you to insert or change information to make it consistent with a particular emphasis or example. These questions can be tricky because the information in the passage will often both sound correct and make sense in context. If you don't pay close attention to the wording of the questions, you can easily assume that things are fine when they're actually not.

Important: with the exception of the NO CHANGE option, you should focus on the answer choices and their "fit" with the emphasis indicated in the question, not on the contextual information in the passage.

The process for answering these questions can be broken into two steps:

1) Underline the key word(s) or phrase – the information indicating what the writer wants to convey.

2) Check each answer against the key information and see whether it matches.

Let's look at an example:

[1] Balanchine then brought Tallchief home to his Ballet Society, the company that would become New York City Ballet. [2] Her immense popularity with the American public grew in part from the intense demands the company made on its phenomenally gifted principal dancer. [3] Tallchief was called upon to dance as many as eight performances a week and <u>learned roles in more than 30 different ballets.</u> [4] Balanchine made use of her artistry to great effect. [5] In fact, audience members did not realize how challenging the part was until much later, when they saw other great ballerinas attempt to perform it. [6] In *Pas de Dix* (1955), for example, she danced the lead role with radiance and **1** impeccable technique.

1

The writer wants to complete the sentence with information **conveying** the sense of effortlessness that characterized Maria Tallchief's dancing in *Pas de Dix*.

A) NO CHANGE
B) many unique qualities.
C) great delicacy.
D) apparent ease.

What follows the word *conveying* in the question? *the sense of effortlessness.* So that's our key phrase. The correct answer must have something to do with **effortlessness**.

Now we're going to check each answer to see if it corresponds to that idea, remembering to start with the version already in the passage.

A) **impeccable technique** – Even if you don't know what *impeccable* means, you can still make an educated guess that it means something like "really great." We're looking for *effortless*, however, and someone can have great technique and still be clearly working very hard. So A) is out.

B) **many unique qualities** – No, this is vague and off-topic. It has nothing to do with effortlessness.

C) **great delicacy** – No, delicacy isn't effortlessness.

D) **apparent ease** – Yes, ease is like *easy*; it means *effortless*. So D) is correct.

Exercise: Adding, Deleting, and Revising Information (answers p. 224)

1. Over the course of the 1950s, as television began to pervade popular culture, game shows quickly became a fixture. Daytime game shows were played for lower stakes to target stay-at-home housewives, while **1** some contestants won prizes worth thousands of dollars. In the late 1950s, viewership of high-stakes games such as *Twenty One* and *The $64,000 Question* began to increase rapidly. However, that popularity proved to be short-lived. In 1959, many of the higher stakes game shows were found to be rigged. **2**

1

Which of the following provides the most effective transition to the information that follows?

A) NO CHANGE
B) people who worked during the day had little interest in game shows.
C) women began to enter the workforce in greater numbers during the 1960s.
D) shows with higher stakes aired in the evening.

2

At this point, the writer is considering adding the following sentence

> As a result, ratings declined, and most of the shows were cancelled.

Should the writer do this?

A) Yes, because it explains the results of the discovery that game shows were rigged.
B) Yes, because it indicates why game shows are less popular today.
C) No, because it does not provide an example of a high-stakes game show.
D) No, because it disturbs the paragraphs' focus on lower-stakes game shows.

2. ▮1▮ The air traffic control system is an organization of people and equipment designed to ensure the safety of private and commercial air travellers. Air traffic controllers are responsible for ensuring a smooth flow of arrivals and departures, and they also monitor all aircraft that enters the airport's airspace. With the assistance of radar and visual observation, these controllers observe and supervise the movements of each plane in order to maintain a safe distance between aircrafts. They also advise pilots of potentially dangerous weather changes such as "wind shear," ▮2▮ sudden, aircraft-affecting changes in wind velocity or direction.

▮1▮

Which choice most effectively establishes the main topic of the paragraph?

A) NO CHANGE
B) Many air traffic controllers are free to carry out their jobs with little supervision.
C) Air traffic controllers possess superior visual memories.
D) Although they are often referred to as flight controllers, most air professionals prefer to be called air traffic controllers.

▮2▮

The writer is considering deleting the information after "wind shear" and ending the sentence with a period. Should that information be deleted?

A) Yes, because it does not explain how different types of aircraft are affected by wind shear.
B) Yes, because air traffic controllers do not actually work as pilots.
C) No, because it defines a term that is likely to be unfamiliar to readers.
D) No, because it explains how changes in wind velocity and direction affect aircrafts.

---

3. In 1883, Theodore Roosevelt traveled to the North Dakota badlands. It was a voyage that changed his life. Roosevelt had always loved the outdoors, but ▮1▮ the voyage convinced him that the natural world deserved protection. After his inauguration as president of the United States in 1901, he became even more dedicated to wilderness conservation. In 1903, he interrupted a national speaking tour to spend two weeks camping in Yellowstone

---

▮1▮

Which choice provides the most effective transition to the information that follows?

A) NO CHANGE
B) he found the trip somewhat unpleasant.
C) he decided to turn his attention to politics. rather than nature.
D) most nineteenth-century politicians preferred more elegant surroundings.

National Park and visited the Grand Canyon to call for its protection. Later, **2** he traveled to Yosemite, where he and the naturalist John Muir slept out under the stars for three nights.

4. For almost 40 years after the end of World War II, the work of Ernest Everett Just, **1** an African-American biologist known for his studies of marine creatures, lay forgotten. Then, in 1983 Kenneth R. Manning, a professor of the history of science at the Massachusetts Institute of Technology, published a prize-winning biography titled *Black Apollo of Science: The Life of Ernest Everett Just.* Since that time, **2** Manning has written several other important books. The United States Post Office issued a stamp commemorating him, numerous conferences were held in his honor, and scientific journals published special issues dedicated to him.

2

The writer wants to include another example to support the idea that Theodore Roosevelt was committed to protecting nature. Which choice most effectively accomplishes that goal?

A) NO CHANGE
B) two of his homes became part of the National Park service.
C) he passed legislation creating 150 National Forests and five National Parks.
D) his face was carved into the side of Mount Rushmore in South Dakota.

1

The writer is considering deleting the underlined phrase (adjusting the punctuation as necessary). Should that information be deleted?

A) Yes, because the paragraph does not focus on Just's research.
B) Yes, because Kenneth Manning was not a professor of marine biology.
C) No, because it explains who Ernest Everest Just was.
D) No, because Ernest Everett Just influenced Kenneth Manning's marine biology research.

2

The writer wants to complete the sentence with information emphasizing the positive impact of Manning's biography on Just's work. Which choice most effectively accomplishes that goal?

A) NO CHANGE
B) a number of events have been organized to bring increased attention to Just.
C) the history of science has become a popular field of study.
D) many important discoveries have been made in marine biology.

5. **1** Paper-making is an ancient art, dating back to second century China. In just a few months, I accumulated piles of books, photos and posters, not to mention stationery and greeting cards, all over my house. I had always been an avid traveler and photographer, but now brightly colored photographs covered my bedroom, my living room, and my office. **2** Then, I discovered the budding world of scrapbooking, **3** an art form that traces its roots to "commonplace" books in fifteenth century England. Suddenly, paper took on a whole new significance for me.

1

Which choice most effectively establishes the main topic of the paragraph?

A) NO CHANGE
B) I recently developed a fascination with paper in all its forms.
C) Some people prefer to keep their homes tidy, but I am not one of them.
D) There are many different kinds of paper at my local crafts store.

2

At this point in the essay, the writer is considering adding the following sentence:

> At times, I even worried that my walls would collapse under their weight.

Should this sentence be added?

A) Yes, because it provides a humorous commentary that emphasizes the main idea of the paragraph.
B) Yes, because the writer's new hobby had potentially damaging consequences.
C) No, because it is irrelevant to the description of the writer's house.
D) No, because it digresses from the idea that the writer enjoyed traveling.

3

The writer is considering deleting the underlined phrase (ending the sentence after *scrapbooking*). Should that information be kept or deleted?

A) Kept, because it explains why scrapbooking became important to the writer.
B) Kept, because it establishes a connection between the writer's interests in art and history.
C) Deleted, because it blurs the paragraph's focus on the writer's love of paper.
D) Deleted, because the writer also refers to photographic prints.

6. Body language is an important form of communication among the members of a wolf pack. For example, wolves may indicate dominate behavior by baring their teeth and pointing their ears forward. Subordinate behavior, on the other hand, may be indicated by closed mouths, narrowed eyes, and ears that are pulled back and held close to the head. And a wolf that stands with its ears sticking straight up or low and out to the side, teeth bared, and a wrinkled snout, clearly communicates a threatening message – all of the surrounding wolves know to stay away. **1** <u>Once they have reached maturity, most wolves leave their birth pack to search for a new territory or to join an existing pack.</u>

1

The writer wants a concluding sentence that restates the main idea of the paragraph. Which choice best accomplishes this goal?

A) NO CHANGE
B) Wolves are highly social animals, and their packs consist of large extended families.
C) These specialized postures have evolved to help reduce aggression, helping the pack members live together more peacefully.
D) When they are between six and eight months old, wolf pups begin to hunt and travel with other members of the pack.

7. Joseph Pulitzer loved politics, but **1** <u>he had difficulty settling on a career.</u> In 1878, the *St. Louis Dispatch* became available at a public auction for only $2,500, and Pulitzer seized the opportunity to purchase it. John A. Dillon, owner of the *Saint Louis Post*, agreed to merge his newspaper with Pulitzer's, and so the *St. Louis Post and Dispatch* was created. The name was soon shortened to the *Post-Dispatch*, and the paper doubled to eight pages.

Although Pulitzer worked on every aspect of his paper, he was particularly involved in attacking corruption, which was rampant in St. Louis. He considered his paper a vehicle for the truth, and he set about finding it with as much energy as he had in the state legislature. His stories exposed tax evasion, gambling rings, and **2** <u>insurance fraud.</u> Readers bought the paper in droves, increasing the paper's circulation by the thousands.

1

Which choice provides the most effective transition to the information that follows?

A) NO CHANGE
B) other fields interested him as well.
C) he became a leading member of the. Democratic Party.
D) journalism was his true passion.

2

The writer would like to give another example of an illegal activity exposed by Pulitzer's paper. Which choice best accomplishes that goal?

A) NO CHANGE
B) local politics.
C) union rallies.
D) artistic events.

8. The twenty-first century is the age of the city. Today more than half the world's population can be found in cities, and megacities—those with populations of 10 million or more—are on the rise. The world's largest megacity is Tokyo-Yokohama, **1** which is also referred to as the National Capital Region of Japan. It also houses a population of over 37.5 million individuals and contains the world's largest metropolitan economy.

2 Severe traffic congestion is one of the common challenges that megacities must confront. While colleges and universities located in small towns may offer many different programs, those located in urban areas are also able to offer their students internships as well as the possibility of gaining experience in a variety of professional fields. Furthermore, unemployment rates in large cities tend to be low because major companies maintain large offices employing hundreds or even thousands of workers. Finally, large cities offer a wide range of entertainment options and cultural institutions such as museums, theaters, and concert venues.

1

Which choice provides a supporting example that reinforces the main point of the sentence?

A) NO CHANGE
B) which is legally classified as a metropolis.
C) which joins two cities and many prefectures to cover 5,200 square miles.
D) which contains a mix of modern skyscrapers and traditional architecture.

2

Which choice most effectively establishes the main topic of the paragraph?

A) NO CHANGE
B) For many people, cities offer economic, educational or social opportunities not available in smaller or more rural areas.
C) In 1900, London became the first city to have more than five million inhabitants.
D) In addition to Tokyo, Mexico City, Beijing, and New York City are also considered megacities.

2. Sentence and Paragraph Order

Sentence and paragraph order questions ask you to identify whether a particular sentence is correctly placed within a paragraph, or whether a particular paragraph is correctly placed within a passage. **The presence of bracketed numbers at the beginnings of sentences signals that a question testing sentence order will appear, and the presence of bracketed numbers at the top of each paragraph signals that a question testing paragraph order will appear.** Whenever you see one of these "clues," pay close attention to the order of sentences or paragraphs as you read. If you are able to notice – and fix – potential errors before you even look at the questions, you can save yourself a lot of time.

Sentence Order

When you encounter a sentence order question, you should first determine the topic of the sentence in question. Then, ask yourself whether it follows logically from the previous sentence and connects to the following sentence. If not, reread the paragraph from the beginning, checking to see where else that specific topic appears. The sentence in question should be placed either before or after.

[1] Balanchine then brought Tallchief home to his Ballet Society, the company that would become New York City Ballet. [2] Her immense popularity with the American public grew in part from the intense demands the company made on its phenomenally gifted principal dancer. [3] Tallchief was called upon to dance as many as eight performances a week and learned roles in more than 30 different ballets. [4] Balanchine made use of her artistry to great effect. [5] In fact, many people did not realize how challenging the part was until much later, when they saw other great ballerinas attempt to perform it. [6] When she danced the lead role in *Pas de Dix* (1955), for example, she dazzled audiences with her radiance and impeccable technique.

1

To make this paragraph most logical, sentence 5 should be placed

A) where it is now
B) after sentence 2
C) after sentence 3
D) after sentence 6

Solution:

1) What is sentence 5 about?

The fact that many people who watched Maria Tallchief perform a part did not realize how difficult it was until later on.

Since sentence 6 does not tell us what specific part is being referred to, we can assume that sentence 5 belongs after the sentence providing that information.

2) What's the topic of the previous sentence?

The fact that Maria Tallchief became popular in part because she gave so many performances. The sentence does not mention a specific part, so we can assume that the sentence does not belong where it is now. A) can therefore be eliminated.

3) What sentence does mention a specific part?

Sentence 6 mentions that Maria danced the lead role in *Pas de Six*. *Role* and *part* are synonyms, and there is no mention of a specific role elsewhere in the paragraph, so those two sentences must be talking about the same role. Since Sentence 5 explains just what *the role* refers to, that sentence should come first. The answer is therefore D).

In addition, if you were to see this question in a complete section, it would build off of the question on p. 19. The correct answer includes the phrase *apparent ease*, setting up a contrast with the idea that Tallchief's part in *Pas de Six* was actually more difficult than it seemed.

Inserting Sentences

It is also possible that you will be asked to identify where in a passage a particular sentence should be added. Unlike Yes/No sentence insertion questions, which normally deal with only a limited section of a passage or paragraph, these questions may ask you to consider various places in multiple paragraphs. Unless you happen to remember the passage exceptionally well, plugging the sentence into each spot listed in the answer choices and working by process of elimination is usually the most effective way to answer these questions. That said, you should still do some very basic work upfront in order to help you recognize the correct location as such.

When you read the sentence to be inserted, take a moment and restate the topic for yourself. This will be the key word or phrase. Then, when you go back to the passage to plug in the sentence, check to see whether the surrounding sentences contain that word or phrase. The sentence will almost certainly have to be placed next to a sentence that includes the topic word or phrase.

Because a full passage is required to look at one of these questions, an example is included on p. 35.

Dividing Paragraphs

You may also be asked to identify the point at which a paragraph should be divided in two. These questions essentially test your ability to recognize where a shift in topic occurs. As is true for sentence order questions, paragraph division questions are always accompanied by numbered sentences.

There are two primary ways that you can approach paragraph division questions. You can check the answer choices one by one, looking at each point in the passage and deciding whether it fits in logically with the information that came before it or begins a new idea; or, you can simply read through the paragraph on your own and identify where a break would logically occur.

While the first option may seem safer and easier, it can also be time consuming and increase the odds that you'll get stuck between two answers. The second option, on the other hand, requires a bit more thought initially but is often faster in the end. It also significantly reduces the chances of your second-guessing yourself.

For an example, let's look at a slightly doctored version of our passage:

[1] "A ballerina takes steps given to her and makes them her own. [2] Each individual brings something different to the same role," the great ballerina Maria Tallchief once said. [3] Tallchief combined great individualism and extraordinary talent, creating a remarkable and vital chapter in American dance. [4] Maria Tallchief was born on an Indian reservation in Oklahoma on January 24, 1925. [5] When Maria was five years old, she began music lessons and soon discovered that she had perfect pitch. [6] But it was dance that captured the young girl's heart. [7] After five years of study, she joined the Ballet Russe de Monte Carlo, where she quickly became a soloist.

1

The best place to begin a new paragraph is

A) sentence 2
B) sentence 3
C) sentence 4
D) sentence 6

In the existing version, the paragraph has two different focuses: it introduces Maria Tallchief and her career, and it provides biographical information. The shift occurs in sentence 4, where the writer first begins to describe Tallchief's early life and background. So the answer is C).

Paragraph Order

Questions about paragraph order test essentially the same skill as those testing sentence order, only on a larger scale. As is true for sentence order questions, you must determine whether a particular paragraph is logically placed, or whether it would make more sense elsewhere in the passage.

While questions testing paragraph order ask you to consider more information than most other question types do, **you do not need to reread the entire passage to determine whether the existing placement of a paragraph is correct; a few key places will usually give you all the necessary information.**

If you can consistently answer paragraph order questions correctly simply by plugging the paragraph in question into the spot indicated by each answer choice, you may feel more comfortable continuing to work this way. That said, doing a few seconds of work upfront (if you can stand it) can as always reduce some of the potential for confusion.

If you are comfortable trying to answer paragraph questions on your own, you should break them into the following steps:

1) Reread the paragraph in question, paying particular attention to the first (topic) sentence. Reiterate the topic for yourself in a word or two, and jot it down quickly.

2) Back up and read the **last sentence** of the previous paragraph, and ask ~~whether~~ yourself whether it leads naturally into the topic of the paragraph in question. If it does, you're done. If not:

3) Skim through each paragraph, looking for a mention of that topic – you do not need to read, just look for the word(s). The paragraph in question should belong next to that paragraph.

Because we really need to look at a complete passage to see how these questions work, a version of our sample passage is reprinted in full, along with a paragraph order question, on the following page.

[1]

"A ballerina takes steps given to her and makes them her own. Each individual brings something different to the same role," the great ballerina Maria Tallchief once said. Tallchief combined great individualism and extraordinary talent, creating a remarkable and vital chapter in American dance.

[2]

Maria Tallchief was born Elizabeth Marie Tall Chief on an Indian reservation in Fairfax, Oklahoma on January 24, 1925. A member of the Osage tribe, she became a trailblazer for Native Americans in the world of ballet. The Osage language is similar to the language spoken by members of the Sioux tribe. When Maria was five years old, she began music lessons and soon discovered that she had perfect pitch. It was dance that captured the young girl's heart, though. After five years of study, she joined the Ballet Russe de Monte Carlo, where she quickly became a soloist. It was during her time with the Ballet Russe that she became known professionally as Maria Tallchief, combining the two parts of her Indian name.

[3]

[1] Balanchine then brought Tallchief home to his Ballet Society, the company that would become New York City Ballet. [2] Her immense popularity with the American public grew in part from the demands the company made on its phenomenally gifted principal dancer: [3] Tallchief was called upon to dance as many as eight performances a week. [4] In fact, many audience members did not realize how technically difficult the part

was until much later, when they saw other great ballerinas attempt to perform it. [5] Audiences were awed by her dedication to her art. [6] When she danced the lead role in *Pas de Dix* (1955), for example, she dazzled audiences with her radiance and impeccable technique. [A]

[4]

In the 1950s, Tallchief became one of the first ballet dancers to make regular appearances on television. [B] They first worked together in Paris in 1947 – the same year Tallchief became the first prima ballerina of the New York City Ballet. Eventually, Tallchief inspired a number of Balanchine's ballets. These included *Orpheus*, *Night Shadow*, and *The Four Temperaments*. In 1954, Balanchine choreographed Tallchief in what would become her most famous role: the Sugar Plum Fairy in *The Nutcracker*. [C]

[5]

In 1965, Maria Tallchief surprised the world by announcing her retirement. [D] She had no intention of dancing past her prime and wanted to pass her love for her art to younger dancers. She was a revolutionary performer who broke many barriers for Native American women.

Solution #1: The topic of the sentence to be added is Tallchief's performance in *The Nutcracker*. The whole passage is about Tallchief, but that ballet is only mentioned in one part, so it's the key phrase. It appears in the last sentence of paragraph 4, so the sentence in question belongs next to it. The answer is therefore C).

Solution #2: Maria Tallchief's collaboration with George Balanchine. More specifically, it is about the start of her collaboration with Balanchine – the second sentence tells us that they **first** worked together in 1947. The last sentence of Paragraph 3 discusses a 1955 collaboration with Balanchine. 1955 is later than 1947, so that information must come later in the passage. The two paragraphs have the same topic, however, so they should be located next to one another. Since Paragraph 4 refers to events that clearly happened before those in Paragraph 3, Paragraph 4 should be placed first (after Paragraph 2). So C) is again correct.

Exercise: Sentence Order* (answers p. 224)

1. [1] Learning to ride a unicycle might seem like a daunting task, but with the right kind of training aids, it doesn't have to be impossible – or even scary. [2] One option is to use a spotter who walks alongside and catches the rider if he or she falls. [3] Another easy way to learn is to find a narrow hallway: riding in a confined space allows the beginning rider to improve balancing from front-to-back and side-to-side. [4] Likewise, riding between two chairs placed back-to-back teaches the rider how to find a proper starting position. [5] On the other hand, props such as ski poles should not be used because they hinder balance and create dependence. [6] If a hallway cannot be found, a fence or clothesline can be used as well.

1

What is the best placement for sentence 6?

A) Where it is now
B) After sentence 1
C) After sentence 2
D) After sentence 3

2. [1] For decades, scientists have hoped for a "solar revolution," a shift from relying on natural gas to heat homes and power cars to harnessing electricity from the sun. [2] The conversion of solar heat into usable energy is accomplished through the use of solar panels – also known as modules – which can be installed directly into the ground, mounted on roofs, or built directly into the walls of a building. [3] It's a tantalizing promise: on sunny days, the sun gives off enormous amounts of energy – enough to power houses, office buildings, and schools. [4] Each module is comprised of cells which convert solar radiation into direct current electricity. [5] Solar-powered buildings can even be very large. [6] In 2011, the world's largest solar-powered office building was constructed, covering over 750,000 square feet.

2

The best placement for sentence 4 is

A) where it is now
B) after sentence 2
C) after sentence 5
D) after sentence 6

*Because paragraph order is tested infrequently, and because of the difficulty involved in creating these questions, they are not included here. An additional example can be found in the practice test, p. 219.

3. [1] Say the word "sushi," and the first thing that comes to mind is usually an image of raw fish. [2] Initially, the rice was only used to help start the fermenting process, but food shortages later made the rice too valuable to be thrown away. [3] But sushi is about rice as well as fish. [4] It's also the original fast food, dating back to 700 A.D. in Japan. [5] At that time, fish was salted, sandwiched between layers of rice, and pressed with heavy stones, a process that fermented and preserved the fish for months or even years. [6] The curing time was also shortened to three or four weeks, so the fish was closer to being raw when it was consumed.

3

To make the paragraph most logical, sentence 2 should be placed

A) where it is now
B) before sentence 4
C) before sentence 5
D) before sentence 6

4. [1] During World War II, Admiral Grace Hopper was stationed at Harvard University, where she worked on IBM's Harvard Mark I computer, the first large-scale computer in the United States. [2] Hopper was only the third person to program this computer, and in 1943, she wrote a manual of operations that lit the path for those that followed her. [3] Then, in the 1950s, she invented the compiler, a device that translated English commands into computer code, allowing programmers to create code more easily and with fewer errors. [4] Hopper's second compiler, the Flow-Matic, was used to program UNIVAC I and II, which were the first computers available commercially. [5] Hopper also oversaw the development of the Common Business-Oriented Language (COBOL), one of the first computer programming languages.

4

The best placement for sentence 4 is

A) where it is now
B) before sentence 1
C) before sentence 2
D) before sentence 5

5. [1] Worldwide awareness of Inuit Art originated with the assistance of James Houston, a noted artist, author and designer for the Stueben Glass Company. [2] In the late 1940s, Houston collected a number of small Inuit carvings, which he then sold to help support the Inuit's economic needs. [3] In 1953, Houston solicited his friend Eugene Power to help him import Inuit art into the United States. [4] Power, who owned and operated University Microfilms in Ann Arbor, Michigan, established a non-profit gallery called Eskimo Art Incorporated in Ann Arbor to import the work. [5] The same year, Power encouraged the Cranbrook Institute of Science to host the first exhibition of Inuit Art in the United States. [6] Later, Houston taught the Inuit to make unique stone cut and seal skin stencil prints, and in 1959, the first collection of Inuit prints was released at Cape Dorset.

5

The most logical place to begin a new paragraph would be at

A) sentence 2
B) sentence 3
C) sentence 4
D) sentence 6

3. Infographics

Infographic questions are essentially "supporting evidence" questions, but because they are presented in such a different format from the rest of the questions test, they deserve a chapter all to themselves.

On every SAT Writing test, one or two passages will be accompanied by an informational graph or chart associated with the passage. The text will contained an underlined statement related to the graphic, and you will be responsible for deciding whether the original statement accurately reflects the information in the graphic or whether it must be changed. **There are essentially two types of questions: "detail" and "big picture." The former will ask you about a specific aspect of the graphic, while the latter will ask you to identify an overall trend.**

While these questions may initially strike you as somewhat exotic, the most important thing is not to become too flustered by them. Unlike grammar questions, which require you to both recall and apply rules, **answers to infographic questions will always be right in front of you.** Furthermore, most graphics will be relatively straightforward and will not require any specialized skills or knowledge.

"Skimming" Graphs

Although infographic questions are formatted differently from other questions, they are still vulnerable to some of the same techniques that can be used elsewhere. For example, you should be careful of relying excessively on the answer choices from the start – as always, incorrect options will be written to sound plausible, and thus to confuse you. As a result, it is very much in your interest to start by doing some basic work upfront. Having a big-picture understanding of the information in the chart may allow you to eliminate several answers upfront, and to identify the correct answer more quickly and with less potential for second-guessing.

Just as you can skim texts to get a general idea of what they are saying, you can also "skim" graphs visually to get a general sense of the information they convey.

Here are some questions to consider:

- What is the shape of the graph? Does the curve go up, down, or both?

- Are changes steady from point to point, or is there a big jump somewhere? If so, where?

- Is there an "outlier" point with a value very different from that of the other points?

Any choice that clearly contradicts the general trend of the graph can be immediately eliminated.

Let's look at some examples:

Biotechnology has become one of the hottest sectors for overall job growth in the United States as well as other developed nations. Because of aging populations and the need for increased drug effectiveness and safety, biotechnology has extended its reach into many medical fields, including biological research, agriculture, and pharmaceutical development. Some regions of the United States, particularly those with strong research sectors, have experienced considerable growth in the number of biotechnology jobs. The Raleigh-Durham "research triangle," home to Duke University and the University of North Carolina-Chapel Hill, saw a significant rise in biotechnology jobs in a variety of areas. For example, **1** the number of biotechnology jobs in the research and laboratory sector tripled between 2002 and 2014. In the coming years, the biotechnology industry will continue to add new sectors, further increasing the demand for workers.

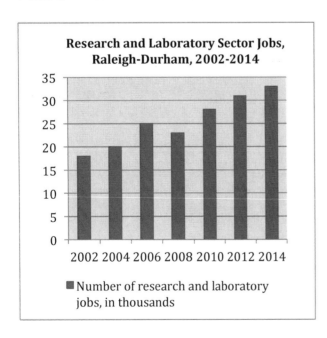

Before we get into the questions, we're just going to stop for a moment and consider the information the graph conveys. That way, we won't have to start figuring things out from scratch at the same time we're trying to answer the questions.

The first thing we're going to do is make sure we understand the pieces of the graph, as well as how they relate to one another. If we have a clear picture of what's going on upfront, we'll be a lot less likely to get confused by the answer choices.

The title indicates that the chart will convey information about the number of **research and laboratory jobs** in the Durham-Raleigh area between 2002 and 2014. That might seem very obvious, but it's actually very, very important because it's giving us the chart's **scope** – that is, how broad or narrow it is.

In this case, the chart is relatively narrow: it is focusing on **one specific field or sector of biotechnology** (research and laboratory jobs), not on all biotechnology sectors, and on one specific region (Raleigh-Durham) rather than on the United States as a whole. That is crucial, because any answer choice that includes information beyond those "boundaries" will be incorrect. We cannot, for example, draw conclusions about research and laboratory jobs in other regions, or in the United States as a whole, or about biotechnology jobs outside the research and laboratory sector. **Incorrect answer choices** may play on those concepts.

The x-axis (horizontal) contains **years** in chronological order. The earliest year is 2002, and the latest is 2014. The points between them represent the interceding years. The graph does not contain information from every single year, however, but rather every other (even) year. So we have information from 2004, 2006, 2008, and 2010, but not from 2005, 2007, 2009, etc.

The y-axis (vertical) is a little bit trickier. It contains numbers in increments of five; however, the information at the bottom of the chart tells us that the bars of the graph represent research and laboratory jobs **in thousands**. So 5 actually means 5,000, 10 means 10,000, and 15 means 15,000. Why not just write the numbers out next to the y-axis? Well, because those are pretty large numbers, and they take up a lot of space. It's easier and clearer without all those zeroes.

Now we consider the overall trend suggested by the graph: the numbers steadily rise from 2002 to 2014, with a quick dip in between (2008). The increase from 2002 to 2014 is significant, but not staggeringly huge.

So now that we have a pretty good idea of what the graph is about, we're going to work through a sample question and see how to apply all that information.

The Raleigh-Durham "research triangle," home to Duke University and the University of North Carolina-Chapel Hill, saw a significant rise in biotechnology jobs in a variety of areas. For example, **1** the number of biotechnology jobs in the research and laboratory sector tripled between 2002 and 2014.

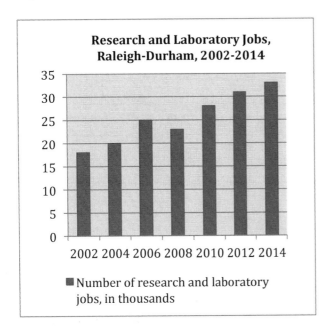

Research and Laboratory Jobs, Raleigh-Durham, 2002-2014

■ Number of research and laboratory jobs, in thousands

1

Which choice offers an accurate interpretation of the data presented in the chart?

A) NO CHANGE
B) the number of biotechnology jobs in all sectors increased between 2002 and 2014.
C) after 2006, the number of research and laboratory jobs increased during every two-year period.
D) around 15,000 more research and laboratory jobs existed in 2014 than existed in 2002.

Let's start with the NO CHANGE option. It states that research and laboratory jobs **tripled** between 2002 and 2014. That's a very large increase. Just by glancing at the graph, we can see that the 2014 bar, while significantly higher than the 2002 bar, isn't three times as high. Upon closer examination, we can observe that the number of jobs in 2002 was somewhere around 18,000, while the number is 2014 was just over 30,000 – a difference of approximately 15,000. The number of jobs almost doubled; it didn't even come close to tripling. So A) is out.

We can, however, use your calculation from A) to identify to the correct answer. D) states exactly what we just figured out, namely that the number of jobs increased by around 15,000. So D) is correct.

Notice the switch in terms: A) is phrased in terms of tripling, while D) provides an actual number. In order to avoid confusion, it is necessary to be able to move between the two types of terminology.

We're also going to look at B) and C), just to see how they work: B) is incorrect because its scope is **too broad**. Remember that the graph only covers the research and laboratory sector, and the answer refers to **all sectors**. C) is wrong because it states that the number of research and laboratory jobs increased during **every** two-year period after 2006, but the number **decreased** in 2008.

Notice the **extreme language** (*every, all*) present in B) and C). You should be suspicious of this type of phrasing because graphs will often reveal **exceptions** to general trends.

Now let's look at a slightly more complex example:

Water is a precious resource. Although it flows freely from the tap, it's not infinite. As institutions housing thousands of students, colleges and universities consume enormous amounts of water in order to maintain lawns, air-condition dorms, and clean plates in dining halls. Now, however, college campuses are becoming home to some of the most innovative water conservation ideas. They are implementing water management technology, smart conservation policies, and more. At Drexel University, for example, rainwater is recycled for non-potable uses, including toilet flushing, landscaping, and gardening. Other schools have had mixed results, however. At the University of Southern California, **1** water consumption at the Health and Sciences campuses declined from 2007 to 2009, while it rose at the University Park campus.

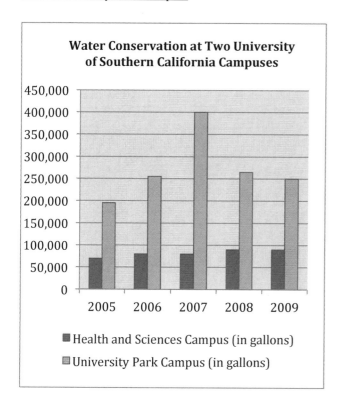

Water Conservation at Two University of Southern California Campuses

■ Health and Sciences Campus (in gallons)
▨ University Park Campus (in gallons)

1

Which choice offers an accurate interpretation of data presented in the chart?

A) NO CHANGE
B) water consumption at the University Park campus decreased from 2007 to 2009, although it rose at the Health and Sciences campus.
C) water consumption at both the University Park and Health and Sciences campuses decreased after peaking in 2007.
D) water usage at the University Park campus decreased every year between 2005 and 2009, while it rose at the Health and Sciences campus.

While the previous graph only asked you to consider how the number of jobs changed over time, this graph requires you to keep track of – and compare – two factors: the amount of water used at the Health and Sciences Campus, and the amount used at the University Park Campus.

If you think that sounds complicated, though, don't worry! You can "skim" this graph too – you just have to make sure not to confuse the information presented in each bar color.

The first thing to notice is that the two sets of bars show two *very* different stories. Any answer choice stating that they are similar will therefore be wrong. That eliminates C).

Next, we can notice that the bars for the Health and Sciences campus (dark gray) are a lot lower than the bars for the University Park Campus. They also go up slightly over time; they do not drop at all. So any answer stating that water usage decreased at the Health and Sciences campus must be wrong. That eliminates A).

We can also notice that the bars for the University Park campus (light gray) go up significantly, then drop. So any answer that mentions water usage there only increasing or decreasing must be wrong. That eliminates D).

We're left with B), which is correct.

Exercise: Infographics (answers p. 224)

1. El Niño is a climate pattern in which water in the Pacific Ocean near the equator becomes hotter than usual, affecting the atmosphere and weather around the world. Although El Niño climate conditions are unpredictable, they typically occur every few years. The climate pattern can change the weather of the United States, particularly in California and the southern states. Although El Niño years do not always bring heavy rains, **1** the wettest winters have occurred when El Niño was strong. In addition, El Niño may bring warmer than normal winter temperatures to the eastern part of the United States.

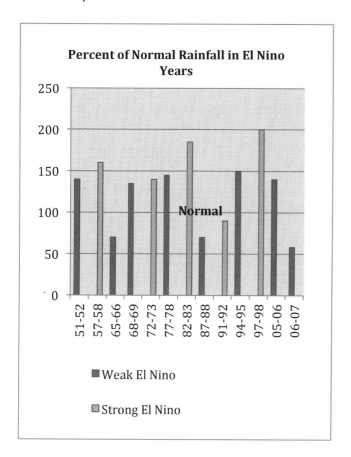

1

Which choice is best supported by the information in the graph?

A) NO CHANGE
B) strong El Niños always create abnormally wet winters.
C) the amount of rainfall in weak El Niño years has increased over time.
D) the amount of rainfall in weak El Niño years has grown closer to the amount of rainfall in strong El Niño years.

2. Because demand for fish cannot be adequately met by wild catch fish, the aquaculture industry makes up market needs. The farmed salmon production represented less than 10% of the total volume 25 years ago, whereas it now accounts for over 70% of the salmon market. Between 1979 and 2011, hatchery-raised salmon **2** grew to a volume of over 3,500 tons, while wild catch salmon has stagnated.

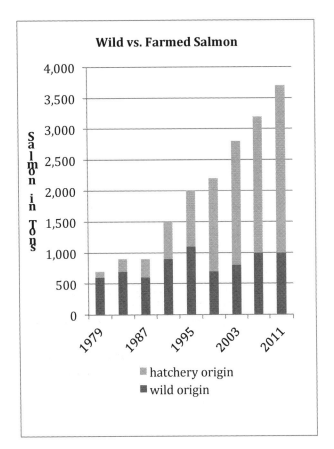

Wild vs. Farmed Salmon

■ hatchery origin
■ wild origin

2

Which choice offers an accurate interpretation of data presented in the chart?

A) NO CHANGE
B) grew to a volume of over 2,500 tons,
C) grew to a volume of 1,000 tons,
D) grew by a volume of over 3,500 tons,

3. A glacier's life is defined by movement and change. Glacier movement most often occurs over hundreds or even thousands of years, but not all glaciers move slowly. For example, surging glaciers can flow quickly, sometimes traveling as much as ten to one hundred times faster than the normal rate of movement. Others may retreat within only a few decades, leaving once glaciated valleys blooming with vegetation again.

Glaciers helped shape the Cascade mountains, but some reports now suggest that they could be gone within a matter of decades. **3** The number of stationary glaciers decreased from 1995 and 2013, and some glaciers have disappeared entirely. Scientists warn that the melting ice could impact everything from tourism to agriculture, forestry, water quality, and underwater ecosystems.

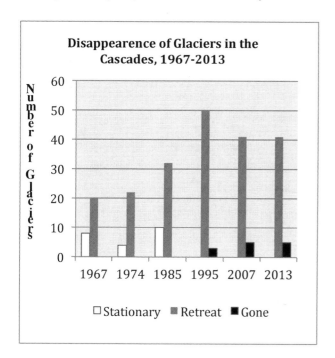

Disappearence of Glaciers in the Cascades, 1967-2013

3

Which choice offers an accurate interpretation of data presented in the chart?

A) NO CHANGE
B) The number of retreating glaciers has decreased since 1995, but
C) The number of stationary glaciers rose from 1967 to 2013, but
D) There were twice as many retreating glaciers in 1995 as there were a decade earlier, and

4.   A few decades ago, wild giant pandas were considered a symbol of wildlife conservation. Large-scale infrastructure projects were destroying the animals' traditional habitat, found only in the Chinese provinces of Sichuan, Shaanxi and Gansu. Now, however, conservationists' efforts seem to be paying off. According to one recent survey, the panda population began to increase during the decade beginning in 2003, **4** rising by several hundred to over 2,000 in 2013. The World Wildlife Federation's 2015-2025 giant panda conservation strategy sets the course for panda protection efforts over the next decade and will focus on improving panda habitat in a manner that balances conservation with local sustainable development.

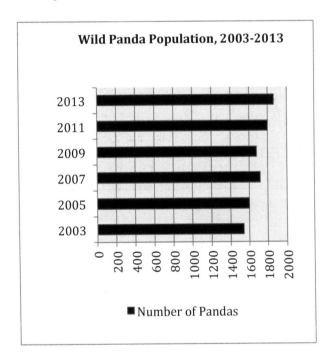

Wild Panda Population, 2003-2013

■Number of Pandas

4

Which choice offers an accurate interpretation of data presented in the chart?

A) NO CHANGE
B) rising by several hundred in each year, for a total of over 1,800
C) declining slightly before rebounding to over 1,800
D) experiencing an initial drop but eventually climbing to 2,000

5.   The process of getting energy from the wind into a home or business is complex and involves many components. A modern wind turbine consists of an estimated 8,000 parts and can be up to 300 feet high. Turbines must be designed, built, transported, and erected before they can start producing energy. This process can be split into three major phases: manufacturing, project development, and operation and maintenance. In a successful project, these phases overlap and there is substantial communication among workers in all three phases. Currently, **5** wind power jobs are evenly distributed between the financial services, construction, and transport sectors. However, as new wind farms are built, existing ones are upgraded, and manufacturers are able to take advantage of returns to scale, the other sectors also are expected to experience rapid growth.

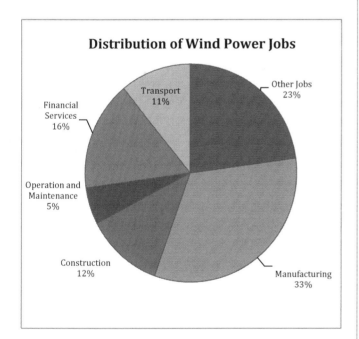

Distribution of Wind Power Jobs

Transport 11%
Other Jobs 23%
Financial Services 16%
Operation and Maintenance 5%
Construction 12%
Manufacturing 33%

5

Which choice offers an accurate interpretation of data presented in the chart?

A) NO CHANGE
B) only half as many people are employed in construction jobs as are employed in manufacturing jobs.
C) there are twice as many jobs in the financial services sector as there are in the transport sector.
D) the highest number of wind power jobs are concentrated in the manufacturing and "other jobs" sectors.

49

4. Shorter is Better

One of the most important concepts that the SAT tests is **conciseness** – that is, clear and to-the-point constructions are preferable to long, wordy ones. As a result, **shorter answers are more likely to be correct.**

This does not mean that the shortest answer will always be correct, or that the longest answer will never be correct. It does, however, mean that **when multiple answer are grammatically acceptable and otherwise the same, the shortest one will pretty much always be right.**

When you do not know the answer to a question immediately and are unsure of how to figure it out, you should **start by checking the shortest answer, then work back to the longest one in order of length**. That also means that **when there is a DELETE or OMIT option, you should always check it first**. If the shortest answer makes sense when you plug it back into the passage (don't forget that step!), you can probably stop right there. Using the framework of the test this way can save you a significant amount of time and energy. It also reduces the chance that you'll second-guess yourself and change right answers to wrong answers.

A. Redundancy

Never use two synonyms to describe something when you can use only one word.

Located in Midland County, Michigan, the

Chippewa Nature Center is one of the most

1 prominent and well-known nature centers in the

United States.

> **1**
>
> A) NO CHANGE
> B) prominently well known
> C) prominent plus being well known
> D) prominent

When you look at the answer choices, you can immediately notice that D) is significantly shorter than the other. Even if you do not know what *prominent* means, you can make a very educated guess. Since *prominent* and *well-known* mean the same thing, only one of them should be used. So D) is in fact correct.

In addition, you must sometimes look at the non-underlined portion of the sentence to identify the redundancy.

Located in Midland County, Michigan, the

Chippewa Nature Center is one of the most

prominent American nature centers **1** that is

known by many people in the United States.

> **1**
>
> A) NO CHANGE
> B) being known by many Americans.
> C) known by many people there.
> D) OMIT the underlined portion (inserting a period after *centers*)

Because there's an OMIT option, we're going to check it first. And indeed, since *prominent* means "known by many people," the underlined portion is unnecessary and D) is correct.

50

B. Wordiness

Wordiness questions do not always include multiple words with the same meaning. Sometimes they simply add in extra words for no other reason than to make the sentence longer. To reiterate: **when you have multiple answer choices that express the same information and differ only in length, the shortest answer will almost always be correct.**

For example:

During the Nimrod Expedition to the South Pole

in 1907, Ernest Shackleton led a group of explorers

explorers on **1** a dangerous voyage.

.

1

A) NO CHANGE
B) a voyage of a dangerous sort.
C) a voyage whose nature was dangerous.
D) a voyage that was dangerous in itself.

While all of the answers express the same information, A) does so in the fewest words and is thus correct. Here, however, there's a slight twist. On the previous page, it was very easy to identify the shortest answer. In this case, the shortest answer is in the passage itself; the difference in length is less obvious. **When considering answer-choice length, don't forget to check the version in the passage!**

C. Passive Voice

In a passive construction, the subject and the object are flipped so that the person or thing performing the action becomes the object, and the person or thing on the receiving end of the action becomes the subject. *X does y* (active) becomes *y is done by x* (passive). The word *by* is often a tip-off that the passive is being used.

Active

William Shakespeare wrote *Hamlet.*

Passive

Hamlet was written by William Shakespeare.

Although it is not absolutely necessary that you master passive constructions since they are always longer than active ones, the ability to recognize them can be helpful. When the shortest answer appears in the passage itself, it can be difficult to identify visually; noticing passive constructions can allow you to eliminate other options.

For example:

During the Nimrod Expedition to the South

Pole in 1907, a group of explorers **were** led on a

dangerous voyage **by** Ernest Shackleton.

1

A) NO CHANGE
B) a group of explorers being led on a dangerous voyage by Ernest Shackleton
C) Ernest Shackleton led a group of explorers on a dangerous voyage
D) a dangerous voyage that Ernest Shackleton led a group of explorers on

It's pretty easy to eliminate B) and D). If you're using your ear, though, you might think that A) and C) sound equally correct, and it isn't immediately obvious which answer is shorter. If you can recognize that A) is passive, however, the question becomes much more straightforward. C) is active, shorter, and correct.

51

Exercise: Shorter is Better (answers p. 224)

1. The issue of free speech as it relates to the First Amendment of the United States Constitution has been a center of controversy **[1]** about free speech since the 1950s. In the **[2]** importantly significant decision Tinker v. Des Moines Independent Community School District (1965), the United States Supreme Court **[3]** formally recognized that freedom of speech and expression do not "end at the schoolyard gate." Unsurprisingly, though, students and school administrators do not always **[4]** concur with one another about what constitutes free speech.

1
- A) NO CHANGE
- B) concerning free speech
- C) in regards to the issue of free speech
- D) DELETE the underlined portion

2
- A) NO CHANGE
- B) important and significant
- C) important while also being significant
- D) significant

3
- A) NO CHANGE
- B) recognized in a formal manner
- C) undertook formal recognition
- D) recognized – doing so formally –

4
- A) NO CHANGE
- B) agree, not to mention concur,
- C) agree and also concurring
- D) agree and concur

2. When Jordan Romero was in elementary school, he became intrigued by a painting that hung in his classroom. The painting **1** showed and depicted seven of the world's highest mountains – one for each continent – and Jordan made up his mind to climb them all. Remarkably, he **2** achieved an attainment of that goal when he reached the top of the Vinson Massif at the age of fifteen years, five months, and twelve days, becoming the youngest climber ever to summit the tallest mountain on each continent. In the process, Romero also became the youngest person to scale Mt. Everest, reaching the top when he was not even fourteen years old **3** and earning the title of the youngest person to climb Mt. Everest.

1

A) NO CHANGE
B) showed a depiction of
C) showed plus depicted
D) depicted

2

A) NO CHANGE
B) achieved as well as attaining that goal
C) attained that goal
D) achieved and attained that goal

3

A) NO CHANGE
B) and he earned the title of the youngest person to climb Mt. Everest.
C) and earning the title of the youngest person to climb Mt. Everest.
D) DELETE the underlined phrase (ending the sentence with a period).

3. Above a hole in the ice, a polar bear lies waiting for a seal to emerge. Food in the frozen Arctic is **1** scarce, in short supply, so the shaggy white hunter must seize every opportunity to pursue its prey. The polar bear is one of the world's largest **2** carnivores that eats meat, rivaled only by the Kodiak brown bear of southern Alaska. Numerous adaptations make the polar bear uniquely suited to life **3** in and around icy habitats. A thick layer of blubber beneath its fur provides **4** insulation, which keeps it warm. Its long neck and narrow skull help it glide through the water, and its front feet are large and flat. Fur even covers its feet, allowing for traction on ice.

1
A) NO CHANGE
B) scarce, and there is not much of it,
C) scarcely difficult to find,
D) scarce

2
A) NO CHANGE
B) carnivorous meat-eater
C) carnivores, which eat meat,
D) carnivores

3
A) NO CHANGE
B) in and also living around
C) in while being around
D) DELETE the underlined portion (ending the sentence with a period).

4
A) NO CHANGE
B) insulation, and this keeps it warm.
C) insulation that keeps it warm.
D) DELETE the underlined portion (ending the sentence with a period).

4. **1** Formerly, in a time that is now past, 3-D printers were expensive tools wielded by professional designers who used them to create prototypes of product such as mobile phones or airplane parts. Now, however, these printers are emerging into the mainstream, and many computer enthusiasts, schools, and libraries are purchasing them. Not only can they **2** design in addition to printing objects, but they can also make copies of physical objects by "scanning" them – using a camera to turn multiple pictures into a three-dimensional model, which can repeatedly be printed **3** again and again.

1

A) NO CHANGE
B) In the past,
C) Formerly, in the past,
D) Formerly in a past time

2

A) NO CHANGE
B) design – also print –
C) design and print
D) design and also printing

3

A) NO CHANGE
B) over and over again.
C) once and again.
D) DELETE the underlined portion (ending the sentence with a period).

5. Rainbows can be observed whenever there are water drops in the air and sunlight shining from behind the observer. They are usually **1** seen in a visible way in the western sky during the morning and in the eastern sky during the early evening. The most spectacular displays occur when half the sky is still dark with rain clouds and the observer is at a spot with clear sky in the direction of the sun. The result is a **2** luminous rainbow that contrasts with the dark background.

The rainbow effect can also be artificially created **3** unnaturally by dispersing water droplets into the air during a sunny day. Rarely, a moonbow, a nighttime rainbow, can be seen **4** during the night. Because human color perception is poor in low light, moonbows are often perceived as white.

1
A) NO CHANGE
B) seen in the western sky
C) seen and perceived visibly in the western sky
D) seen visibly in the western sky

2
A) NO CHANGE
B) luminously light-filled rainbow
C) luminous rainbow, full of light
D) luminous and light-filled

3
A) NO CHANGE
B) unnaturally, by
C) unnaturally and
D) DELETE the underlined portion.

4
A) NO CHANGE
B) in the nighttime.
C) at night.
D) DELETE the underlined portion (ending the sentence with a period).

5. Diction, Idioms, and Register

The term *diction* simply refers to an author's choice of words. Diction errors involve words that are incorrect in a particular context, either because they have the wrong meaning or because they do not follow the conventions of standard written English.

English contains many fixed phrases, known as **idioms. Idioms are not correct or incorrect for any logical reason; they simply reflect the fact that certain phrases have evolved to be considered standard usage.** As a result, there is essentially no way to study for these types of questions other than reading. English contains far too many idioms to memorize, and there is no way to predict which one(s) will appear on any given test.

For example, consider the following:

In 1585, Captain Ralph Lane and 108 colonists, including the scientist Thomas Hariott, built a small settlement on Roanoke Island, off the coast of North Carolina. From this base, they explored parts of eastern North Carolina, obtained samples of various metals, and tested them at the site. In less than a year, however, they **1** exhausted their supplies and were forced to return to England.

1

A) NO CHANGE
B) expended
C) diluted
D) undermined

To "exhaust" supplies means to use them up completely – it is a fixed phrase, and the verb *exhaust* cannot be replaced by any of the other verbs listed, even though their meanings are similar.

Some verbs and nouns must always be followed by specific **prepositions**.

A familiarity **1** in the most common programming languages is useful for anyone who wants to pursue a career in information technology.

1

A) NO CHANGE
B) with
C) to
D) for

The phrase *a familiarity* always requires the preposition *with*; any other preposition is idiomatically unacceptable. B) is therefore correct.

Although memorizing idioms should not be your priority, some common ones are listed on the next page.

Common Idioms with Prepositions

Serve as
Known as/to be
(Pre)occupation with
Consistent/inconsistent with
Sympathize with
Correlate with
Identify with
Familiar/unfamiliar with
In contrast to (BUT: contrast with)
Be native to (BUT: be a native of)
Have a tendency toward
Biased toward
Recommend x to y
Listen to
Prefer x to y
Devoted to
A threat to/threaten to
Central to
Unique to
Similar to
Enter into
Have insight into
Interested in
Succeed in/at
Adept in/at
Have confidence in
Engage in/with
Take pride in
Insist on
Focus on
Rely on
Reflect on
Dwell on
Draw (up)on
Based on
Suspicious of
Devoid of
A proponent of
A command of
A source of
An offer of
An understanding/knowledge of
Take advantage of

Approve/disapprove of
In the hope(s) of
Characteristic/typical of
Convinced of
Consist of
Composed/comprised of
In recognition of
Capable/incapable of
A mastery of
Have an appreciation of/for
Criticize for
Necessary for
Prized for
Endure/last for
Wait for
Watch/look (out) for
Responsible for
Compensate for
Strive for
Famous/Celebrated for
Recognized/known for
Named for/after
Worry about
Complain about
Wonder/ be curious about
Think about
Bring about
Be particular about
Protect from/against
Defend from/against
Followed by
Confused/puzzled/perplexed by
Accompanied by
Encouraged by
Outraged by
Surprised/stunned/shocked by
Amazed by
Awed by
Impressed by
Known as/to be
Differ(ent) from
Refrain from
Have power/control over

Commonly Confused Words

The SAT also tests your ability to distinguish between commonly confused pairs of words. Sometimes the words tested will be spelled differently but pronounced identically. Other times the words may have slightly different spellings and pronunciations. Either way, you are responsible for recognizing whether the underlined word is being used correctly based on the context of the passage.

As always, these questions have the potential to test other concepts (e.g. prepositions or commas) simultaneously, but the correct answer will most likely depend on the ability to recognize which version of the word is correct.

For example:

For centuries, scientists believed in the existence of planets beyond the solar system but had no way of knowing how common they were or how similar they might be to better-known planets. Beginning in the 1900s, many people insisted that they had discovered exoplanets; however, their claims had little affect on the scientific community until 1992, when the first exoplanet was positively identified.

1
A) NO CHANGE
B) affect to the scientific community
C) effect on the scientific community
D) effect, on the scientific community

Affect is a verb, but here the underlined word should be a noun. So that eliminates both A) and B). Note that the preposition *to* in B) is a decoy – you don't actually need to worry about the preposition at all if you know that *affect* is wrong.

Both C) and D) correctly contain *effect*, but the comma before the preposition *on* makes D) incorrect. That leaves C), which is the answer.

The chart on the next page provides some commonly confused pairs of words, along with their definitions.

Commonly Confused Words

A lot – a large quantity	vs.	**Allot, v.** – to give out a specific amount.
Accept – to receive	vs.	**Except** – with the exception of
Advice, n. – counsel	vs.	**Advise, v.** – to give advice
Affect, v. – to have an impact on	vs.	**Effect, n.** – an impact
Allude – make a reference to	vs.	**Elude** – to evade, be unable to be caught
Allusion – a reference	vs.	**Illusion** – something not real
Cite – attribute	vs.	**Site** – location, **Sight** – the ability to see
Device, n. – a machine	vs.	**Devise, v.** – to come up with
Lay – Followed by a noun, e.g. *He lay the book down on the table.*	vs.	**Lie** – Not followed by a noun, e.g. *He lies down every evening after dinner.*
Perspective – point of view	vs.	**Prospective** – possible or potential, e.g. a prospective student
Precede – come before (pre = before)	vs.	**Proceed** – to move along
Than – used for comparisons	vs.	**Then** – next; used to indicate sequence of events
To – indicates direction, e.g. *she went to work.*	vs.	**Too** – also

In addition, **know the following**:

- Could, should, would, might **have**, NOT could, should, would, might **of**

- Suppose**d**, use**d** to, NOT suppose, use to

Other commonly confused words that could potentially be tested:

Access vs. Excess	Averse vs. Adverse	Imply vs. Infer
Addition vs. Edition	Collaborate vs. Corroborate	Ingenious vs. Ingenuous
Adopt vs. Adapt	Conscious vs. Conscience	Precedent vs. President
Afflict vs. Inflict	Council vs. Counsel	Principal vs. Principle
Anecdote vs. Antidote	Descent vs. Dissent	Respective vs. Respectful vs. Respected
Assent vs. Ascent	Elicit vs. Illicit	Simulate vs. Stimulate
Assure vs. Ensure	Emit vs. Omit	Their vs. They're vs. There

Gerunds vs. Infinitives

On the SAT, gerunds and infinitives may be incorrectly switched with one another.

Infinitive = TO form of a verb

Gerund = -ING form of a verb

Again, gerunds are considered correct in certain situations while infinitives are considered correct in other simply because of how the English language has evolved. There is no logical reason why one rather than the other is considered correct in a given situation, and you will have no choice but to rely on your ear.

Note that when replacing an infinitive with a gerund, you may need to insert a preposition as well (e.g. *to make* may need to be replaced by *for making*, not simply *making*).

Let's look at a test-style example:

Deactivated viruses form the basis of many vaccines known for their effectiveness **1** to prevent disease. As a result, people can be safely injected with genetic material from a virus without becoming ill themselves.

1

A) NO CHANGE
B) in preventing
C) with preventing
D) preventing

Because the idiomatic phrase is *effectiveness in making*, B) is correct.

Note when both a gerund and an infinitive are acceptable, you will not be asked to choose between them.

Correct: Soon, the members of the dance company will begin **to rehearse** for the performance.

Correct: Soon, the members of the dance company will begin **rehearsing** for the performance.

While I again do not advocate trying to memorize all the expressions that require gerunds vs. infinitives, it may be helpful to know some of the most common expressions. On the next page, I have therefore included a chart with common instances of idioms with both gerunds and infinitives.

Idioms with Gerund	Idioms with Infinitive
Accused of being	Agree to be
Accustomed/used to being	Allow to be
Admired for being	Appear/seem to be
Admit to being	Arrange to be
After being	Aspire to be
Avoid being	Attempt to be
Banned from being	Choose to be
Before being	Claim to be
(In)Capable of being	Consider to be
Consider being	Decide to be
Deny being	Decline to be
Describe being	Deserve to be
Discuss being	Encourage to be
Effective in/at being	Expect to be
Enjoy being	Fail to be
Famous for being	Have the ability to be
Imagine being	Inclined to be
In charge of being	Inspire (someone) to be
In the hope(s) of being	Intend to be
Insist on being	Known to be (+ noun)
Known as/for being	Manage to be
Mind being	Neglect to be
Postpone being	Offer to be
Praised for being	Prepare to be
Prevent from being	Promise to be
Regarded as being	Refuse to be
Report being	Reluctant to be
Resent being	Require to be
Risk being	Seek/strive to be
Seen as being	Shown to be
Stop being	Struggle to be
Succeed in/at being	Tend to be
Viewed as being	Threaten to be
Without being	Want/wish to be

Register

Register refers to how **formal** or **informal** an author's language is. Most SAT passages are written in a straightforward, moderately serious tone and are unlikely to contain extremely formal or casual language.

The type of language you use when talking to your friends is most likely very different from the language you use when writing a paper for school. In the former situation, you're likely to speak casually, using slang phrases such as *really cool* or *lots of stuff*.

If you were writing a paper, however, you'd be much more likely to say *extremely interesting* or *many different things*. (You could, of course, write *really cool* in an English paper, but chances are your teacher wouldn't be very, uh, cool with that.)

You also wouldn't – or at least shouldn't – write things like *a plethora of enthralling objects*. Used selectively and precisely, ten-dollar words are perfectly relevant and acceptable in certain situations, but if you're just using them to show off, chances are you'll make it a lot harder for readers to follow what you're actually saying. Unless you read non-stop and have a phenomenal vocabulary, there's also a pretty good chance you'll misuse some of them and will end up sounding pretty silly.

The point the SAT is trying to make is that you shouldn't go around using big words simply for the sake of doing so – the goal of writing is to communicate your ideas to your readers, and you should aim to be as clear and direct as possible.

As a result, answers to register questions will typically be either too casual and slangy or excessively formal, whereas correct answers will be somewhere in the middle.

For example:

During the Nimrod Expedition to the South Pole in 1907, Ernest Shackleton led a group of explorers on a voyage to the South Pole. Shackleton and the members of his expedition endured a great number of hardships, but when they finally arrived, they **1** saw a bunch of awesome stuff.

1
A) NO CHANGE
B) perceived myriad captivating visuals.
C) were greeted by many fascinating sights.
D) noticed some pretty interesting things.

A) and D) are both more casual and less specific than the rest of the passage, and B) is too formal, while C) correctly matches its neutral, moderately serious tone.

Like diction questions, register questions are difficult to study for because they require you to be familiar with linguistic conventions and to distinguish between informal, moderately formal, and extremely formal writing – skills that can only be acquired from consistent, long-term exposure to a variety of styles and types of writing.

Exercise: Diction, Idioms, and Register (answers p. 225)

1.   Mt. Kilimanjaro. Like the mountain, which is
[1] swept in clouds, the name Kilimanjaro is a mystery. It
might mean Mountain of Light, Mountain of Greatness, or
Mountain of Caravans. Locals refer to it simply as Kipo.
Not only is Mt. Kilmanjaro the highest mountain on the
African continent, but at nearly 20,000 feet, it is also the
tallest free-standing mountain in the world. Although Mt.
Kilmanjaro was once a volcano that erupted regularly, it
has [2] exhibited a dearth of activation for thousands of
years.

1

A) NO CHANGE
B) surfaced
C) cloaked
D) varnished

2

A) NO CHANGE
B) stayed kind of quiet
C) been pretty cool
D) lain dormant

2.   Just a few decades from now, the days of sitting in a
standard forward-facing seat may be air travel history. As
the health of the travel industry has improved, airlines have
shifted their focus [1] at the flying experience. A recent
wave of aircraft deliveries has [2] spurred demand for
seats, and manufacturers around the world are working
overtime in order to keep up. All this business has led to a
frenzy of innovation not seen in the skies since the jet-set
era of the 1960s. While airlines [3] seek impressing
passengers with futuristic amenities, design teams are hard
at work problem-solving for the needs of travelers in the
years to come.

1

A) NO CHANGE
B) on
C) in
D) to

2

A) NO CHANGE
B) exploded
C) excited
D) goaded

3

A) NO CHANGE
B) seek to impress
C) seek in impressing
D) seek for impressing

3. Some people call the durian "the king of fruit." Others can't stand to be within a mile of it. **1** <u>Elevated</u> throughout Southeast Asia, the durian resembles a cross between a porcupine and a pineapple, and it can weigh as much as seven pounds. Its most striking feature, however, is its odor. The flesh **2** <u>emits</u> a pungent smell, even when the husk is intact. While durian fans regard the fruit as having a pleasantly sweet fragrance, others find the aroma overpowering and even revolting. The smell can **3** <u>illicit reactions ranging from</u> deep appreciation to intense disgust: people claim that it is similar **4** <u>with</u> the smell of rotten onions, turpentine, or sewage. On the other hand, the durian's taste has been compared to that of custard or caramel. Some people even **5** <u>claim</u> to call it sublime.

1

A) NO CHANGE
B) Perpetuated
C) Activated
D) Cultivated

2

A) NO CHANGE
B) offers
C) omits
D) stimulates

3

A) NO CHANGE
B) illicit reactions ranging, from
C) elicit reactions that range from
D) elicit reactions ranging from:

4

A) NO CHANGE
B) from
C) to
D) in

5

The writer of this essay would like to call attention to the fact that praising the durian can have negative consequences. Which of the following best accomplishes that goal?

A) NO CHANGE
B) dare
C) want
D) intend

4. According to the United States Library of Congress, the majority of American feature films from the silent era are crumbling; fewer than 20 percent remain **1** intact. Meanwhile, half of the movies produced in the United States before 1950 have already been lost. The good news, however, is that both researchers and film buffs are working to **2** revive and preserve the movies that still exist. In addition, new archives are being established to house these films.

1

A) NO CHANGE
B) inert
C) entire
D) integrated

2

A) NO CHANGE
B) restore
C) regulate
D) relieve

5. The making of wooden sculptures has been extremely widely practiced. Many of the most important sculptures of China and Japan are in wood, as are the great majority of African sculptures. Wood is light, so it suitable **1** in masks and other sculptures intended to be carried, and can take very fine detail. It is also much easier to carve than stone. However, wood sculptures are **2** vulnerable to decay, insect damage, and fire. As a result, they **3** hang around much less often than sculptures made out of more durable materials such as stone and bronze. Wood thus forms an important hidden element in the art history of many cultures. For example, wooden totem poles have traditionally been displayed outdoors, but researchers have little idea of how the totem pole tradition **4** accumulated.

1

A) NO CHANGE
B) for
C) with
D) from

2

A) NO CHANGE
B) inferior
C) accessible
D) eligible

3

A) NO CHANGE
B) hang out
C) survive
D) remain extant

4

A) NO CHANGE
B) encroached.
C) developed.
D) amplified.

6. Sentences and Fragments

Before you read any further, try the exercise below. When you look at its title, you might roll your eyes and think, "Well *duh*, of course I know what a sentence is," but you might also be surprised – sometimes it isn't nearly as obvious as you might think.

Knowing how to distinguish between sentences and fragments is absolutely crucial to being able to correctly use the types of punctuation discussed in the following chapters. If you cannot tell when a statement is and is not a complete sentence, you will find it extremely difficult to know when to use periods, commas, semicolons, and colons.

Is it a Sentence?

For each statement below, circle "Sentence" if it can stand alone as an independent sentence and "Fragment" if it cannot. Once you have read the statement carefully, spend no more than a couple of seconds deciding on your answer. Try to complete the entire exercise in under two minutes.

1. Louis Armstrong was one of the greatest jazz musicians of the twentieth century.

    Sentence   Fragment

2. He was one of the greatest jazz musicians of the twentieth century.

    Sentence   Fragment

3. Louis Armstrong, who was one of the greatest jazz musicians of the twentieth century.

    Sentence   Fragment

4. Who was one of the greatest jazz musicians of the twentieth century.

    Sentence   Fragment

5. Louis Armstrong, who was one of the greatest jazz musicians of the twentieth century, was a vocalist as well as a trumpet player.

    Sentence   Fragment

6. Today, he is considered one of the greatest jazz musicians of the twentieth century.

    Sentence   Fragment

7. He is, however, considered one of the greatest jazz musicians of the twentieth century.

    Sentence   Fragment

8. He is now considered one of the greatest jazz musicians of the twentieth century.

    Sentence   Fragment

9. Because of his virtuosic trumpet skills, Louis Armstrong is considered one of the greatest jazz musicians of the twentieth century.

    Sentence   Fragment

10. Although he was one of the most virtuosic trumpet players of his generation.

    Sentence   Fragment

11. Many people considering Louis Armstrong the greatest jazz musician of all time.

    Sentence   Fragment

12. Many of them consider him the greatest jazz musician of all time.

    Sentence   Fragment

13. Many consider him the greatest jazz musician of all time.

    Sentence   Fragment

14. Many of whom consider him the greatest jazz musician of all time.

    Sentence   Fragment

15. Having shown an unusual gift for music early in his childhood, Louis Armstrong, who was born in New Orleans on August 4, 1901.

    Sentence   Fragment

16. Having shown an unusual gift for music early in his childhood, Louis Armstrong, who was born in New Orleans on August 4, 1901, went on to become one of the greatest jazz musicians of the twentieth century.

    Sentence   Fragment

17. Moreover, Armstrong, who spent much of his early life in poverty, went on to become one of the greatest jazz musicians of the twentieth century.

    Sentence   Fragment

18. Nicknamed "Satchmo," Louis Armstrong, who was born in New Orleans on August 4, 1901, grew up to become one of the greatest jazz musicians of the twentieth century and, perhaps, one of the greatest musicians of all time.

    Sentence   Fragment

68

You might be wondering how much that exercise really has to do with the SAT – after all, questions are always presented in the context of a passage, and those are just random sentences. But if you can't consistently recognize when any given statement is and is not a sentence, you won't know what sort of punctuation to use when separating them from other sentences. In fact, dealing with sentences like the ones above in context can often make things *harder*, not easier, because you have all sort of other information that can distract you.

For example, let's say you weren't sure about #13 (*Many consider him the greatest jazz musician of all time*). If you saw the following question, you might get stuck.

In the decades since Armstrong retired from performing, his fame has continued to grow. Jazz fans and scholars now unanimously consider him one of the greatest jazz musicians of the twentieth century, many consider him to be among the greatest jazz musicians of all time.

1

A) NO CHANGE
B) century many consider
C) century. Many consider
D) century; many considering

Unfortunately, there's simply no way to answer this question for sure without knowing whether you're dealing with one sentence or two. You might recognize that B) and D) sound awkward and eliminate them on that basis, but with A) and C), you're stuck. If you think the second clause is a sentence, you'll want to put in a period and choose C). But if it isn't a sentence, then the comma must be ok, and the answer must be A).

You stare at the question for a while, thinking it over. *Many consider him to be among the greatest jazz musicians of all time…* That sounds kind of weird. Besides, what sort of sentence would just say *many*, without explaining many of *what?* You can say *many people*, that's fine, but not just *many*. It just sounds wrong. You don't even know who the sentence is talking about. You can't start a sentence like that. Unless it's some kind of trick… But C) is just too weird. No way can that be the answer.

So you pick A).

But actually, the answer *is* C).

You've just fallen into a classic trap – you thought that because *Many consider him the greatest jazz musician of all time* didn't make sense out of context, it couldn't be a sentence. But guess what: **whether a statement is or is not a sentence has absolutely nothing to do with its meaning.**

Beginning on the next page, we're going to take a very simple sentence and look at the various elements that can get added onto it without changing the fact that it's a sentence. We're also going to look at some common types of fragments and how they get formed.

Building a Sentence

Every sentence must contain two things:

1) A **subject**

2) A **conjugated verb** that corresponds to the subject.

A sentence can contain only one word (*Go!* is a sentence because the subject, *you*, is implied) or consist of many complex clauses, but provided it contains a subject and a verb, it can be considered grammatically complete regardless of whether it makes sense outside of any context.

A. Simple Sentence

Sentence: The tomato grows.

This is known as a simple sentence because it contains only a subject (*the tomato*) and a verb (*grows*), which tells us what the subject does. Because it can stand on its own as a sentence, it can also be called an **independent clause**.

B. Prepositional Phrase

If we want to make our sentence a little longer, we can add a **prepositional phrase**. A prepositional phrase is a phrase that begins with a preposition, a **time** or **location** word that comes **before a noun**. Common prepositions include *in, to, with, from, for, at, by,* and *on*. (For a complete list, see p. 11.)

Sentence: The tomato grows **around the world.**

Sentences can contain many prepositional phrases, sometimes one after the other.

Sentence: The tomato grows **in many shapes and varieties in greenhouses around the world**.

A prepositional phrase can also be placed between the subject and the verb. When that is the case, the prepositional phrase starts at the preposition and ends right before the verb.

Sentence: The tomatoes **in the greenhouse** grow in many varieties and colors.

A prepositional phrase can also be placed at the **beginning** of a sentence:

Sentence: **In the greenhouse,** the tomatoes grow in many varieties and colors.

A prepositional phrase **cannot**, however, stand alone as a complete sentence:

Fragment: In the greenhouse

Fragment: In many shapes and varieties in greenhouses around the world

C. Pronoun as a Subject

Nouns can also be replaced by **pronouns** – words such as *it*, *she*, and *they*. In the above sentence, we can replace the subject, the singular noun *tomato*, with the singular pronoun *it* and rewrite the sentence this way:

Sentence: It grows.

This is actually still a sentence because it still has a subject (*it*) and a verb that corresponds to the subject (*grows*). The only difference between this version and the original version is that we don't know what the subject, *it*, is.

This is where a lot of people run into trouble. They assume that if a statement doesn't make sense out of context, then it can't be a sentence. But again, those two things are not necessarily related.

As is true for the original version, we can rewrite the longer versions of our sentence using pronouns:

Sentence: **It** grows around the world.

Sentence: **It** grows in many shapes and varieties in greenhouses around the world.

If we wanted to make the subject plural, we could replace it with the plural pronoun *they*.

Sentence: Tomatoes grow.

Sentence: **They** grow.

Sentence: **They** grow in many shapes and varieties in greenhouses around the world.

It and *they* are the most common **subject pronouns** (pronouns that can replace a noun as the subject of a sentence), but there are a number of other pronouns that can be used as subjects as well. Some of them can refer to people only, while others can refer to both people and things. The chart below lists some of the most common pronouns as well as what they can refer to.

People	Groups of People or Things
I You She/He/It We They	One Each Few Both Some Several Many Most Other(s) A number of The majority

"Group" Pronouns

One very common point of confusion often involves **"group" pronouns** such as *some, several, few, many,* and *others*. These pronouns can be used to begin clauses in two different ways, one of which creates an independent clause and the other of which creates a dependent clause.

Let's start with these two sentences:

Sentence: Many tomatoes are grown in greenhouses around the world.

Sentence: Most people believe that the tomato is a vegetable.

People generally don't have too much trouble recognizing that these are sentences. They have pretty clear subjects (*many tomatoes, most people*) and verbs (*are, believe*), and they make sense by themselves. The problem arises when we take away the nouns *tomatoes* and *people,* and start to deal with the pronouns on their own.

Pronoun (of them) = sentence

In this usage, the pronoun simply acts as a subject and is used to replace a noun. It is often followed by the phrase *of them,* but it can be used by itself as well.

Sentence: **Many (of them)** are grown in greenhouses around the world.

Sentence: **Most (of them)** believe that the tomato is a vegetable.

Taken out of any context, the above examples don't make much sense, nor do they provide any real information. Regardless of how odd you find these examples, however, **they are still sentences** because each one contains a subject (*many, most*) and a verb (*are, believe*) that corresponds to it.

Pronoun + "of which" or "of whom" = fragment

When an indefinite pronoun is followed by *of which* or *of whom,* it creates a **dependent clause,** which by definition cannot stand alone as a full sentence.

Fragment: **Many of which** are grown in greenhouses around the world.

Fragment: **Most of whom** believe that the tomato is a vegetable.

Which means:

Incorrect: The tomato is used by cooks around the **world, most of them** believe that it is a vegetable rather than a fruit.

Correct: The tomato is used by cooks around the **world. Most of them** believe that it is a vegetable rather than a fruit.

Correct: The tomato is used by cooks around the **world, most of whom** believe that it is a vegetable rather than a fruit.

D. Adverbs

Adverbs **modify verbs** and **clauses**. Most adverbs are created by adding –*ly* onto adjectives. For example:

Slow	→	Slowly
Current	→	Currently
Important	→	Importantly

A second type of adverb, however, does not end in –*ly*. Some of these adverbs are **adverbs of time**, which tell you **when** or **how often** something occurs. Others are **transitions** that indicate relationships between ideas.

Again	Meanwhile	Next	Often	Then
Consequently	Moreover	Never	Still	Today
Furthermore	Nevertheless	Now	Sometimes	Yesterday

Important: adverbs have <u>no grammatical effect whatsoever</u> on a sentence. A sentence to which an adverb is added will continue to be a sentence, regardless of where the adverb is placed.

Sentence: <u>Now</u>, the tomato grows in many shapes and varieties in greenhouses around the world.

Sentence: The tomato **currently** grows in many shapes and varieties in greenhouses around the world.

Sentence: The tomato grows in many shapes and varieties in greenhouses around the world **today**.

E. Non-Essential Clauses

Information can be inserted between the subject and the verb in the form of a **non-essential clause**:

Sentence: The tomato**, which is one of the most popular salad ingredients,** grows in many shapes and varieties in greenhouses around the world.

Non-essential clauses describe nouns (usually the subject). They often begin with **"w-words"** such as *who(se)*, *which*, and *where*, and they are usually **followed by a verb**. They can consist of lengthy phrases or single words:

Sentence: The tomato**, however,** grows in many varieties in greenhouses around the world.

These clauses or words are called "non-essential" because when they are removed, the sentence still makes grammatical sense.

Fragment: The tomato~~, which is one of the most popular salad ingredients,~~ and it grows in many shapes and varieties in greenhouses around the world.

Sentence: The tomato~~, which is one of the most popular salad ingredients,~~ grows in many shapes and varieties in greenhouses around the world.

Appositives

Although non-essential clauses frequently begin with "w-words" (also known as **relative pronouns**), they are not required to do so. You could also see a non-essential clause that looks like this:

> The tomato, **one of the most popular salad ingredients,** grows in many shapes and varieties in greenhouses around the world.

A non-essential clause that does not begin with a "w-word" is known as an **appositive**. Appositives can also appear as descriptions at the beginnings or ends of sentences, as in the examples below.

> Beginning: **One of the most popular salad ingredients,** the tomato grows in many shapes and varieties in greenhouses around the world.

> End: In greenhouses around the world grow many shapes and varieties of the tomato, **one of the most popular salad ingredients**.

A non-essential clause cannot stand alone as a complete sentence. As a **shortcut**, know that a statement (not a question) beginning with a "w-word" like *which, who(se),* or *where* will not be a complete sentence.*

> Fragment: Which is one of the most popular salad ingredients

> Fragment: Who think that the tomato is a vegetable

> Sentence: One of the most popular salad ingredients, the tomato grows in many shapes and varieties in greenhouses around the world.

In addition, a sentence cannot **stop** right after a non-essential clause. If it does, it is no longer a complete sentence but rather a fragment, and it should not have a period or semicolon placed after it.

> Fragment: The tomato, which is one of the most popular salad ingredients

> Fragment: The tomato, one of the most popular salad ingredients

Although the first version does contain the verb *is*, that verb does not correspond to the subject, *the tomato*. Instead, it corresponds to the pronoun *which* at the beginning of the new clause. In order to create a sentence, we must either remove *which* from the sentence, restoring the verb to the subject, *the tomato*:

> Sentence: The tomato **is** one of the most popular salad ingredients.

or we must place a main verb after the non-essential clause and complete the sentence with more information:

> Sentence: The tomato, (which is) one of the most popular salad ingredients, **grows** in many shapes and varieties in greenhouses around the world.

*The only exception to this rule involves cases in which a "w-word" functions as a subject, e.g. *Where the meeting would be located was a subject of intense debate.* Although this usage is rare, you should be aware that it is acceptable.

F. Participles and Gerunds

Every verb has two **participles**:

1) Present participle

The present participle is formed by adding *–ing* to the verb

Talk	→	talking
Paint	→	painting
Throw	→	throwing

2) Past participle

The past participle is usually formed by adding *–ed* or *–n* to the verb

Talk	→	talked
Paint	→	painted
Throw	→	thrown

A **participial phrase begins with a participle** and can be in either the **present** or the **past**. While participial phrases will occasionally involve past participles, the vast majority will involve present participles (*–ing* form).

Let's get back to our sentence – now we're going to add a participial phrase at the beginning:

> **Originating in South America**, the tomato, one of the most popular salad ingredients, grows in many shapes and varieties in greenhouses around the world.

To form the past tense, we can use the present participle *having* + past participle of the main verb (*originated*):

> **Having originated in South America**, the tomato, one of the most popular salad ingredients, grows in many shapes and varieties in greenhouses around the world.

We can also use the past participle of the verb *grow*.

> **Grown originally in South America**, the tomato, one of the most popular salad ingredients, is now produced in many shapes and varieties in greenhouses around the world.

Participial phrases can appear in the beginning (as in the above examples), middle, or end of a sentence.

Middle:	The tomato**, cultivated initially in South America during the first millennium B.C.,** is now grown in many shapes and varieties in greenhouses around the world.
End:	The tomato is now grown in greenhouses around the world, **having first been cultivated in South American in the first millennium B.C.**

Participial phrases **cannot** stand alone as sentences, however:

Fragment: Originating in South America

Fragment: Having first been cultivated in South America in the first millennium B.C.

Fragment: Grown originally in South America

Fragment: Grown originally in South America, the tomato, one of the most popular salad ingredients

Gerunds are identical in appearance to present participles: they are created by adding *–ing* to the verb. (At this point, you do not need to worry about the grammatical distinction between gerunds and participles.)

Important: a word that ends in *–ing* is <u>not a verb</u>. A phrase that contains only an *-ing* word and no conjugated verb is a **fragment**.

Fragment: Tomatoes **growing** in many shapes and varieties in greenhouses around the world.

In order to turn the fragment into a sentence, we must eliminate the gerund by **conjugating** the verb.

Sentence: Tomatoes **grow** in many shapes and varieties in greenhouses around the world.

Important: Answer choices that contain BEING (gerund of *to be*), are usually wrong. In addition to creating fragments, *being* often leads to wordy and awkward constructions. *Being* is also **irregular** – the conjugated forms of the verb look completely different from the gerund form. In order to easily correct errors with *being*, you should make sure to know all of the conjugated (third person) forms of the verb *to be*.

	Present	**Past**
Singular	Is	Was
Plural	Are	Were

Present

Fragment: Today, the tomato **being** grown in greenhouses around the world.
Sentence: Today, the tomato **is** grown in greenhouses around the world.

Past

Fragment: Originally, tomatoes **being** cultivated only in South America.
Sentence: Originally, tomatoes **were** cultivated only in South America.

G. Conjunctions

There are two main types of conjunctions:

1) **Coordinating conjunctions** join two independent clauses.

2) **Subordinating conjunctions** join an independent clause and a dependent clause.

Coordinating Conjunctions

There are seven coordinating conjunctions, collectively known by the acronym **FANBOYS**.

For, And, Nor, But, Or, Yet, So

The most common FANBOYS conjunctions are **AND & BUT**, so they should be your primary focus. We'll talk a lot more about FANBOYS in the next chapter, but for now, you need to know that a complete sentence **cannot** begin with a FANBOYS conjunction, regardless of how many clauses it contains.

In real life, this rule is sometimes broken for stylistic reasons, but if the SAT directly asks you to choose between a version of a sentence that begins with a FANBOYS conjunction and one that does not, the latter will almost certainly be correct.

Incorrect: And today, tomatoes are cultivated in greenhouses around the world.

Correct: Today, tomatoes are cultivated in greenhouses around the world.

Subordinating Conjunctions

Somewhere around third grade, you probably learned that you should never start a sentence with *because*. While this rule is taught with the best of intentions, it's unfortunately only half right. In reality, it's perfectly acceptable to begin a sentence with *because* – sometimes.

Here's the rule: *Because* is a type of conjunction known as a **subordinating conjunction**. A clause that begins with a subordinating conjunction **cannot stand on its own as a sentence** and is therefore **dependent**.

Sentence: Tomatoes are brightly colored and full of flavor.

Fragment: **Because** tomatoes are colorful and full of flavor.

If, however, we add that dependent clause to an independent clause (a complete sentence), it is perfectly acceptable to begin the whole sentence with the word *because*:

Sentence: **Because tomatoes are brightly colored and full of flavor,** they are one of the most popular salad ingredients.

Other common subordinating conjunctions include the following:

When	Although	Until	If
Whenever	Though	Whatever	Whether
Before	Despite	Because	Whereas
After	Unless	Since	While

Any of these words can be used to begin a sentence, as long as that sentence contains an independent clause after the dependent clause begun by the subordinating conjunction.

In the examples below, the incorrect first version of each sentence contains only a dependent clause, while the correct version that follows contains a dependent clause followed by an independent clause.

Incorrect: **Although** tomatoes have been cultivated since the first millennium B.C.

Correct: **Although** tomatoes have been cultivated since the first millennium B.C., they did not become popular in the United States until the mid-nineteenth century.

Incorrect: **When** tomatoes were first brought to Europe from South America.

Correct: **When** tomatoes were first brought to Europe from South America, many people believed that they were poisonous.

Incorrect: **Despite** the fact that many people believe that the tomato is a vegetable.

Correct: **Despite** the fact that many people believe that the tomato is a vegetable, it is actually a fruit.

Exercise: Sentences and Fragments (answers p. 225)

Label each of the following phrases as either a sentence or a fragment. Rewrite all fragments as sentences by changing, adding, or eliminating <u>one word only</u>.

1. Since 2009, physicists having been intrigued by possible evidence of dark matter in the center of the Milky Way galaxy.

2. Only around 25 percent of the variation in the human life span is influenced by genes, with the rest depending on other factors, including accidents, injuries, and exposure to substances that accelerate aging.

3. When they catch sight of their prey, and peregrine falcons drop into a steep, swift dive at more than 200 miles an hour.

4. After publishing her acclaimed novel *The God of Small Things*, author Arundhati Roy turning her attention to writing works of non-fiction and working as a political activist.

5. Each spring, students who gather from around the world for the FIRST Robotics Competition, an experience that can change lives.

6. The forestry industry has met and continuing to meet the growing change required to stay competitive within a rapidly transforming economy.

7. They enjoy national popularity, with the average person in the United States consuming over 25 pounds of them each year.

8. Findings from one recent study about meteorites suggesting that water has been present on Earth since the planet was formed.

9. Usually structured differently from autobiographies, but memoirs follow the development of an author's personality rather than the writing of his or her works.

10. Chicago's metropolitan area, sometimes called Chicagoland, which is home to 9.5 million people and is the third-largest in the United States.

11. She began adding elements of gospel music into her songs in early 1961, releasing her first gospel-influenced album later that year.

12. Because of increased financial regulations, there is now more demand than ever for qualified candidates to fill positions in fields such as accounting, bookkeeping, financial analysis, and auditing.

13. The Great Lakes being a major highway for transportation, migration, and trade as well as home to a large number of aquatic species.

14. Today, graduates of avionics programs – programs that teach students to install, maintain, and repair modern airplanes – have the opportunity to work for both airlines and government agencies.

15. Cities around the world once maintained extensive cable car systems, most of them have been replaced by more modern forms of transportation.

7. Combining & Separating Sentences: Periods, Semicolons, Commas, and Conjunctions

There are three ways to separate complete sentences (independent clauses) from one another:

1) Period

2) Semicolon

3) Comma + conjunction

A. Period = Semicolon

Periods and semicolons are **grammatically identical**: both are used to separate two complete sentences. The only difference is that the first letter after a period should be capitalized, while the first letter following a semicolon should be lower case, but you do not need to worry about this distinction for the SAT.

Correct:	Tomatoes are used in many different types of **cooking. Farmers** around the world grow them in both fields and greenhouses.
Correct:	Tomatoes are used in many different types of **cooking; farmers** around the world grow them in both fields and greenhouses.

"Strong" Transitions

Certain transitions (technically known as conjunctive adverbs) are considered "strong" enough to begin a sentence. The ones on which you are most likely to be tested include *however, therefore, thus, consequently, moreover,* and *nevertheless.*

When used to begin a clause, these transitions should never follow a comma.

Incorrect:	The tomato is one of the most popular salad **ingredients, however,** it is actually a fruit.
Correct:	The tomato is one of the most popular salad **ingredients; however,** it is actually a fruit.
Correct:	The tomato is one of the most popular salad **ingredients. However,** it is actually a fruit.

Very important: No matter where a sentence starts, make sure to read from the beginning all the way through to the period. Otherwise, you might not notice that there are two sentences rather than one. A phrase that makes sense at the end of one sentence might actually be the start of the following sentence.

Let's look at an example:

Since the early nineteenth century, doomsayers have gloomily predicted that increasing populations would exhaust their food **1** supplies in only a few decades, they claimed food shortages would result in catastrophic famines. Yet the world currently produces enough food to feed 10 billion people, and there are only 7 billion of us.

A) NO CHANGE
B) supplies. In only a few decades, they claimed,
C) supplies, in only a few decades, they claimed
D) supplies in only a few decades they claimed,

Because the underlined phrase initially seems to make sense where it is, most test-takers will immediately pick NO CHANGE and move on to the next question without a second thought. (If you did that, don't worry – it just means you're normal.) What they will not do is read all the way to the period at the end of the paragraph.

Take a moment now and just read the entire sentence in isolation:

Since the early nineteenth century, doomsayers have gloomily predicted that increasing populations would exhaust their food supplies in only a few decades they claimed food shortages would result in catastrophic famines.

Can you spot the problem now? If we leave the phrase *in only a few decades* without any punctuation, the sentence is way too long. In fact, there are two sentences, not one:

Sentence #1:   Since the early nineteenth century, doomsayers have gloomily predicted that increasing populations would exhaust their food supplies in only a few decades.

Sentence #2:   They claimed food shortages would result in catastrophic famines.

As discussed, two complete sentences must be divided by a period or a semicolon, not a comma (more about that in a little bit). The only answer that divides the sentence into two is B). When the underlined phrase is attached to the beginning of the second sentence rather than the end of the first, the sentences make perfect sense – even if it would never have occurred to you to divide the sentences there in the first place:

Sentence #1:   Since the early nineteenth century, doomsayers have gloomily predicted that increasing populations would exhaust their food supplies.

Sentence #2:   In just a few decades, they claimed, food shortages would result in catastrophic famines.

So B) is correct.

It is a good idea to check answer choices that contain periods <u>first</u>. When you are given the option to use a period, there is a good chance there are two sentences, and thus answers with periods are likely to be right.

B. Comma + FANBOYS

As discussed in the previous chapter, complete sentences can also be joined by comma + coordinating (FANBOYS) conjunction: **F**or, **A**nd, **N**or, **B**ut, **O**r, **Y**et, **S**o.

The two most commonly used FANBOYS conjunctions are *and* + *but*. They should be your primary concern, but you should be aware of the others as well.

When a FANBOYS conjunction is used without a comma to join two sentences, the result is a **run-on sentence**. Note that a sentence does not have to be long to be a run-on.

Run-on: Tomatoes are used in many different types of **cooking and they** are grown around the world in both fields and greenhouses.

Correct: Tomatoes are used in many different types of **cooking, and they** are grown around the world in both fields and greenhouses.

Likewise, a FANBOYS conjunction should never be used after a period or a semicolon.* Any answer choice that contains a FANBOYS conjunction after a period or semicolon can be automatically eliminated.

Incorrect: Tomatoes are used in many different types of **cooking. And they** are grown around the world in both fields and greenhouses.

Incorrect: Tomatoes are used in many different types of **cooking; and they are** grown around the world in both fields and greenhouses.

When the subject is the same in both clauses and is **not** repeated in the second clause, do **not** use a comma:

Incorrect: Tomatoes are used in many different types of **cooking, and are** grown around the world in both fields and greenhouses.

Correct: Tomatoes are used in many different types of **cooking and are** grown around the world in both fields and greenhouses.

Important: you can also think of the above rule this way. Since *comma* + *and* = period, simply replace *comma* + *and* with a period and see if you have two complete sentences:

Incorrect: Tomatoes are used in many different types of **cooking. Are** grown around the world in both fields and greenhouses.

Since the information after the period is not a sentence, no comma should be used before *and*.

*It is possible that you will see a sentence that begins with a FANBOYS conjunction for stylistic effect. In that case, you will *not* be tested on the conjunction, although you may be tested on another aspect of the sentence.

Very Important: Semicolon = Period = Comma + FANBOYS

Because a period, semicolon, and "comma + FANBOYS" are grammatically identical, you will never be asked to choose between them. When more than one of these constructions appear as answer choices, you can eliminate all of them since no question can have more than one right answer.

The most common FANBOYS conjunctions are AND & BUT.

For example:

If you grow tomatoes to sell at a **1** market, remember that it will take about 70 to 80 days from the time you set plants in the field until you can pick ripe tomatoes from them.

1

A) NO CHANGE
B) market, and remember
C) market. Remember
D) market; remember

Since B), C), and D) are grammatically equivalent, all of them can be eliminated. When you encounter this pattern, you should of course double-check the remaining answer to make sure that it makes sense, but in general, you can assume that it will be right. In this case, A) is correct because it places a comma between a dependent clause and an independent clause.

For example:

There are many good varieties of tomatoes available to **1** growers – each grower should try a few plants of several varieties to determine which performs best.

1

Which of the following would NOT be an acceptable alternative to the underlined portion?

A) growers. Each grower
B) growers, each grower
C) growers; each grower
D) growers, and

Solution: Don't get too concerned about the dash (we'll talk about those later). If you know that the period in A), the semicolon in C), and the *comma + and* in D) are the same, you can instantly eliminate all of those answers. Only B) remains. Since it forms a comma splice, it is NOT an acceptable alternative to the underlined portion of the sentence.

Comma Splices

When a comma alone is used to separate two independent clauses, the result is known as a **comma splice**. **Comma splices are always incorrect.**

Shortcut: commas splices are often signaled by the construction *comma + pronoun* (e.g. *it, he, she, they, I*). When you see this construction underlined, you should immediately be on your guard.

Comma Splice:	Tomatoes are used in many different types of **cooking, farmers** around the world grow many varieties of them in both fields and greenhouses.

Remember from the previous chapter that an independent clause can start with a pronoun (*it, they, she, many, some*), as in the first example below, or with an adverb, as in the second sentence below. Remember also that an independent clause does not need to make sense out of context to be a grammatically complete sentence.

Sentence:	Tomatoes are used in many different types of cooking.
Sentence:	**They** are grown in both fields and greenhouses around the world.
Comma Splice:	Tomatoes are used in many different types of **cooking, they** are grown in both fields and greenhouses around the world.
Sentence:	The ramparts of Old Quebec were constructed during the seventeenth century.
Sentence:	**Today**, they still stand in their original location.
Comma Splice:	The ramparts of Old Quebec were constructed during the seventeenth century, today they still stand in their original location.

Fixing Comma Splices

There are a number of ways to fix comma splices, and no method is inherently preferable to any other method. Some questions will require you to fix comma splices with a period, while others will require you to fix them using a semicolon, a comma + FANBOYS conjunction, or even another construction entirely. As a result, you should be comfortable fixing comma splices in a variety of ways.

Comma splice:	Tomatoes were originally small and **multicolored, they** are mostly large and red today.
Correct:	Tomatoes were originally small and **multicolored. They** are mostly large and red today.
Correct:	Tomatoes were originally small and **multicolored; they** are mostly large and red today.

We can also leave the comma and add either a FANBOYS conjunction or *semicolon + however.*

Correct:	Tomatoes were originally small and **multicolored, but/yet** they are mostly large and red today.
Correct:	Tomatoes were originally small and **multicolored; however,** they are mostly large and red today.

Another option is to turn one of the independent clauses into a **dependent clause**, often by adding a subordinating conjunction such as *because*, *while*, or *although* (for a more extensive list, see p. 78).

When a dependent clause is joined with an independent clause to form a complete sentence, then a comma alone can be placed between the clauses. In the sentences below, the dependent clause is in bold.

Correct: **While tomatoes were originally small and multicolored,** they are mostly large and red today.

Correct: **Originally small and multicolored,** tomatoes are mostly large and red today.

Correct: Tomatoes are one of the most popular cooking ingredients, **used in soups, stews, and salads in many different cuisines**.

Joining Sentences with Participles

Earlier we saw how answers ending in –ING are often incorrect because they either lead to wordy/awkward constructions or create fragments. When it comes to fixing comma splices, however, answers containing -ING are **often correct** because they create dependent clauses and thus prevent commas from separating two complete sentences.

For example:

Incorrect: Tomatoes were originally small and multicolored, **they became** large and red only during the nineteenth century.

Correct: Tomatoes were originally small and multicolored, **becoming** large and red only during the nineteenth century.

In the context of a passage, this type of answer could show up in several ways:

Choreographer and dancer Savion Glover aims to restore the African roots of **1** tap dance, he eliminates hand gestures to focus on the feet as the primary source of movement.

1

A) NO CHANGE
B) tap dance; and he eliminates
C) tap dance, consequently he eliminates
D) tap dance, eliminating

Or:

Choreographer and dancer Savion Glover aims to restore the African roots of **1** tap dance. He eliminates hand gestures to focus on the feet as the primary source of movement.

1

What is the best way of joining the sentences at the underlined portion?

A) tap dance, for this reason he eliminates
B) tap dance; and he eliminates
C) tap dance, consequently, he eliminates
D) tap dance, eliminating

Although the questions are asked in slightly different ways, both are testing fundamentally the same thing. In both cases, B) can be eliminated because the FANBOYS conjunction *and* should only follow a comma, never a semicolon. C) can be eliminated because *consequently* is not a FANBOYS conjunction and should only follow a semicolon or period.

In the first example A) can be eliminated because it contains a comma splice (note the tipoff: *comma + he*).

In the second example, A) can be eliminated because it contains a comma splice and is wordy.

In both examples, D) correctly joins the sentences using the participle *eliminating*. Notice that in both cases, the correct answer is the shortest answer. The SAT tests conciseness, and so shorter is usually better.

Exercise: Periods, Semicolons, and Commas + FANBOYS (answers p. 226)

1. Many common substances found in household items are dangerous to people's **1** health, however, experts insist that they are harmless in very small amounts. In addition, factors such as temperature or length of exposure may affect substances' potential to cause harm.

1

A) NO CHANGE
B) health; however, experts insist
C) health, but experts insisting
D) health, nevertheless, experts insist

2. Universities have historically offered a wide variety of continuing education **1** classes, some of them are now offered over the Internet as well as in traditional classrooms. In fact, the number of classes offered electronically has skyrocketed over the past decade and is expected to continue to increase.

1

A) NO CHANGE
B) classes, some of them that are
C) classes. Some of which are
D) classes, some of which are

3. Gwendolyn Knight painted throughout her **1** life, she did not start seriously exhibiting her work until relatively late. Her first gallery exhibit took place when she was in her fifties, and her first retrospective exhibit occurred when she was nearly eighty years old. Entitled "Never Too Late for Heaven," it took place at the Tacoma Museum of Art in Tacoma, Washington in 2003.

1

A) NO CHANGE
B) life, however, she did not start
C) life but did not start
D) life; but she did not start

4. African-American life during the 1920s was documented in great detail by the writers and artists of the Harlem Renaissance. Far less is known about it during the **1** Depression in the 1930s, the market for their work disappeared virtually overnight when the stock market crashed.

1

A) NO CHANGE
B) Depression in the 1930s the market
C) Depression. In the 1930s, the market
D) Depression, in the 1930s the market

5. The geologic instability known as the Pacific Ring of Fire has produced numerous **1** faults. They cause approximately 10,000 earthquakes annually. Roughly 90% of all earthquakes occur along the Ring of Fire, and the ring is dotted with three quarters of all active volcanoes on Earth.

1

Which of the following would NOT be an acceptable alternative to the underlined portion?

A) faults, they cause
B) faults; they cause
C) faults that cause
D) faults, which cause

6. The Mid-Autumn Festival, a popular harvest festival celebrated in Asia, dates back 3,000 years to China's Shang **1** Dynasty, it is traditionally held on the fifteenth day of the eighth month. The celebration is also known as the Mooncake Festival, Lantern Festival, and Children's Festival.

1

A) NO CHANGE
B) Dynasty, and it is
C) Dynasty. And it is
D) Dynasty it is

7. Frank Lloyd Wright (June 8, 1867 – April 9, 1959) was many **1** things in addition to being an architect who designed more than 1,000 buildings, he was also an interior designer and writer. His architectural philosophy held that buildings should be designed in harmony with people and their surrounding environments. This idea, which became known as organic architecture, was best exemplified by his design for the Fallingwater home (1935): a house built into the side of a hill and balanced over a waterfall. Used as Wright's summer **2** residence, and it is considered a masterpiece of American architecture.

1

A) NO CHANGE
B) things, in addition to being an architect
C) things. In addition to being an architect
D) things in addition to being an architect,

2

A) NO CHANGE
B) residence. It is considered
C) residence; it is considered
D) residence, it is considered

8. When it came to food, a pirate's life could be **1** difficult living at sea, far from major seaports, meant that hunger was a normal part of daily living. The absence of warm, dry storage spaces put normal pantry staples such as flour and dried beans at a high risk of mold. Climate also presented preservation **2** problems, keeping fresh fruits and meats was next to impossible in warmer waters. Moreover, fresh water was difficult to keep during long sea voyages because it could easily be contaminated by algae and microbes.

1

A) NO CHANGE
B) difficult. Living at sea
C) difficult, living at sea,
D) difficult, living at sea

2

A) NO CHANGE
B) problems keeping fresh fruits
C) problems, keeping fresh fruits,
D) problems; keeping fresh fruits

9. Norman Rockwell's paintings depicting everyday life appealed to a vast **1** audience in the 1950s, Rockwell became one of the most popular artists in the United States. Rockwell is most famous for the cover illustrations he created for *The Saturday Evening* **2** *Post*, he published hundreds of images over the course of four decades.

1

A) NO CHANGE
B) audience, in the 1950s,
C) audience in the 1950s
D) audience. In the 1950s,

2

A) NO CHANGE
B) *Post*; publishing
C) Post, having published
D) *Post* he published

8. Transitions

In the previous chapter, we looked at various ways of joining sentences from a grammatical standpoint. Now, however, we're going to look at joining sentences from a meaning standpoint. On the SAT, you will be responsible not only for recognizing when a given transition (aka conjunction) can be used grammatically to join two parts of a sentence, but also whether that transition creates a logical relationship between them.

In practice, this means that you are likely to encounter questions with more than one answer that is grammatically correct. When that is the case, you must consider the meaning of the sentence as well as the grammar in order to select the option that makes the most sense in context.

Let's start by looking at an example:

Architects don't often become as famous as other types of artists, such as painters, so their work can have a greater effect in the long term. Architecture is essentially the art we live in. Buildings shelter and protect us throughout our lives for home, work, and play. Even if we've never stood in any of the buildings designed by master architects, we've probably been in plenty of buildings that incorporate their influences.

1

A) NO CHANGE
B) painters, however, their work can have
C) painters, and their work can have
D) painters, but their work can have

When we look at the look at the various answer choices, we can notice that they contain different types of transitions, indicating different types of relationship between the two parts of the sentence. In addition, A), C), and D) are all grammatically acceptable, using comma + FANBOYS to join two complete sentences.

This answer choice pattern tells us that the question isn't just testing grammar – it's also testing meaning. So that means we need to stop and think about the **relationship** between the two statements.

The first statement indicates that architects *don't often become as famous other types of artists;* the second indicates that architects' work has a *greater effect.* Those are contrasting ideas, so a transition indicating that a contrast is necessary.

Now we need to think about punctuation. *However* must come after a period or semicolon at the start of a clause, so B) can be eliminated. In D), the FANBOYS conjunction *but* correctly follows a comma, so D) is correct.

Types of Transitions

Continuers indicate that two sentences are expressing similar ideas.

Correct: The tomato is one of the most popular salad ingredients. **Moreover**, it is used in many hot dishes, including soups and stews.

Correct: Tomatoes are among the oldest crops grown in the New World. **In fact**, they were cultivated as far back as 500 B.C.

Contradictors indicate that two sentences are expressing different ideas.

Correct: Martha Graham retired from dancing when she was 70 years old; **however,** she continued to choreograph for many years afterward.

Cause and Effect words indicate that one action is the **result** of another.

Correct: The tomato is one of the most popular salad ingredients, **so** many people believe mistakenly believe that it is a vegetable.

The chart below includes some common transitions. For definitions, see the glossary at the end of the chapter.

Continuers	Contradictors	Cause and Effect
Add Information And Also Furthermore Moreover In addition **Give Example** For instance For example **Define** That is **Emphasize** In fact Indeed **Compare** Similarly Likewise **Sequence of Events** Then Next Finally	But Yet However (Al)though While Whereas Despite/In spite of Still Even so Nevertheless Meanwhile Otherwise Instead **Contrast** In contrast On the contrary On the other hand	So Thus Therefore Consequently As a result Because Since Accordingly As such

How to Work Through Transition Questions

Important: As soon as you encounter a transition question, pick up your pencil and physically cross out the transition in the original sentence. Do not just draw a line in your imagination. If you need to erase the line later to look at the original version… well, that's why you work in pencil.

The simple fact that a particular transition is already there in the passage means that you are likely to be unconsciously biased toward it. Even if it doesn't really make sense, you're more likely to try to see a relationship that isn't there. The problem, however, is that **transition questions are about what words mean, not how they sound. A word that sounds completely fine to you might in reality create a completely illogical relationship.** Crossing out the transition makes it easier for you to focus on what each sentence is saying. If you forget this step, sooner or later you are likely to get confused and miss a question you could have gotten right.

Once you have crossed out the transition, you must **reread the entire sentence or sentences**. Then, determine whether the parts before and after the transition express **similar** or **different ideas**. If they express similar ideas, you can automatically eliminate any contradictor, e.g. *but* or *however*. If they express different ideas, you can automatically eliminate any continuer, e.g. *and* or *therefore*.

Important: If two or more answers contain synonyms and are grammatically identical, those answers can be automatically eliminated because no question can have more than one right answer. So, for example, if choice A) is *but* and choice C) is *yet*, you can immediately eliminate both.

Let's look at an example:

Conditions in the interior of Antarctica are inhospitable to many forms of life: sub-zero temperatures, high winds, and extreme dryness make it impossible for most animals to survive. The Antarctic Peninsula and the surrounding islands have milder temperatures and liquid water, **1** whereas more animals can thrive there.

> **1**
> A) NO CHANGE
> B) when
> C) since
> D) so

The first thing we need to do is cross out the underlined transition so that we don't get distracted by it:

> **The Antarctic Peninsula and the surrounding islands have milder temperatures and liquid water, ~~whereas~~ more animals can thrive there.**

Now, we need to consider what each half of the sentence is saying, looking at the paragraph for context:

1) Weather conditions on the Antarctic Peninsula are milder than those in the Antarctic interior.

2) More animals can thrive on the Antarctic Peninsula.

The second statement is the **result** of the first. The only transition that correctly conveys that cause/effect relationship is *so*. *Since* would indicate that the first statement resulted from the second. The answer is thus D).

Sometimes you may need to supply a transition at the beginning of the sentence. In such cases, the process is the same: cross out the transition (if there is one), determine whether the two clauses express similar or different ideas, and find the answer that expresses the correct logical relationship.

Important: When the beginning of a sentence is underlined, make sure you read all way through to the period. Otherwise, you may not notice a comma splice or illogical relationship.

For example:

Conditions in the interior of Antarctica are inhospitable to many forms of life: sub-zero temperatures, high winds, and extreme dryness make it impossible for most animals to survive. The Antarctic Peninsula and the surrounding islands have milder temperatures and liquid water, more animals can thrive there.

A) NO CHANGE
B) Because the Antarctic Peninsula
C) Although the Antarctic Peninsula
D) Whereas the Antarctic Peninsula

The beginning of the sentence might seem fine, but if read all the way through, you'll notice that there's actually a comma splice. In addition, the presence of different types of transitions should clue you in to the fact that this is a question about transitions. Because the second statement is the **result** of the first, (B) is the only option. You could also recognize that C) and D) are synonyms and can thus be eliminated immediately.

You could also be asked to revise part of a sentence so that it corresponds logically to a transition.

For example:

Conditions in the interior of Antarctica are inhospitable to many forms of life: sub-zero temperatures, high winds, and extreme dryness make it impossible for most animals to survive. The Antarctic Peninsula and the surrounding islands have milder temperatures and liquid water, but more animals can thrive there.

A) NO CHANGE
B) they were discovered in the 1840s.
C) they lie close to the Antarctic continent.
D) most of them are still covered in ice.

The first part of the sentence talks about the relatively *mild* climate of the Antarctic Peninsula, and the contradictor *but* indicates that what follows must convey the **opposite** idea. D) fulfills that requirement because of the phrase *still covered in ice*. The other options do not create the correct contrast.

Still other transition questions will give you two sentences and ask you to identify the best way to combine them. For example, the question above could also be asked this way:

Healthy arctic marine mammals have a thick layer of fat beneath the **1** skin. Tropical marine mammals have very few fat reserves in their bodies. As a result, many of them dwell primarily in the warm waters that surround coral reefs.

1

What is the best way to join the sentences at the underlined portion?

A) skin, however tropical marine mammals have
B) skin, so tropical marine mammals have
C) skin, but tropical mammals having
D) skin, whereas tropical marine mammals have

Again, the two sentences convey opposite ideas, so a contradictor is required. A) uses the contradictor *however* but incorrectly places a comma rather than a semicolon before it. B) correctly places a comma before a FANBOYS conjunction, but *so* indicates a cause-and-effect relationship.

C) correctly uses the contradictor *but* after a comma, but the gerund *having* turns the second clause into a fragment. That leaves D), which correctly uses the contradictor *whereas* to convey the contrasting relationship between the two parts of the sentence.

Double Transitions

Only one transition should be used to indicate the relationship between two clauses.

Incorrect: **Although** the tomato is actually a fruit, **but** many people believe that it is a vegetable.

Correct: **Although** the tomato is actually a fruit, many people believe that it is a vegetable.

Correct: The tomato is actually a fruit, **but** many people believe that it is a vegetable.

If two different types of transitions (e.g. a continuer and a contradictor) are used, you must not only eliminate one of the transitions but also recognize which one creates a logical meaning between the parts of the sentence.

Incorrect: **Although** the tomato is actually a fruit, **and** many people believe that it is a vegetable.

Incorrect: The tomato is actually a fruit, **and** many people believe that it is a vegetable.

Correct: **Although** the tomato is actually a fruit, many people believe that it is a vegetable.

Transitions Between Sentences

Although questions testing transitions between sentences require the same skills as those testing transitions within a sentence, they are more challenging because you are responsible for backing up and reading the previous sentence in order to determine the correct relationship. They also involve a wider variety of transitions.

Let's reconsider this passage from a slightly different angle:

Conditions in the interior of Antarctica are inhospitable to many forms of life: sub-zero temperatures, high winds, and extreme dryness make it impossible for most animals to survive. Therefore, the Antarctic Peninsula and its surrounding islands have milder temperatures and liquid water, allowing more animals to thrive there.

A) NO CHANGE
B) In contrast,
C) In fact,
D) Despite

The fact that the first word is an underlined transition indicates that you must back up and consider the relationship between this sentence and the previous sentence. First, though, you need to forget about the existing transition and consider what the two sentences are saying independently.

1) Antarctica has a very extreme climate, so animals can't live there.

2) The Antarctic Peninsula and its islands have a milder climate, so animals can live there.

Clearly these two sentences express opposite ideas, so we're looking for a transition indicating that contrast.

A) is out because *therefore* is used to indicate a result. C) is out because *in fact* is a continuer, and D) is out because *despite* is ungrammatical when it is plugged into the sentence. B) is correct because *in contrast* clearly indicates that an opposing idea is being introduced.

In the question we just looked at, the placement of the transition at the beginning of the sentence made it pretty clear that you needed to back up and read the previous sentence. Sometimes, however, the transition may appear in the middle of a sentence. **Although these questions may initially appear to only test one sentence, they are actually testing your ability to identify the relationship between <u>two</u> sentences: the sentence in question and the sentence <u>before</u> it.**

Compare these two versions of the following sentence:

Version #1: **Therefore**, tropical marine mammals have very few fat reserves in their bodies.

Version #2: Tropical marine mammals, **therefore**, have very few fat reserves in their bodies.

These two sentences have **exactly the same meaning**. The only difference is that the first version places the transition at the beginning of the sentence, whereas the second version places the transition in the middle of the sentence. In both cases, the purpose of the transition is to connect the sentence to the previous sentence. It is necessary to back up and read the previous sentence in order to determine the relationship between them.

Let's look at how that works in context:

Healthy arctic marine mammals have a thick layer of fat beneath the skin. Tropical marine mammals, therefore, have very few fat reserves in their bodies. As a result, many of them dwell primarily in the warm waters that surround coral reefs.

1
A) NO CHANGE
B) likewise
C) however
D) for example

Let's start by eliminating the transition and considering the information before and after the transition separately. What we get is something very different from what we got in the previous question.

1) Tropical marine mammals

2) have very few fat reserves in their bodies

What should immediately jump out here is that there is no logical relationship between these two statements; they simply make no sense when read separately.

So why would we want to put a transition between them in the first place? Because the transition clarifies the relationship between that sentence and the previous one. Now we're going to back up and consider those two sentences, again **without the transition**.

1) Healthy arctic marine mammals have a thick layer of fat beneath the skin.

2) Tropical marine mammals, ~~therefore,~~ have very few fat reserves in their bodies.

The two sentences express contrasting ideas: a *thick layer* of fat vs. *very few* fat reserves. So a contradictor is required. *Therefore*, *likewise*, and *for example* are not contradictors, leaving C) as the only option.

It is also possible that no transition will be required. The presence of an answer choice without a transition means that a transition may be unnecessary. In such cases, you should **check that option first**.

Let's look at an example:

Conditions in the interior of Antarctica are inhospitable to many forms of life. Therefore, sub-zero temperatures, high winds, and extreme dryness make it impossible for most animals to survive.

1
A) NO CHANGE
B) On the other hand, sub-zero temperatures
C) Nevertheless, sub-zero temperatures
D) Sub-zero temperatures

Since D) contains no transition, it is especially important that we cross out *therefore* in the original version and examine the two statements without any transition.

1) Conditions in the interior of Antarctica are inhospitable to many forms of life.

2) Subzero temperatures, high winds, and extreme dryness make survival impossible for most animals.

The two sentences discuss similar ideas, but the second sentence simply provides more detailed information to support the first sentence. It is not a **result** of the first sentence. So A) is out. B) and C) can be eliminated because *on the other hand* and *nevertheless* are reversers, and the two sentences express similar ideas. In fact, no transition is necessary here at all. So the answer is D).

Glossary of Transitions

Accordingly
Consequently
— Therefore, as a result

Correct: Dolphins are social animals. **Consequently**, they live in pods of up to a dozen animals.

Correct: Dolphins are social animals. **Accordingly**, they live in pods of up to a dozen animals.

Furthermore
Moreover
— In addition

Correct: Dolphins are social animals. **Furthermore**, they are highly intelligent.

Correct: Dolphins are social animals. **Moreover**, they are highly intelligent.

In fact
Indeed
— Used to emphasize a preceding statement

Correct: Dolphins are highly intelligent. **In fact**, they are one of the smartest mammals.

Correct: Dolphins are highly intelligent. **Indeed**, they are one of the smartest mammals.

Even so
Still
Nevertheless
— Despite this

Correct: Dolphins are descended from land-dwelling animals. **Nevertheless**, they can only survive in water.

Correct: Dolphins are descended from land-dwelling animals. **Even so**, they can only survive in water.

Correct: Dolphins are descended from land-dwelling animals. **Still**, they can only survive in water.

While
Whereas
} Although, but

> Correct: **While** dolphins are commonly thought of as fish, they are actually mammals.

> Correct: A salmon is a type of fish, **whereas** a dolphin is a type of mammal.

As such – *As a + noun*

As such is one of the trickier transitions, and it's best explained with an example.

Let's start with this sentence:

> Correct: Dolphins are social animals, and because they are social animals, they live in pods of up to a dozen animals.

We can also write the sentence this way:

> Correct: Dolphins are social animals, and as social animals, they live in pods of up to a dozen animals.

The sentence is fine as is, but it's a little wordy because the words *social animals* are repeated. To eliminate the repetition, we can replace the phrase *as social animals* with *as such*.

> Correct: Dolphins are social animals, and as such, they live in pods of up to a dozen animals.

Likewise – Similarly

> Correct: As mammals, dolphins are warm blooded. **Likewise**, they nourish their young with milk.

Meanwhile – At the same time

> Correct: Many people think of dolphins as fish. **Meanwhile**, they ignore scientific research, which long ago established that dolphins are actually mammals.

That is – In other words

That is indicates that the writer is providing a definition or explanation/clarification. It often follows a dash.

> Correct: Dolphins are mammals – **that is**, they are warm blooded and nourish their young with milk.

Transition Exercise I (answers p. 226)

From the three options, circle the one that correctly indicates the logical relationship between each set of statements. Then, choose the transition that best connects the statements. Remember that the placement of the transition does not affect the relationship between the statements.

1. In the past, coffees were blended to suit a homogenous popular taste, _____ many different coffee flavors are now being produced.

Step 1: Continue   Contrast   Cause-and-Effect

Step 2:
    A) for
    B) but
    C) and
    D) because

2. _____ researchers are unable to drill into the Earth's core, its chemical composition remains a mystery.

Step 1: Continue   Contrast   Cause-and-Effect

Step 2:
    A) While
    B) Because
    C) Despite
    D) Although

3. The Taj Mahal is regarded as one of the eight wonders of the world. _____, some people believe that its architectural beauty has never been surpassed.

Step 1: Continue   Contrast   Cause-and-Effect

Step 2:
    A) On the other hand
    B) For example
    C) Indeed
    D) However

4. Music serves no obvious purpose. It has, _____, played a role in every known civilization on earth.

Step 1: Continue   Contrast   Cause-and-Effect

Step 2:
    A) however
    B) therefore
    C) in fact
    D) moreover

5. _____ modern technology offers remarkable opportunities for self-expression and communication, it also offers many possibilities for distraction.

Step 1: Continue   Contrast   Cause-and-Effect

Step 2:

    A) Because
    B) Despite
    C) Since
    D) While

6. In order to save an endangered species, preservationists must study it in detail. _____, scientific information about some endangered animals is scarce.

Step 1: Continue   Contrast   Cause-and-Effect

Step 2:

    A) However
    B) Therefore
    C) In fact
    D) Likewise

7. Pyramids are most commonly associated with ancient Egypt. _____, many people are surprised to learn that the Nubians, who lived in modern-day Sudan, constructed a far greater number of pyramids than the Egyptians did.

Step 1: Continue   Contrast   Cause-and-Effect

Step 2:

    A) Consequently
    B) In fact
    C) In addition
    D) For example

8. _____ modern chemistry keeps insects from ravaging crops, removes stains, and saves lives, constant exposure to chemicals is taking a toll on many people's health.

Step 1: Continue   Contrast   Cause-and-Effect

Step 2:

    A) Because
    B) Although
    C) Despite
    D) Since

9. In the Middle Ages, fairs often attracted large crowds and led to rioting. _____, authorities were reluctant to grant permission for fairs to be held.

Step 1: Continue   Contrast   Cause-and-Effect

Step 2:

    A) In fact
    B) Nevertheless
    C) Therefore
    D) Furthermore

10. Skilled managers are in high demand. _____, management professionals with the right experience and credentials are some of the most sought-after professionals in the world.

Step 1: Continue   Contrast   Cause-and-Effect

Step 2:

    A) Nevertheless
    B) Indeed
    C) Besides
    D) However

Transition Exercise II (answers p. 226)

1. On the screen, three people walk in a garden. The image is black-and-white, and the figures move in a jerky way. After a few seconds, they disappear. Filmed in 1888, *Roundbay Garden Scene* seems primitive in comparison to the slick, sophisticated Hollywood films of today. **1** Therefore, it is the oldest surviving film in existence.

1
A) NO CHANGE
B) Therefore
C) In fact
D) Instead

2. In 1959, Project Mercury became the first human spaceflight program led by the National Aeronautics and Space Administration (NASA). The project was aimed at putting an American into orbit before the Soviet Union could accomplish that goal. **1** However, the program ran until 1963 and involved seven astronauts flying six solo trips.

1
A) NO CHANGE
B) In addition, the program
C) Nevertheless, the program
D) The program

3. Chimpanzees and bonobo monkeys resemble each other physically, but their social behaviors differ greatly. Chimpanzees have an omnivorous diet, a troop hunting culture, and complex social relationships. Bonobo monkeys, **1** on the other hand, eat mostly fruit, rarely hunt, and do not have a strict social hierarchy.

1
A) NO CHANGE
B) therefore
C) moreover
D) consequently

4. A gamelan is a traditional musical ensemble from Indonesia, typically from the islands of Java and Bali. Gamelans typically feature a variety of instruments, including xylophones, gongs, and bamboo flutes. Some ensembles also include vocalists. **1** Nevertheless, gamelan music is an integral part of Indonesian culture.

1
A) NO CHANGE
B) Thus, gamelan music
C) For example, gamelan music
D) Gamelan music

5. Many people fear or dislike spiders, but spiders are mostly beneficial because they prey on insects and other pests. The spiders commonly seen out in the open during the day are usually harmless and unlikely to bite people. **1** For instance, poisonous spiders generally spend most of their time in woodpiles, corners, or boxes and rarely come into contact with human beings.

1

A) NO CHANGE
B) In contrast
C) Therefore
D) Nevertheless

6. **1** Although computerized fingerprint scanners have been a staple of spy movies for decades, but until recently, they were rarely found in the real world. Over the last few years, **2** therefore, scanners have become common in many different locations, including police stations, high-security buildings, and even computer keyboards. The price of a scanner has also decreased significantly. **3** However, it is now possible to purchase a USB fingerprint scanner for under $100.

1

A) NO CHANGE
B) While computerized
C) Since computerized
D) Computerized

2

A) NO CHANGE
B) in fact
C) however
D) for example

3

A) NO CHANGE
B) Next
C) In fact
D) Likewise

7. Executive editors play one of the most important roles at a newspaper or magazine: they oversee assistant editors and generally have the final say about which stories are published. **1** Meanwhile, if a writer covering local news proposed a piece about the candidates in a city election, the executive editor would decide whether to approve the article and determine what angle the writer should take. Executive editors also plan budgets and negotiate contracts

1

A) NO CHANGE
B) For instance
C) Similarly
D) Instead

with freelance writers, sometimes called "stringers." Although many executive editors work for newspaper publishers, some also **2** work for television stations or advertising firms.

2
A) NO CHANGE
B) work extremely long hours.
C) find their jobs challenging.
D) collaborate with their colleagues.

8. Straw has been used as a building material for centuries. Contrary to popular belief, it is not easily destroyed. **1** In fact, it can actually be quite hardy. In the nineteenth century, settlers in the Nebraska Sandhills used straw to build houses when wood and clay were scarce; some of the structures are still standing today. Builders are hoping such longevity is a trend, but new homes that use straw do have some updates. In the updated structures, **2** however, the straw is pressed into panels and framed with timber for reinforcement. The panels are then covered in brick so that no straw remains exposed to the elements.

1
A) NO CHANGE
B) Therefore
C) For example
D) However

2
A) NO CHANGE
B) meanwhile
C) for example
D) moreover

9. The Silk Road acquired its name from the lucrative trade in Chinese silk carried out along its 4,000 miles, beginning during the Han dynasty (206 BC – 220 AD). The Chinese took great interest in the safety of their **1** goods, and they extended the Great Wall of China to ensure the protection of their trade routes.

Trade on the Silk Road was a significant factor in the development of China, India, Persia, Europe, and Arabia, opening long-distance political and economic interactions. **2** Because silk was certainly the major trade item from China, numerous other types of goods also traveled along the Silk Routes. The Silk Road facilitated cultural trade among many different cultures.

1
A) NO CHANGE
B) goods, they
C) goods, but they
D) goods, therefore they

2
A) NO CHANGE
B) While silk
C) Despite Silk
D) Silk

10. By turning the camera on herself, Cindy Sherman established her reputation as one of the most respected photographers of the late twentieth century. **1** Despite the majority of her photographs are pictures of herself, these photographs are most definitely not self-portraits. Rather, Sherman uses herself as a vehicle for commentary on a variety of issues of the modern world: the role of the woman, the role of the artist, and many more. It is through these ambiguous and eclectic photographs that Sherman has developed a distinct signature style. **2** Moreover, she has raised challenging and important questions about the role and representation of women in society, the media and the nature of the creation of art.

1
A) NO CHANGE
B) For
C) Since
D) Although

2
A) NO CHANGE
B) Therefore
C) However
D) Consequently

9. Non-Essential and Essential Clauses

As discussed earlier, non-essential words and phrases can be removed from sentences without affecting their essential meaning. When these words or phrases are eliminated, the sentence still makes grammatical sense.

For example:

> Correct: The Tower of London, **which was begun by William the Conqueror in 1078,** is one of the largest and most imposing fortifications in England.

The sentence contains a clause that is surrounded by commas and that begins with the word *which*. If we cross out that clause, we are left with:

> Correct: The Tower of London…is one of the largest and most imposing fortifications in England.

The sentence that remains makes complete sense on its own.

Non-essential clauses must always be surrounded by commas; if one or both of the commas are removed, the sentence is incorrect.

> Incorrect: The Tower of London, **which was begun by William the Conqueror in 1078** is one of the largest and most imposing fortifications in England.

> Incorrect: The Tower of London **which was begun by William the Conqueror in 1078,** is one of the largest and most imposing fortifications in England.

> Incorrect: The Tower of London **which was begun by William the Conqueror in 1078** is one of the largest and most imposing fortifications in England.

In order to fix the sentence, you must recognize that it will still make sense if the clause *which was begun by William the Conqueror in 1078* is removed. Commas must therefore be added around that clause.

> Correct: The Tower of London, **which was begun by William the Conqueror in 1078,** is one of the largest and most imposing fortifications in England.

Sometimes non-essential clauses can be very long. In such cases, you must make sure to look all the way back to the beginning of the sentence in order to identify the start of the non-essential clause. In such cases, you will need to cross out a lot of information to test out whether a non-essential clause is present.

To reiterate: if a sentence still makes sense when a clause is crossed out, two commas must be placed around that clause.

You should also make sure to look for key words such as *which*, *who(se)*, and *where*, which often – but not always – signal the start of a non-essential clause. In addition, you should think carefully about where in the sentence it is logical for the clause to begin and end. This is particularly important when only the end of the non-essential clause is underlined.

For example:

London, which was originally built by the Romans along the banks of the Thames more than two thousand years **1** ago contains some extremely modern neighborhoods.

A) NO CHANGE
B) ago; contains
C) ago, containing
D) ago, contains

If you focus only on the underlined portion of the sentence, you're likely to get confused. You might be able to sense that a comma isn't really necessary there, but you won't know quite why. The key is to go back to the beginning of the sentence and recognize that it contains a non-essential clause, as signaled by the word *which*.

Important: Do not "cross out" information mentally. Take your pencil and draw a line; you can always erase it later. If you don't physically cross out the words, you're likely to miss something important.

Crossed Out:

London, ~~which was originally built by the Romans along the banks of the Thames more than two thousand years ago~~ **1** contains some extremely modern neighborhoods.

1

A) NO CHANGE
B) ago; contains
C) ago, containing
D) ago, contains

Logically, the non-essential clause ends at *ago*. When the clause from *which* to *ago* is crossed out, the sentence that remains makes sense. It is thus necessary to insert a comma after *ago*, making D) correct.

Crossing out non-essential clauses can also help you identify fragments. When you are confronted with a exceptionally long statement, you can easily get "lost" and end up unable to determine whether it is a sentence.

For example:

London, ~~which was originally built by the Romans along the banks of the Thames more than two thousand years ago~~ and contains some extremely modern neighborhoods.

1

A) NO CHANGE
B) ago, and which contains
C) ago, containing
D) ago, contains

With the non-essential clause removed, it is much clearer that A), B), and C) will all produce fragments when plugged into the sentence. Only D) correctly places a verb immediately after the comma, supplying a main verb that corresponds to the subject.

Two Commas vs. Semicolon/Period

Many of the transition words and phrases that are used to **begin** clauses can also be used non-essentially **within** clauses. Some common examples include *however, therefore, in fact, indeed, for example,* and *moreover.* (We actually saw some of these transitions used non-essentially in the previous chapter.)

As discussed earlier, these transitions should follow a period or semicolon when they are used to begin a clause. In the following sentence, for example, the transition *however* is used to begin the second clause.

> Correct: The Tower of London was built during the Norman Conquest; **however,** nearly a thousand years later, it still remains standing.

That transition can also be used non-essentially in the middle of a sentence. Compare this version of the sentence to the first version:

> Correct: The Tower of London was built during the Norman Conquest. Nearly a thousand years later, **however,** it still remains standing.

The commas around *however* tell us that if we cross that word out, the sentence will still make sense. And sure enough, when we eliminate it, we are left with a grammatically acceptable sentence:

> Correct: Nearly a thousand years later…it still remains standing.

What we **cannot** do is this:

> Incorrect: The Tower of London was built during the Norman Conquest, **however,** nearly a thousand years later, it still remains standing.

In the above version of the sentence, the two commas imply that the word *however* can be removed without affecting the sentence's essential meaning. But if we remove those commas, we end up with two independent clauses placed back-to-back without any punctuation between them.

> Incorrect: The Tower of London was built during the Norman Conquest nearly a thousand years later, it still remains standing.

The need for two commas vs. a semicolon is determined solely by context. If you are unsure which type of punctuation should be used, cross out the word or phrase in question and read the sentence without it.

If the sentence makes sense, the word or phrase is being used non-essentially, and two commas must be used.

If the sentence does **not** make sense, or a comma splice is created, a semicolon or period is required.

Important: two commas do not always equal a non-essential clause!

One common mistake is to assume that the presence of two commas in a sentence automatically indicates a non-essential clause. Compare the following two sentences:

Sentence #1:   London, which was one of the largest and most important cities in Europe during the Middle Ages, remains an important financial and cultural center today.

This sentence contains a non-essential clause that can be removed without altering its basic meaning:

Correct: London, ~~which was one of the largest and most important cities in Europe during the Middle Ages,~~ remains an important financial and cultural center today.

Now take a look at this sentence:

Sentence #2:   During the Middle Ages, London was one of the largest and most important cities in Europe, and today it remains an important financial and cultural center.

If we cross out the information between the commas, we get this:

Incorrect: During the Middle Ages, ~~London was one of the largest and most important cities in Europe,~~ and today it remains an important financial and cultural center.

The remaining sentence does not make sense, indicating that the information between the two commas does not constitute a non-essential clause.

In addition, some sentences that contain commas setting off non-essential clauses <u>also</u> contain commas that serve unrelated purposes. In such cases, it can be difficult to quickly tell where non-essential clauses are located.

Correct: Sumo wrestling, a full-contact sport in which competitors attempt to force one another out of a circular ring, originated in Japan, which remains the only country in the world where it is practiced.

The above sentence contains only one non-essential clause that can be removed without creating a problem:

Correct: Sumo wrestling, ~~a full-contact sport in which competitors attempt to force one another out of a circular ring,~~ originated in Japan, which remains the only country in the world where it is practiced.

If the information between a different set of commas is removed, however, we are left with nonsense:

Incorrect: Sumo wrestling, a full-contact sport in which competitors attempt to force one another out of a circular ring, ~~originated in Japan,~~ which remains the only country in the world where it is practiced.

If you cannot hear where the non-essential clause belongs, take your pencil (not a pen!), draw a line through the section you want to test, and read the sentence without it. If that doesn't work, erase the line, cross out a different section, and try again. It is very important that you go through this process because it is the only means you have of figuring out the answer logically.

Exercise: Identifying Non-Essential Words and Phrases (answers p. 227)

In the following sentences, place commas around non-essential phrases as necessary. If you are unsure whether a phrase is non-essential, cross it out and read the sentence without it. Note that some sentences contain additional unrelated commas.

1. The cesium fountain atomic clock, the most precise form of timekeeper available, is expected to become inaccurate by less than a single second over the next 50 million years.

2. Frank Gehry's buildings, often cited as being among the most important works of contemporary architecture, have become popular tourist attractions in many cities.

3. The most common types of coral, which are usually found in clear, shallow waters, require sunlight in order to grow.

4. Used in some martial arts, the Red Belt, one of several colored belts intended to denote a practitioner's skill level and rank, originated in Japan and Korea.

5. The Iditarod dog sled race, an annual event in Alaska, commemorates the dogsled teams that delivered a life-saving serum during the 1925 diphtheria epidemic.

6. New Zealand, one of the last lands to be settled by humans, developed distinctive animal and plant life during its long isolation.

7. Forensic biology, the application of biology to law enforcement, has been used to identify illegal products from endangered species and investigate bird collisions with wind turbines.

8. Human computers, who once performed basic numerical analysis for laboratories, were behind the calculations for everything from the first accurate prediction of the return of Halley's Comet to the success of the Manhattan Project.

9. Simone Fortini, a choreographer born in Italy but a resident of the United States since a young age, rapidly became known for a style of dancing based on improvisation and everyday movements.

10. The Rochester International Jazz Festival, which takes place in June of each year, typically attracts more than 100,000 fans from across the United States.

11. The unusually large size of the komodo dragon, the largest species of lizard, has been attributed to its ancient ancestor, the immense varanid lizard.

12. Illegal logging in forests, once nearly responsible for destroying the monarch butterfly's winter habitat, has declined in recent years, but the species is still threatened.

13. Fashioned from Russian folk tales, *Swan Lake*, one of the most popular ballets, tells the story of Odette, a princess turned into a swan by an evil sorcerer's curse.

Essential Clauses With and Without "That"

Clauses beginning with *that* are always essential to the meaning of a sentence and should **never be set off by commas** (or any other form of punctuation, for that matter). The use of a comma before or after *that* is always **incorrect**.

Incorrect: Parrots are one of the most difficult **pets, that** a person can have because they are intelligent, demanding, and live for up to 50 years.

Incorrect: Parrots are one of the most difficult **pets that,** a person can have because they are intelligent, demanding, and live for up to 50 years.

Correct: Parrots are one of the most difficult **pets that** a person can have because they are intelligent, demanding, and live for up to 50 years.

In the above sentence, the word *that* is optional. The sentence can be correctly written both with and without it.

Correct: Parrots are one of the most difficult **pets that** a person can have because they are intelligent, demanding, and live for up to 50 years.

Correct: Parrots are one of the most difficult **pets a** person can have because they are intelligent, demanding, and live for up to 50 years.

If the word *that* is deleted, however, no comma should be used in its place. When *that* is optional and is not used, it is always **incorrect** to insert a comma in its place.

Incorrect: Parrots are one of the most difficult **pets, a** person can have because they are intelligent, demanding, and live for up to 50 years.

The Case of "Who:" Non-Essential vs. Essential Clauses

Clauses beginning with *who* can be either non-essential (using commas) or essential (no commas). Both versions are grammatically acceptable, but they have different meanings. For example, it is possible to write the following sentence two different ways.

Correct: People, **who attend large open air events such as sporting matches and music festivals,** often turn to camping as a cheap form of accommodation.

The commas in the above sentence imply that the clause between them is not central to the meaning of the sentence. The focus of the sentence is on **people in general**; the fact that they attend large open air events such as sporting matches and music festivals is secondary.

Correct: People **who attend large open air events such as sporting matches and music festivals** often turn to camping as a cheap form of accommodation.

The lack of commas in this version of the sentences indicates that it is not discussing people in general but rather **a specific group of people**: those who attend large open air events such as sporting matches and music festivals. While the first version of the sentence is grammatically correct, this version simply makes more sense.

Independently, these sentences can be written either way without a problem; the focus of the sentence merely shifts depending on whether the commas are used. When a sentence that can be written either with or without commas is tested in the context of a paragraph, however, only one version will be correct.

For example, consider the following:

The store where I work has a return policy I have always found amusing. Normally, customers have one year from the purchase date to return unwanted or defective item; however, **1** customers, who make purchases on February 29th, have *four* years to return their items. The store's owner reasons that customers should have the right to return an item until the next occurrence of the date on which they bought it. Since February 29th occurs only once every four years, customers should thus be allowed nearly 1,500 days to decide whether they truly want a toaster or pair of shoes.

1

A) NO CHANGE
B) customers, who make purchases on February 29th
C) customers who make purchases on February 29th,
D) customers who make purchases on February 29th

Solution: The commas around the phrase "who make purchases on February 29th" imply that it could be crossed out without affecting the meaning of the passage. In this case, however, the phrase does provide crucial information: it specifies *which* particular customers, and the remainder of the paragraph talks *only* about these particular customers.

Without the phrase, the passage would also contradict itself because the previous sentence states that customers normally only have one year to return unwanted items. The underlined portion introduces an exception to that rule, which is then discussed in the rest of the passage. So A) is incorrect.

B) is incorrect because the clause in question must either have two commas, indicating that it is non-essential, or no commas, indicating that it is essential. Having only one comma is not an option.

C) is incorrect for the same reason as B), except that in this case the single comma is placed at the end of the clause rather than at the beginning. This answer is a little trickier because the complete subject, *customers who make purchases on February 29th*, is quite long, and it might seem that a pause is needed after it. In reality, however, a comma should never be placed between a subject and a verb, regardless of how long that subject may be.

D) is correct because the lack of commas indicates that the underlined information is essential to the meaning of the sentence, and does not separate the subject from the verb.

Let's look at another example:

The hexacopter, a lump of steel propellers and lenses, is both camera and flying machine. This contraption is revolutionizing the way news is reported. In the past, journalists, who wanted to obtain aerial shots of events to accompany their stories, were forced to rely on conventional helicopters, which often flew too high to capture detailed images. The hexacopter, however, can catapult itself into the air and hover right above the scene the photographer wishes to record.

1

A) NO CHANGE
B) journalists who wanted to obtain aerial shots to accompany their stories,
C) journalists, who wanted to obtain aerial shots to accompany their stories
D) journalists who wanted to obtain aerial shots to accompany their stories

Solution: B) and C) can be eliminated pretty quickly because our options are two commas or no commas. If we were to cross out the information between the commas, the sentence would still make perfect grammatical sense (*In the past, journalists…were forced to rely on conventional helicopters*).

The problem is that by definition, the commas imply that the information between them is not essential – and in this case, the information is important. Based on the context, it is clear that the sentence is not talking about journalists in general, as the commas would imply, but rather about **specific** journalists: those who wanted to obtain aerial shots to accompany their stories. Because that information is necessary to define the type of journalists being discussed, no commas should be used. D) is therefore correct.

It is also possible that you will encounter **other types of clauses that can be either essential or non-essential**. When this is the case, you may have to think very carefully about whether commas are required. Such questions are unlikely to appear often, but you should be prepared for the possibility of encountering them.

For example, consider the following:

In 2004, while rummaging in a Seattle basement, historian and journalist J. Pennelope Goforth came across a silver shopping bag with **an envelope** inside. [1] The envelope marked "Alaska Commercial Company" immediately caught her attention. For years, Goforth had researched the company, which had controlled Alaska's waters in the late nineteenth century.

1

A) NO CHANGE
B) The envelope marked "Alaska Commercial Company,"
C) The envelope, marked "Alaska Commercial Company,"
D) The envelope, marked "Alaska Commercial Company"

Solution: The key to answering this question is to recognize that the sentence is referring to one specific envelope. The previous sentence clearly states that Gofoth found a big shopping bag *with an envelope inside*. That's <u>one</u> envelope.

The next sentence can therefore only be referring to that single envelope, not implying that the envelope Goforth found was one of many envelopes. Because the clause *marked "Alaska Commercial Company"* describes that one particular envelope, commas must be used. C) is therefore correct.

On the other hand, consider this version of the passage:

In 2004, while rummaging in a Seattle basement, historian and journalist J. Pennelope Goforth came across a silver shopping bag **filled with envelopes**. [1] The envelope marked "Alaska Commercial Company" immediately caught her attention. For years, Goforth had researched the company, which had controlled Alaska's waters in the late nineteenth century.

1

A) NO CHANGE
B) The envelope marked "Alaska Commercial Company,"
C) The envelope, marked "Alaska Commercial Company,"
D) The envelope, marked "Alaska Commercial Company"

Solution: In this version, the passage clearly indicates that Goforth found many envelopes. The description *marked "Alaska Commercial Company*" is essential because it specifies which one of the envelopes Goforth found. No commas are therefore needed, making A) correct.

Commas with Names and Titles

Names and titles can be either essential or non-essential. While you may have learned in school that a comma should always be placed before a name or title, that is not the whole story. Commas should *sometimes* be placed before – and after – names and titles. Other times no commas at all should be used. It depends on the context.

Important: When a name or title appears in the middle of a sentence (that is, not as the first or last words), there are generally only two correct options: 1) two commas, before and after the name/title, or 2) no commas at all. (In rare instances, a single comma may be required after the name or title for other reasons, as discussed later in the chapter.)

The simplest way to determine whether commas are necessary is to treat the name or title like any other non-essential word or clause – take your pencil, cross it out, and see if the rest of the sentence makes sense **in context** without it. If the sentence makes sense, the commas are necessary; if the sentence does not make sense, the commas are not necessary.

Let's look at how this rule would play out in some test-style questions:

Ada Lovelace and her **1** acquaintance, Charles Babbage, were two of the most influential figures in the history of computer science. After Babbage sketched out his ideas for an "analytical engine," Lovelace demonstrated that the machine might be able to carry out a variety of complex tasks.

1

A) NO CHANGE
B) acquaintance Charles Babbage
C) acquaintance Charles Babbage,
D) acquaintances, Charles Babbage

Solution: Because the name *Charles Babbage* appears in the middle of a sentence, our options are two commas or no commas, eliminating C) and D). To decide between A) and B), we're going to cross out the name:

> **Ada Lovelace and her acquaintance were two of the most influential figures in the history of computer science.**

At this point, we need to be careful and consider the context. The sentence is still grammatically acceptable, but a crucial piece of information is lost: we do not know who Lovelace's acquaintance was. As a result, the reference to Babbage in the following sentence does not make sense. So the name is essential, and no commas are required. The answer is therefore B).

Another way to think of this rule is as follows:

- Commas around a name or title imply that it is the **only** person or thing.

- No commas around a name or title imply that it is **one of many** people or things.

Placing commas around *Charles Babbage* would imply that Babbage was Ada Lovelace's **only** acquaintance. Is that possible? Yes, theoretically. But it's probably not what the writer intended to say. Without the commas, the sentence implies that Ada Lovelace had multiple acquaintances, one of whom was Charles Babbage. That version simply makes more sense.

Let's look at another example:

Caribbean-American **1** author, Jamaica Kincaid is also known for being an enthusiastic essayist and gardener. She was born Elaine Potter Richardson in St. John's, Antigua but came to the United States at the age of 17 to work as an au pair in Westchester County, New York. She eventually won a scholarship to Franconia College in New Hampshire but returned to New York City to write. In 1985, she published the novel, *Annie John*, a semiautobiographical story of a young girl growing up in Antigua.

1
A) NO CHANGE
B) author Jamaica Kincaid
C) author, Jamaica Kincaid,
D) author Jamaica Kincaid,

Solution: Once again, we're going to start by crossing the name out of the sentence.

Caribbean-American author…is also known for being an enthusiastic essayist and gardener.

No, that makes no sense whatsoever. In addition to being ungrammatical, it doesn't tell us who the Caribbean-American novelist is. The name is clearly essential here, so no commas are necessary. The answer is B).

Now, however, consider this:

I've always been interested in gardening, but until recently, I didn't have room for flowers or plants. When I moved into a new house last summer, however, I was thrilled to discover that there was enough space in the yard for a garden. There was just one problem – I'd never actually planted one. So I called a friend who had a lot more gardening experience than I did. Luckily, that **1** friend, Jane, agreed to come over the next day.

1
A) NO CHANGE
B) friend, Jane
C) friend Jane,
D) friend Jane

Solution: Once again, the name is located within the sentence, indicating that our options are two commas or no commas. When we cross out *Jane*, the resulting sentence still makes sense: *Luckily, that friend agreed to come over the next day.* The commas are therefore necessary, making the answer A).

Let's look at an example of a question involving a title. We're going to revisit this passage, but from a slightly different angle:

Jamaica Kincaid (born May 25, 1949) is a novelist, essayist, and gardener. She was born Elaine Potter Richardson in St. John's, Antigua but came to the United States at the age of 17 to work as an au pair in Westchester County, New York. She eventually won a scholarship to Franconia College in New Hampshire but returned to New York City to write. In 1985, she published **1** the novel, *Annie John,* a semiautobiographical story of a young girl growing up in Antigua.

A) NO CHANGE
B) the novel *Annie John,*
C) the novel, *Annie John*
D) the novel *Annie John*

Solution: As always, we're going to start by crossing the title out of the sentence and reading the sentence without it.

In 1985, she published the novel…a semiautobiographical story of a young girl growing up in Antigua.

No, this does not make sense in context because we do not know which novel the sentence is referring to. The information is therefore essential, meaning that commas should not be placed around the title.

But wait, there's a twist! This is the rare **exception** to the "two commas or no commas" rule. A comma is required to separate the independent first clause from the dependent second clause (*In 1985, she published the novel Annie John, a semiautobiographical story of a young girl growing up in Antigua*). Without the comma, we just get a big jumble. So the answer is B).

Exercise: Essential and Non-Essential Clauses (answers p. 227)

The following questions test your understanding of commas and non-essential/essential clauses. If you are uncertain whether a clause is essential or non-essential, follow these steps:

1) Cross out the phrase, name, or title.

2) Determine whether the sentence makes sense in context without it.

3) Determine whether commas are necessary.

1.   Along with her **1** husband Martin Luther King, Coretta Scott King played an important role in the Civil Rights Movement. She was most active after 1968, when she took on the leadership of the struggle for racial equality herself and became a key figure in the women's movement.

1

A)   NO CHANGE
B)   husband Martin Luther King;
C)   husband, Martin Luther King,
D)   husband, Martin Luther King

2.   Some animal trainers claim that most obedience programs consist of no more than teaching a dog tricks. A **1** dog, that has undergone obedience training, may understand commands such as "sit," "down," and "heel" but may still engage in destructive and aggressive behaviors such as chewing shoes or digging up flowers.

1

A)   NO CHANGE
B)   dog that has undergone obedience training
C)   dog that, has undergone obedience training
D)   dog, that has undergone obedience training

3.   Lisa See, author of the **1** best-selling novel, *Snow Flower and the Secret Fan,* has always been intrigued by stories that have been lost, forgotten, or deliberately covered up. To research the book, See traveled to a remote area of China **2** that, she was told, only one foreigner before her had ever visited. While there, See was able to investigate a secret type of writing that women had kept hidden for over a thousand years.

1

A)   NO CHANGE
B)   best-selling novel *Snow Flower and the Secret Fan*
C)   best-selling novel, *Snow Flower and the Secret Fan*
D)   best-selling novel *Snow Flower and the Secret Fan,*

2

A)   NO CHANGE
B)   that she was told,
C)   that, she was told
D)   that; she was told

119

4. Alfred Mosher Butts, the American **1** architect, who created Scrabble™, intended it to be a variation on the existing word game Lexiko. The two games had the same set of letter tiles and point values, which Butts had worked out by analyzing the frequency with which letters appeared in newspapers and magazines. He decided the new game should be called "Criss-Crosswords" and added the 15 x 15 game board. Butts created a few sets **2** himself, but the first manufacturers who inspected them did not think that the game was likely to become very popular.

1

A) NO CHANGE
B) architect, he created Scrabble™,
C) architect who created Scrabble™,
D) architect; who created Scrabble™

2

A) NO CHANGE
B) himself, but the first manufacturers, who inspected them,
C) himself, but the first manufacturers, who inspected them
D) himself; however, the first manufacturers who inspected them

5. In November 1895, German **1** physicist Wilhelm Roentgen accidentally discovered an image created by rays emanating from a vacuum tube. Further investigation showed that the rays penetrated many kinds of matter. A week after his discovery, Roentgen photographed the hand of his **2** wife, Anna, clearly revealing her wedding ring and bones. The image, which electrified the general **3** public aroused great scientific interest in the new form of radiation.

1

A) NO CHANGE
B) physicist Wilhelm Roentgen,
C) physicist, Wilhelm Roentgen
D) physicist, Wilhelm Roentgen,

2

A) NO CHANGE
B) wife, Anna clearly revealed
C) wife Anna; clearly revealing
D) wife Anna, this clearly revealed

3

A) NO CHANGE
B) public, aroused
C) public, and aroused
D) public; aroused

6. Grant Wood's best known **1** painting, *American Gothic*, is one of the few images to reach the status of universally recognized cultural icon. It was first exhibited in 1930 at the Art Institute of Chicago, where it is still located. Photographs of the painting, which was awarded a $300 **2** prize appeared in newspapers country-wide and brought Wood immediate recognition. Since then, it has been borrowed and satirized endlessly for advertisements and cartoons.

1

A) NO CHANGE
B) painting *American Gothic*,
C) painting *American Gothic*,
D) painting, *American Gothic*,

2

A) NO CHANGE
B) prize, and appeared
C) prize, appeared
D) prize, appearing

7. Certification for school **1** librarians also known as school media specialists, varies by state. Some states require school media specialists to be certified teachers, while others require they have only a Masters of Library Science. Some require a Masters Degree in Education with a specialization in library science. In contrast, almost all states require **2** librarians, who work in local libraries, to obtain professional certification.

1

A) NO CHANGE
B) librarians. Who are also known
C) librarians, they are also known
D) librarians, also known

2

A) NO CHANGE
B) librarians who work in local libraries,
C) librarians who work in local libraries
D) librarians and work in local libraries

8. Although Mt. Everest is the highest mountain in the world, it is less challenging to climb than some of the other mountains in the Himalayas. High elevations and low temperatures **1** do, however, create a difficult and dangerous trek. **2** Mountain climbers, who want to trek to the summit of Mt. Everest, are advised to ensure that they are properly equipped and physically capable of making the journey.

1

A) NO CHANGE
B) do; however,
C) do however
D) do, however

2

A) NO CHANGE
B) Mountain climbers, who want to trek to the summit of Mt. Everest
C) Mountain climbers who want to trek to the summit of Mt. Everest
D) Mountain climbers who want to trek, to the summit of Mt. Everest,

9. First recorded in 1835, the **1** disease, polio, baffled scientific researchers for decades. It **2** was in fact, the most serious public health problem of the mid-20th century, and scientists were frantic for a cure. During the 1940s, President Franklin D. Roosevelt was the world's most recognized polio victim. In 1938, he founded the **3** organization, March of Dimes to fund the development of a cure. Before a vaccine was finally discovered by an American **4** scientist Jonas Salk in 1955, more than 80 percent of polio patients received help from the foundation.

1

A) NO CHANGE
B) disease polio
C) disease, polio
D) disease polio,

2

A) NO CHANGE
B) was, in fact,
C) was in fact;
D) was, in fact

3

A) NO CHANGE
B) the organization March of Dimes,
C) the organization March of Dimes
D) the organization, March of Dimes,

4

A) NO CHANGE
B) scientist Jonas Salk,
C) scientist, Jonas Salk
D) scientist, Jonas Salk,

10. Additional Comma Uses and Misuses

Note: While the following rules may be tested on occasion, they are **not** a primary focus of the test; therefore, I have not included separate exercises for them.

Commas <u>should</u> be used:

A. To Separate Items in a List

In any list of three or more items, each item must be followed by a comma. The comma before *and* is optional. You will not be asked to choose between a version with the comma and a version without the comma.

Correct:	The museum's new open-storage display brings some 900 vintage World's Fair souvenirs out of attics, desk drawers, **shoeboxes, and museum** archives for visitors to view.
Correct:	The museum's new open-storage display brings some 900 vintage World's Fair souvenirs out of attics, desk drawers, **shoeboxes and museum** archives for visitors to view.

No comma should ever be used **after** the word *and*.

Incorrect:	The museum's open-storage display brings over 900 vintage World's Fair souvenirs out of attics, desk drawers, **shoeboxes, and, museum** archives for visitors to view.
Incorrect:	The museum's open-storage display brings over 900 vintage World's Fair souvenirs out of attics, desk drawers, **shoeboxes and, museum** archives for visitors to view.

B. To Separate Adjectives Whose Order Could be Reversed

When the order of the adjectives does not matter, then a comma should be used. You can also try placing the word *and* between the adjectives; if they can be separated that way, then the comma is correct.

Correct:	One of the Queens Museum's recent exhibits featured works by contemporary artists from Japan, Taiwan, and Ireland, offering patrons the chance to see a kind of **innovative, passionate** art that larger museums often ignore.
Correct:	One of the Queens Museum's recent exhibits featured works by contemporary artists from Japan, Taiwan, and Ireland, offering patrons the chance to see a kind of **passionate, innovative** art that larger museums often ignore.
Correct:	One of the Queens Museum's recent exhibits featured works by contemporary artists from Japan, Taiwan, and Ireland, offering patrons the chance to see a kind of **innovative and passionate** art that larger museums often ignore.

If the first adjective modifies the second adjective, or if the adjectives could not normally be separated by the word *and*, no comma should be used:

Incorrect: Columbian artist Maria Fernanda Cardoso often makes use of **colorful, plastic objects** in her paintings and sculptures.

Incorrect: Columbian artist Maria Fernanda Cardoso often makes use of **colorful and plastic objects** in her paintings and sculptures.

Correct: Columbian artist Maria Fernanda Cardoso often makes use of **colorful plastic objects** in her paintings and sculptures.

In the above sentence, *colorful* describes *plastic objects*, so a comma should not be used between them.

C. After a Close-Parenthesis Where a Comma Would Normally be Necessary

Sentences that test both commas and parentheses simultaneously are likely to be rare, but it is possible they will appear. The best way to approach such sentences is to simply cross out the parenthetical material.

Correct: The Tower of London was constructed as a prison in the eleventh century (1078 to be exact), but over the centuries it has been used as everything from an armory to a treasury.

If we eliminate the parentheses, we are left with two independent clauses joined by a FANBOYS conjunction:

Correct: The Tower of London was constructed as a prison in the eleventh **century ~~(1078 to be exact)~~, but** over the centuries it has been used as everything from an armory to a treasury.

No comma should be used **before** an open-parenthesis, however:

Incorrect: The Tower of London was constructed as a prison in the eleventh **century, (1078 to be exact),** but over the centuries it has been used as everything from an armory to a treasury.

Two commas indicate non-essential information, and the parentheses *already* serve that function. If we eliminate the parentheses, we get two commas next to one another – a result that is never correct:

Incorrect: The Tower of London was constructed as a prison in the eleventh **century,, but** over the centuries it has been used as everything from an armory to a treasury.

D. After Introductory Words and Phrases

Introductory words and phrases (e.g. *in fact*, *moreover*, *as a result*) should be set off by commas. For example:

Correct: **At first,** it looked as if the storm was going to miss us by a few hundred miles.

Correct: **Nevertheless,** Armstrong persisted and became an extraordinary musician.

Note: When a set of choices consists of introductory words/phrases, all will typically include commas. The focus will be on meaning, not grammar.

Commas should <u>NOT</u> be used:

A. Before or After Prepositions

To review, prepositions are **location** and **time** words such as *of, for, from, to, in, with, by, before,* and *after*. Do not use a comma **before or after** a preposition.

Incorrect:	Ada Lovelace and Charles Babbage were two of the most influential **figures, in** the history of computer science and mathematics.
Incorrect:	Ada Lovelace and Charles Babbage were two of the most influential **figures in,** the history of computer science and mathematics.
Correct:	Ada Lovelace and Charles Babbage were two of the most influential **figures in** the history of computer science and mathematics.

The only **exception** to this rule occurs when a preposition is used to begin a non-essential clause.

Correct:	Although Ada Lovelace lived nearly a century before the first computer was built, she**, in a way that was unique among nineteenth century mathematicians,** predicted many of the modern computer's capabilities.

B. Between Adjectives and Nouns

This is a particularly important rule when you are dealing with multiple adjectives or lists. Although commas are required between the items of the list, no comma should be placed between the final adjective and the noun.

Incorrect:	Headquartered in New York City, the National Academy of Television Arts and Sciences (NATAS) is a well-known **national, organization** with local chapters in cities around the United States.
Correct:	Headquartered in New York City, the National Academy of Television Arts and Sciences (NATAS) is a well-known **national organization** with local chapters in cities around the United States.

C. Before or after "That"

Incorrect:	Puzzle-solving, an ancient and universal practice, depends on the kind of creative **insight, that** ignited the first campfires thousands of years ago.
Incorrect:	Puzzle-solving, an ancient and universal practice, depends on the kind of creative **insight that,** ignited the first campfires thousands of years ago.
Correct:	Puzzle-solving, an ancient and universal practice, depends on the kind of creative **insight that** ignited the first campfires thousands of years ago.

D. Between Subjects and Verbs

Unless a subject and verb are separated by a non-essential clause, no comma should be placed between them.

Incorrect: <u>Ada Lovelace and Charles Babbage</u>, **were** two of the most influential figures in the history of computer science and mathematics.

Correct: <u>Ada Lovelace and Charles Babbage</u> **were** two of the most influential figures in the history of computer science and mathematics.

This rule holds true even when subjects are extremely long and complex:

Incorrect: <u>What is particularly remarkable about Ada Lovelace's work on Babbage's "analytical engine,"</u> **is** that she foresaw many of the ways in which computers are used today.

Correct: <u>What is particularly remarkable about Ada Lovelace's work on Babbage's "analytical engine"</u> **is** that she foresaw many of the ways in which computers are used today.

Even though you may feel that a pause is necessary before the verb (and even though it is acceptable to use one informally in order to break up long sentences), in strict grammatical terms, no comma should be used.

E. Between Compound Nouns, Verbs, or Adjectives

When two or more nouns, verbs, or adjectives are joined by the word *and*, do not use a comma.

The easiest way to approach this rule is as follows: because *comma + and* = period, plug in a period in place of *comma + and*. Since there clearly will not be two full sentences, no comma is needed.

Compound Subject

Incorrect: **Ada Lovelace, and Charles Babbage** were two of the most influential figures in the history of computer science and mathematics.

Plug in: **Ada Lovelace. Charles Babbage** were two of the most influential figures in the history of computer science and mathematics.

Correct: **Ada Lovelace and Charles Babbage** were two of the most influential figures in the history of computer science and mathematics.

Compound Object

Incorrect: Ada Lovelace and Charles Babbage were two of the most **important, and influential** figures in the history of computer science and mathematics.

Plug in: Ada Lovelace and Charles Babbage were two of the most **important. Influential** figures in the history of computer science and mathematics.

Correct: Ada Lovelace and Charles Babbage were two of the most **important and influential** figures in the history of computer science and mathematics.

F. Before or Around "Self" Words

"Self" words (technically known as **emphatic pronouns**) are used to emphasize that a particular person or people is being referred to. Each object pronoun has an emphatic counterpart.

Me	→	Myself
You	→	Yourself
It	→	Itself
One	→	Oneself
Her/Him	→	Her/himself
Us	→	Ourselves
Them	→	Themselves

Although constructions containing these words may sound strange to you, there is nothing inherently wrong with them. In fact, the only thing you need to know is that it is **incorrect** to place a comma before them, or before and after them. For example:

Incorrect: The tower of London, which lies within the Borough of Tower Hamlets, is separated from the **city, itself (or: city, itself,)** by a stretch of open space.

Correct: The tower of London, which lies within the Borough of Tower Hamlets, is separated from the **city itself** by a stretch of open space.

In most cases, it is also incorrect to place a comma after an emphatic pronoun.

Incorrect: The tower of London, which lies within the Borough of Tower Hamlets, is separated from the city **itself,** by a stretch of open space.

However, when a comma would normally be necessary (e.g. before a FANBOYS conjunction or to set off a non-essential clause), it is acceptable to place one after an emphatic pronoun.

Correct: The tower of London is separated from the city **itself, but** it is nevertheless one of London's most popular tourist attractions.

In the sentence above, *comma + but* is used to separated two complete sentences. The first sentence just happens to ends with the word *itself*.

11. Colons and Dashes

Colons should be used in two situations:

1) Before a list

2) Before an explanation

A colon must follow a sentence that can stand alone as a complete thought, but it can come before either a sentence or a fragment. In the examples below, the information before the colon in the first version does not make sense on its own, while the information before the colon in the second version can stand by itself.

Shortcut: you can assume that any answer that places a colon before *such as* or *including* is **incorrect**; under normal circumstances, there is no way to create a standalone statement ending with these words.

Colon before a list

Incorrect:	Photographer and filmmaker George Picker chronicled artists **such as/including:** folk singers, jazz musicians, and visual artists.
Correct:	Photographer and filmmaker George Picker chronicled a wide variety of **artists:** folk singers, jazz musicians, and visual artists were all among his subjects.

Colon before an explanation

Incorrect:	The Amazon parrot does not make an ideal pet for most people **because: it** requires much more attention and entertainment than many other animals do.
Correct:	The Amazon parrot does not make an ideal pet for most people **for one major reason: it** requires much more attention and affection than many other animals do.

When a colon precedes an explanation, a complete sentence typically follows. For this reason, there are instances in which a colon, a semicolon/period, and a dash (see next page) are all grammatically acceptable:

Correct:	The Amazon parrot does not make an ideal pet for most **people: it** requires much more attention and affection than many other animals do.
Correct:	The Amazon parrot does not make an ideal pet for most **people; it** requires much more attention and affection than many other animals do.
Correct:	The Amazon parrot does not make an ideal pet for most **people. It** requires much more attention and affection than many other animals do.

When a colon, semicolon, or period is acceptable, you will not be asked to choose between them.

While **dashes** are typically the most unfamiliar punctuation mark for many test-takers, mostly because they are used more frequently in British English than in American English, they are fairly straightforward.

Dashes have three major uses:

1) Set off a non-essential clause

2) Introduce a list or explanation

3) Create a deliberate pause

The vast majority of ACT questions that test dashes test the first usage. Questions testing the second usage appear occasionally, and questions testing the third appear only rarely.

A. Non-Essential Clause: 2 dashes = 2 commas

When used this way, two dashes are exactly equivalent to two commas. If one dash appears, so must the other. Another punctuation mark such as a comma cannot be used in place of it.

Incorrect: London **– which is a very old city,** has many new buildings.

Correct: London **– which is a very old city –** has many new buildings.

The choice to use two dashes rather than two commas is purely a stylistic one, and the ACT will never require you to choose between the two. The only rule is that dashes must go with dashes and commas with commas. One of the ACT's favorite errors is to mix and match commas and dashes.

For example:

The Norman Conquest – which occurred in

1066, marked an important step in the

development of the English language.

1

A) NO CHANGE
B) 1066 – marked
C) 1066. Marked
D) 1066: marked

If you know that a dash must only be paired with another dash, you can immediately choose B).

B. Before a List or Explanation: Dash = Colon

When used this way, a dash is the exact equivalent of a colon and must come after a full, stand-alone statement. The dash vs. colon distinction is purely stylistic; you will not be asked to choose between them.

List: Photographer and filmmaker George Picker chronicled a wide variety of **artists – folk** singers, jazz musicians, and visual artists were all among his subjects.

Explanation: The Amazon parrot does not make an ideal pet for most **people – it** requires much more attention and affection than many other animals do.

C. Create a Pause

A dash can also be used for stylistic reasons: to deliberately interrupt a statement or to create a dramatic pause or sense of suspense.

Create a pause: After eight hours of driving, we finally arrived **home – and** that was when we discovered that we had forgotten to close all of the windows.

This use of a dash is unlikely to be a major focus of the new SAT. You do not need to spend a lot of time focusing on it; you should simply be aware that it exists.

Exercise: Colons and Dashes (answers p. 228)

1. Wrangell-St. Elias National Park, the largest national park in the United States, represents everything compelling about Alaska. It is immense – larger, in fact, than Belgium. It showcases towering mountains – Mount St. Elias stands **1** over 18,000 feet tall as well as glaciers. Alaska's human history is also displayed in the mining towns of McCarthy and Kennicott. Just getting there is an **2** adventure: it's a long day's drive through miles of wilderness to reach the park's entrance.

1
A) NO CHANGE
B) over 18,000 feet tall –
C) over 18,000 feet tall,
D) over 18,000 feet tall;

2
A) NO CHANGE
B) adventure; it being a long day's drive
C) adventure, but it's a long day's drive
D) adventure. Its a long day's drive

2. A dentist's job includes tasks **1** such as: filling cavities, examining X-rays, and applying protective sealant. Dentists, who receive medical training similar to that of **2** doctors – can also perform oral surgery on patients and write prescriptions. They also educate patients about caring for teeth and gums by encouraging them to follow a variety of healthy habits: taking fluorides, flossing, brushing, and abiding by a healthy diet.

1
A) NO CHANGE
B) such as filling cavities; examining
C) such as filling cavities, examining
D) such as: filling cavities examining

2
A) NO CHANGE
B) doctors, can
C) doctors can
D) doctors; can

3. A novel method of air **1** conditioning – which is taking root among some of the world's most powerful corporations, uses the simple power of ice. Not only is the system more environmentally friendly but it also saves millions of dollars in utility bills. The system **2** works by: making ice at night, when lower power usage means energy is cheaper and lower temperatures require less power to freeze water. The larger the difference between nighttime and daytime temperatures, the greater the energy savings.

1
A) NO CHANGE
B) conditioning. Which
C) conditioning, which
D) conditioning which

2
A) NO CHANGE
B) works, by making ice at night
C) works by making ice at night,
D) works by making ice at night –

4. The northern snakehead is a fish that lives up to its **1** name: its head tapers to a point, making it look as if **2** someone, perhaps a mad scientist – had grafted a snake's head and several inches of scaly body onto a fish. Its fins hang unevenly from its body, as though they were tacked on as an afterthought. Given the fish's wild appearance, it's hardly a surprise that scientists have given it a **3** nickname – Frankenfish.

1

A) NO CHANGE
B) name. It's head tapers to a point
C) name, its head tapers to a point;
D) name its head tapers to a point

2

A) NO CHANGE
B) someone perhaps
C) someone. Perhaps
D) someone – perhaps

3

Which of the following would be an acceptable alternative to the underlined portion?

A) NO CHANGE
B) nickname Frankenfish
C) nickname: Frankenfish
D) nickname; Frankenfish

5. The appearance of mosaic **1** murals, pictures made of many small pieces – has remained unchanged for thousands of years. However, the last few decades have seen the emergence of a new **2** style. Colorful three-dimensional stone wall murals. One such mural was produced by Janna Morrison in 2005. She combined the piecework of mosaic murals with traditional soap stone slab carving **3** to produce: lifelike tropical plants, flowers, and sea life scenes ranging in size from a few inches to life-size plants inlaid along entire walls.

1

A) NO CHANGE
B) murals – pictures
C) murals, pictures,
D) murals. Pictures

2

A) NO CHANGE
B) style, colorful, three-dimensional
C) style: colorful, three-dimensional
D) style; colorful three-dimensional

3

A) NO CHANGE
B) to produce; lifelike, tropical plants, flowers,
C) to produce – lifelike tropical plants, flowers,
D) to produce lifelike tropical plants, flowers,

12. Apostrophes: Possessive vs. Plural

Plural and Possessive Nouns

Singular	Plural (-s, -es)	Singular Possessive (-'s)	Plural Possessive (-s')
Artist	Artists	Artist's	Artists'
Business	Businesses	Business's	Businesses'

To form the **plural** of a noun, add *–s*. When a singular noun ends in *–s*, add *–es*. Do **not** add an apostrophe.

    Correct: The **birds** are flying. (= More than one bird is flying.)

    Correct: The **businesses** are open. (= More than one business is open.)

To form the **possessive** of a singular noun, add *apostrophe + –s*, even for nouns whose singular ends in *–s*.*

    Correct: The **bird's** wings are red. (= The wings of the bird are red.)

    Correct: The **business's** policy is new. (= The policy of the business is new.)

To form the **possessive** of a plural noun, add an apostrophe after the *–s* or *–es*.

    Correct: The **birds'** wings are red. (= The wings of the birds are red.)

    Correct: The **businesses'** policies are new. (= The policies of the businesses are new.)

Contraction with Verb

The construction *–s + apostrophe* can also be used to form a **contraction** between a noun and the verb *is*.

    Incorrect: The **birds** flying over the city.

    Correct: The **bird's** flying over the city. (= The **bird is** flying over the city.)

The second sentence is correct because *apostrophe + –s* stands in for the verb *is*. The first sentence is incorrect because the lack of an apostrophe makes the word *birds* plural and eliminates the verb from the sentence.

*Note: For well-known individuals whose names end in *–s*, it is permissible to form the possessive by adding only an apostrophe (e.g. Dickens' works = the works of Dickens). While this usage accounts for much of the confusion about where to place apostrophes, you do NOT need to worry about it for the SAT.

Shortcut: When there are two nouns in a row, the first noun should generally contain an apostrophe. For example, <u>horse's tail</u> is correct because the first noun contains an apostrophe, whereas <u>horses tail</u> is incorrect because the first noun does not contain an apostrophe.

To simplify the process of determining whether and/or where to use an apostrophe, you can also ask yourself two questions:

1) Singular or plural? If singular, cross out plural answers and vice-versa.

2) Possessive or not possessive? If not possessive, cross out any answer with an apostrophe.

For two-noun questions, check each noun separately, starting with the one you're more certain about. In some cases, one noun will give you all the information you need to answer a question.

Let's look at an example. Break each question down, making sure to cross out incorrect answers as you go.

An artists' colony is a place where creative **1** practitioner's live and interact with one another. Colonies often select their artists through an application process, and residencies range from a few weeks to over a year. Since colonies such as MacDowell and Yaddo were founded in the early 20th century, they have exhibited hundreds of **2** artist's works and provided important spaces for collaboration and experimentation.

1
A) NO CHANGE
B) practitioners
C) practitioners'
D) practitioner's,

2
A) NO CHANGE
B) artists works
C) artist's work's
D) artists' works

Question 1: Singular or Plural? _____ Possessive? _____

Question 2: Noun 1: Singular or Plural? _____ Possessive? _____

Noun 2: Singular or Plural? _____ Possessive? _____

1) The word after *practitioners* is *live*, which is a verb. Since a possessive noun cannot come before a verb, no apostrophe is needed. That eliminates A), C), and D), making B) correct.

2) The word after *works* is *and. And* is not a noun, so *works* does not require an apostrophe. That eliminates C). Now look at the first word. *Works* is a noun, so the word before it requires an apostrophe. That eliminates B). Now the question is whether the word is singular or plural. The phrase *hundreds of* indicates that the passage is talking about more than one artist. So A) can be eliminated as well. D) is correct because the passage is referring to the works **of** the artists.

Plural and Possessive Pronouns

To review: a pronoun is a word such as *it(s)* and *they/their* that can replace a noun in a sentence. For example, the sentence *I.M. Pei is a well-known architect* can be rewritten as <u>He</u> *is a well known-architect.*

Apostrophes are used differently for pronouns than they are for nouns.

- To form the possessive, add *–s*. **Do not add an apostrophe.**

- To form a contraction with the verb *is* or *are*, add *apostrophe + –s* or *–re.*

A. It's vs. Its

It's = it is, it has

Its = possessive of *it*

Its', Its's = do not exist

The easiest way to choose between *its* and *it's* is simply to plug in *it is*. If *it is* makes sense in context, you need the apostrophe. If *it is* does not make sense, the apostrophe is incorrect.

Incorrect:	Some critics of the Internet have argued that it is a danger because **it's (it is)** vastness threatens people's intellectual health.
Incorrect:	Some critics of the Internet have argued that it is a danger because **its'** vastness threatens people's intellectual health.
Correct:	Some critics of the Internet have argued that it is a danger because **its** vastness threatens people's intellectual health.

B. They're, Their, and There

Although the same rules apply to *they're vs. their* as apply to other pronouns, an extra degree of confusion is often present because of a third identical-sounding pronoun: *there*.

They're = they are

Their = possessive of *they*. Used before a noun.

There = a place

In general, it's easiest to think of *there* as separate from *they're* and *their*, which both involve *they*. For *their vs. they're*, check whether you could plug in *they are*. If you can plug it in, you need the apostrophe; if you can't plug it in, you don't need the apostrophe.

They're

Incorrect: Although **their** usually powered by rowers, canoes may also contain sails or motors.

Incorrect: Although **there** usually powered by rowers, canoes may also contain sails or motors.

Correct: Although **they're** usually powered by rowers, canoes may also contain sails or motors.

Since you would say, *Although they are usually powered by rowers*, the apostrophe is required.

Their

Incorrect: Deactivated viruses form the basis of many vaccines known for **they're** effectiveness in preventing disease.

Incorrect: Deactivated viruses form the basis of many vaccines known for **there** effectiveness in preventing disease.

Correct: Deactivated viruses form the basis of many vaccines known for **their** effectiveness in preventing disease.

Since you would not say *Deactivated viruses form the basis of many vaccines known for they are effectiveness*, no apostrophe is needed. Since the sentence does not describe a place, *there* is not correct either.

There

Incorrect: Because the city of Denver is located close to the Rocky Mountains, snow often falls **they're**.

Incorrect: Because the city of Denver is located close to the Rocky Mountains, snow often falls **their**.

Correct: Because the city of Denver is located close to the Rocky Mountains, snow often falls **there**.

Since the sentence is clearly talking about a place, *there* is required.

C. You're vs. Your

You're = you are

Your = possessive form of *you*.

To determine which version is correct, plug in the phrase *you are*.

Incorrect: The first few hours of the workday can have a significant effect on **you're** level of productivity over the following eight hours.

Correct: The first few hours of the workday can have a significant effect on **your** level of productivity over the following eight hours.

Since you would not say *The first few hours of the workday can have a significant effect on you are level of productivity*, no apostrophe should be used.

D. Who's vs. Whose

Who's = who is, who has

Whose = possessive form of *who*. Unlike *who*, *whose* can be used to refer to both people and things.

To determine which version is correct, plug in the phrase *who is*.

Incorrect: Jessye Norman is an American opera singer **whose** known for her moving performances.

Correct: Jessye Norman is an American opera singer **who's** known for her moving performances.

Since you would say *Jessye Norman is an American opera singer who is known for her moving performances*, the apostrophe is necessary.

On the other hand:

Incorrect: Jessye Norman is an American opera singer **who's** performances many people find moving.

Correct: Jessye Norman is an American opera singer **whose** performances many people find moving.

Since you would also not say *Jessye Norman is an American opera singer who is performances many people find moving*, *whose* rather than *who's* must be used.

It is also possible that you will see questions testing possessive and plural with other pronouns. The same rule applies to those pronouns as applies to the ones discussed throughout this chapter: *apostrophe + –s or –re = pronoun + is or are*, while no apostrophe = possessive.

	Pronoun + is/has, are	Pronoun + would	Possessive
That	That's	That'd	Thats = does not exist
She, He	She's, He's	She'd, He'd	Shes, hes = does not exist, pl. is *her/ his*
They	They're	They'd	
Her, Him	Her's, hers' = does not exist His's, his' = does not exist	N/A	Hers His
Their	Their's = does not exist	N/A	Theirs

Exercise: Apostrophes with Nouns and Pronouns (answers p. 228)

Identify any plural or possessive error involving the pronouns, and write the correct version of the word on the line to the right of the question. Some of the underlined words may not contain an error.

1. Despite <u>it's</u> brilliance and power, the sun grew out of tiny particles suspended in enormous clouds of dust and gas.

_____

2. The British scientist J.D. Bernal believed that human beings would eventually be replaced by creatures <u>who's</u> bodies were half-human and half-machine.

_____

3. Instrument-makers have tried to reproduce a Stradivarius violin's precise sound for hundreds of years, but all of <u>they're attempts</u> have been unsuccessful.

_____

4. Bats can perceive and stalk <u>their</u> prey in complete darkness, using a system of ultrasonic sounds to produce <u>echo's that identify it's</u> location.

_____

5. A computer program devoted to facial recognition can determine people's emotions by following <u>there</u> faces' movements and linking <u>its</u> readings with a database of expressions.

_____

_____

6. George Westinghouse was an electrical industry pioneer <u>who's</u> first major invention, the rotary steam engine, earned him many <u>scientists'</u> admiration when he was still a young man.

_____

_____

7. Although Los Angeles has long been famous for <u>it's</u> <u>traffic jam's</u>, pedestrians are now able to walk in the <u>cities</u> center with much greater ease.

_____

8. The woolly mammoth's appearance and behavior have been studied more than those of most prehistoric animals because <u>there</u> bones have been discovered in many different locations.

_____

9. Individuals <u>whose</u> goal is to obtain an advanced degree in speech-language pathology must first receive <u>they're</u> undergraduate degree in a related field.

_____

_____

10. If the idea of traveling across the United States in an 18-wheeler, flying a commercial jet, or crossing the Atlantic in a cargo vessel appeals to you, then a career in transportation might be just what <u>your</u> looking for.

_____

11. The peacock is a bird <u>who's</u> penchant for showing off <u>its</u> bright, multicolored plumage has made it a symbol of vanity and pride in many different cultures.

_____

12. The gray wolf, which once lived throughout much of North America, is now rarely spotted because <u>it's</u> habitat has been almost entirely destroyed.

_____

13. Every spring, New Orleans receives thousands of tourists for Mardi Gras, the <u>years</u> most important festival. Visitors arrive <u>their</u> from around the world.

_____

13. Pronoun and Noun Agreement

Many questions that test apostrophes will also test pronoun agreement simultaneously. As a result, it is impossible to discuss one without discussing the other.

A pronoun must agree with the noun to which it refers, i.e. its **antecedent** or **referent**. Singular pronouns (e.g. *she*, *it*) must agree with singular nouns, and plural pronouns (e.g. *they*) must agree with plural nouns.

For example:

The cacao bean is the dried and fully fermented fatty bean of the cacao tree (Theobroma cacao). **1** Their the source of cocoa butter and solids, including chocolate, as well as an ingredient in many Mesoamerican dishes such as molé and tejate.

1
A) NO CHANGE
B) It's
C) Its
D) They're

When a lot of people look at a question like this, they notice immediately that *their* is possessive and doesn't make sense in context. Happy to have identified the error, they leap to pick D). *They're = they are*, which makes perfect grammatical sense. But unfortunately, D) is not the right answer.

When we look at the various options, we can see that they contain both singular (*it*) and plural (*they*) options. That distribution indicates that we need to figure out what noun the pronoun is supposed to refer to, and whether that noun is singular or plural. For the moment, we're going to forget the possessive issue.

The underlined pronoun is at the start of the sentence, and antecedents typically come before pronouns (*ante* = before). So we need to look at the previous sentence to figure out what noun the pronoun refers to:

The cacao bean is the dried and fully fermented fatty bean of the cacao tree (Theobroma cacao).

Now we're going to think through the problem, step-by-step.

- What is logically the source of cocoa butter and solids? The cacao bean.

- Is *the cacao bean* singular or plural? Singular. We know because there is no *–s* on the end of *bean*.

- Is *they* singular or plural? Plural.

So we have a mismatch. The pronoun *it* should be used to refer to singular nouns. *Its* is possessive, whereas *it's* means *it is*, which makes sense in context. The answer is therefore B). *They're vs. their* was only a distraction. Note that it does not matter that the pronoun *they* would logically refer to the plural noun *cacao beans*. Only the singular *cacao bean* appears, and **a pronoun must refer to a word that actually appears**.

Pronouns can refer to either people or things. Some pronouns can refer only to people, some can refer only to things, and some can refer to both.

A. Things

The pronouns *it(s)* and *they/their* are used to refer to singular and plural things (e.g. cities, books, paintings). Note that the plural of *it* can be either *they* or *them*, not *its*.

Singular		Plural
It	$\rightarrow$	They/Them
Its	$\rightarrow$	Their

A singular noun must be replaced with a singular pronoun.

Incorrect: While **the tomato** is botanically a fruit, **they** are considered a vegetable for culinary purposes.

Correct: While **the tomato** is botanically a fruit, **it** is considered a vegetable for culinary purposes.

Likewise, a plural noun must be replaced with a plural pronoun.

Incorrect: While **tomatoes** are botanically fruits, **it** is considered a vegetable for culinary purposes.

Correct: While **tomatoes** are botanically fruits, **they** are considered a vegetable for culinary purposes.

An antecedent may appear in the same sentence in which an underlined pronoun appears. It may also appear in the previous sentence (as in the example on the previous page) or, on rare occasions, in the following sentence.

Important: When you see a set of answer choices that includes both singular and plural pronouns, you should always take a moment to determine which noun the underlined pronoun refers to. Otherwise, you are very likely to be confused by answers that are grammatically correct but that create disagreements when plugged back into the passage.

B. People

Singular Nouns		Plural Nouns
She, He	→	They
Her, His	→	Their

Errors involving these pronouns are often easier to catch than those involving *it* and *they* for the simple reason that it is generally clear whether a passage is discussing one person or more than one person.

For example:

Mae Jemison became the first African-American woman to travel into space when she went into orbit aboard the Space Shuttle Endeavour on September 12, 1992. After **1** one's medical education and a brief general practice, Jemison served in the Peace Corps for two years.

A) NO CHANGE
B) her
C) Its
D) They're

Since the underlined pronoun can only refer to Mae Jemison, who is clearly female, *her* is the sole possibility, and the answer must be B).

Important: When it is unclear whether a singular noun (e.g. an artist, an architect, a cook) refers to a male or a female, the phrase *he or she* or *his or her* should be used.

For example:

When an artist works with oil paints, **1** they should allow at least a week for paintings to dry. During that time, paintings should be stored in a safe, dry place, away from objects that could brush against them and smear the paint. Drying times for oil paintings vary from a few days to several months. Some types of oil paintings take up to a year to "cure" before they can be varnished.

1

A) NO CHANGE
B) one
C) he or she
D) we

Because *an artist* is singular, the phrase *he or she* rather than *they* is required. C) is therefore correct.

Note: the word *each* is singular (it's short for *each one*) and must agree with the singular pronouns *it* and *he or she*.

Incorrect:	Each of the artists will exhibit **their** work at the museum next year.
Correct:	Each of the artists will exhibit **his or her** work at the museum next year.

C. Noun Agreement

Nouns themselves must also agree in number: singular subjects must be paired with singular nouns, and plural subjects must be paired with plural nouns.

Singular noun agreement

Incorrect: Orville Wright, along with his brother Wilbur, are considered **inventors** of the airplane.

Correct: Orville Wright, along with his brother Wilbur, is considered **an inventor** of the airplane.

If the non-essential clause is removed, the error reveals itself: *Orville Wright...are considered inventors of the airplane.* Clearly that does not make sense. Since Orville Wright was one person, he must have been *an inventor*.

Plural noun agreement

Incorrect: Capitalizing on the national bicycle craze of the early 1890s, Orville and Wilbur Wright decided to open a shop and become **a bicycle seller**.

Correct: Capitalizing on the national bicycle craze of the early 1890s, Orville and Wilbur Wright decided to open a shop and become **bicycle sellers**.

Since Orville and Wilbur Wright were two people, they must have become bicycle sellers, plural.

D. One vs. You

You   →   You
One   →   One

While both *one* and *you* can be used to talk about people in general, the two pronouns cannot be mixed and matched within a sentence or paragraph but must remain consistent throughout. In addition, they should not be matched with any other pronoun.

Remember that context is important. While all four of the answers to a given question may be grammatically correct and make sense out of context, only one will make the sentence **parallel** to the surrounding sentences.

If you have been reading the passage carefully, not just skipping from question to question, it is likely you will remember which pronoun was used in the previous couple of sentences. If you are unsure, however, go back to the passage and read the surrounding sentences to see which pronoun is used.

For example:

If **you** want to protect your home from insect invasions, **you** should avoid leaving crumbs lying on the floor. **You** should also avoid leaving dirty dishes in the sink since ants and mice are attracted to leftovers. Finally, one should make sure that cracks in the floor and walls are sealed because pests can often enter homes by wriggling through tiny spaces.

1
A) NO CHANGE
B) we
C) they
D) you

If you were just to read the sentence with the underlined pronoun on its own, you probably wouldn't see anything wrong. When we look at the surrounding sentences, however, we can see that they contain the pronoun *you*. That means that the pronoun in this sentence must match. D) is therefore correct.

Emphatic Pronouns

Words such as *herself*, *itself*, and *themselves* can correctly be used to emphasize either people or things. Just make sure that they agree with the noun they emphasize.

Incorrect: What has been criticized is the author's refusal to discuss her work publicly, not the quality of <u>the writing</u> **herself**.

Correct: What has been criticized is the author's refusal to discuss her work publicly, not the quality of <u>the writing</u> **itself**.

Because *the writing* (thing) rather than *the author* (person) is the noun being emphasized, *itself* should be used.

E. Missing or Ambiguous Antecedent

When the noun that a pronoun refers to is missing or unclear, it is necessary to include the specific name of the person, place, or thing that the pronoun refers to.

For example:

Daniel Liebeskind and Frank Gehry are among the most celebrated architects in the world. **1** He is known for using unconventional building materials such as corrugated metal to create tilted geometrical structures.

A) NO CHANGE
B) Their
C) Gehry
D) He would be

Because *Daniel* and *Frank* are both male names, it is unclear which one *he* refers to. Only C) supplies the name.

Important: given the choice between a pronoun such as *it* or *they* and a noun naming a specific person or thing, the noun will virtually always be correct – even when it appears in the <u>longest</u> answer.

For example:

Some sources claim that Spanish conquistador Hernán Cortés was the first person to bring the tomato to Europe in 1521. Others say that Christopher Columbus took it back as early as 1493. Regardless of which version is true, reports from that time period all agree that **1** they were intensely suspicious when they first encountered the small yellow fruit.

A) NO CHANGE
B) members of the Spanish court
C) some of them
D) those people

Since the passage describes how two explorers brought the tomato back to Europe, it makes sense that *they* would refer to the Europeans who first encountered it; however, the noun *Europeans* doesn't actually appear. Only B) supplies the noun indicating who was suspicious.

This and That

The pronoun *this* and *that* (and their plural forms, *these* and *those*) should be followed by a noun. When they appear alone, they are frequently ambiguous.

For example:

> Over the last several decades, the Internet has fundamentally changed how we live, work, and play. From virtual classrooms to electronic banking to online gaming, many of our daily actions and interactions are now governed by the web. While this has numerous benefits, it has some drawbacks as well.

 1

A) NO CHANGE
B) that
C) these
D) this technology

Although the reader can reasonably assume that the word *this* refers to the Internet or conducting daily activities online, the sentence does not actually spell it out. D) is correct because it includes a specific noun, and **more specific is always better**.

Sometimes, you may also be tested on the noun following the pronoun. The right answer will correctly rephrase information from the previous sentence, or previous part of a sentence, in a more general way. Incorrect answers will provide a general noun that does not correspond to the specific information provided earlier.

> Over the last several decades, the Internet has fundamentally changed how we live, work, and play. From virtual classrooms to electronic banking to online "gaming," many of our daily actions and interactions are now governed by the web. While these have numerous benefits, they have some drawbacks as well.

 1

A) NO CHANGE
B) some things
C) such exceptions
D) these innovations

In the paragraph above, *Internet, virtual classrooms, electronic banking,* and *online "gaming"* are all examples of things that have developed over the past few decades – that is, they are *new*. *Innovations* are new things (the root *nov–* means "new"), so D) is correct. A) incorrectly uses the pronoun *these* without a noun afterward. In B), the register of the word *things* is too casual, and *some* is vague. And in C), there is no mention in the paragraph of an "exception." The pronoun *such* is a decoy – it is simply a stylistic alternative to *these* and does not affect the answer.

Exercise: Pronoun/Noun Agreement and Apostrophes (answers p. 228)

1. New types of digital technology have allowed acoustic engineers to create sophisticated noise-filtering devices. As a result, **1** he or she can now eliminate unwanted noise with a precision never before possible.

1
A) NO CHANGE
B) one
C) we
D) they

2. Hidden between a bookstore and a café, San Francisco's Jack Kerouac Alley is easy to overlook. Once a place to throw garbage, **1** they've been transformed into an inviting pedestrian-only thoroughfare, complete with decorative lampposts and poetry in English and Chinese lining the walkway.

1
A) NO CHANGE
B) they'd
C) it's
D) he's

3. Deserts are found on every continent including Antarctica. **1** Its often the site of unusual rock formations and, in some cases, amazing archaeological finds. Many of the largest ones, including the Gobi Desert, the Great Basin Desert, and the Patagonian Desert, are located in the shadows of immense mountain ranges that block moisture from nearby oceans or bodies of water.

1
A) NO CHANGE
B) They're
C) Their
D) It's

4. The most common movements we make while asleep are rapid eye movements. When we dream, our eyes move in accordance with what we are dreaming about. If, for example, we dream about watching a game of tennis, **1** one's eyes will move from left to right with each volley. These movements, generated in the dream world, escape from normal sleep paralysis and leak into the real world. Seeing a sleeping person's eyes move is the strongest sign that **2** he or she is dreaming.

1
A) NO CHANGE
B) our eyes
C) their eye's
D) they're eyes

2
A) NO CHANGE
B) they're
C) there
D) one

5.   You're up to your knees in mud and weeds, getting bitten by things you can't identify. **1** One's surroundings seem to grow more hostile by the minute. Meanwhile, you search for a creature that probably ran away hours ago and couldn't care less about communing with you. And as you open your notebook, the sky opens and drenches **2** them. Welcome to the world of nature writing.

1

A) NO CHANGE
B) You're surroundings
C) Your surroundings
D) Their surrounding's

2

A) NO CHANGE
B) the pages.
C) that.
D) this.

6.   Miles Dewey Davis III (May 26, 1926 – September 28, 1991) was an American jazz musician, trumpeter, bandleader, and composer. Known for creating a unique sound and style through the use of non-traditional instruments such as the French horn, Davis joined Ella Fitzgerald and Duke Ellington as **1** the most renowned performers in the United States during the mid-twentieth century.

1

A) NO CHANGE
B) the most renowned performers,
C) one of the most renowned performers
D) one of the more renowned performers –

7.   According to author Nadine Gordimer, the process of writing fiction is unconscious, emerging from what people learn and how **1** they live. Gordimer, who was born in South Africa in 1923, was an authority on that subject. **2** They received the Nobel Prize in Literature in 1991, having attained international recognition for her work. At the time she won **3** that, she had published 10 novels, dozens of short stories, essay collections, and a play.

1

A) NO CHANGE
B) one lives.
C) you live.
D) we live.

2

A) NO CHANGE
B) This
C) One
D) She

3

A) NO CHANGE
B) the award
C) them
D) that thing

8. Webs allows spiders to catch prey without having to expend energy chasing it around. However, [1] it's a tiring dilemma because of the large amount of protein required, in the form of silk. In addition, silk quickly loses its stickiness and become inefficient at capturing prey. As a result, spiders often eat [2] it's own webs daily to regain some of the energy used in spinning. The silk proteins are thus recycled.

[1]
A) NO CHANGE
B) spinning a web is a tiring process
C) its a tiring process
D) they're process is tiring

[2]
A) NO CHANGE
B) its own web's
C) there own webs'
D) their own webs

9. There are over 3,000 lizard species, but the Komodo dragon, a reptile with ancestors that date back more than 100 million years, wins the prize for being the largest living lizard in the world. [1] They're name came from rumors of a large dragon-like lizard inhabiting the warm, hilly islands of Indonesia. Indeed, the yellow color of its long, forked tongue reminds people of a mythical fire-spitting dragon. Despite its ancient roots, the Komodo dragon was unknown to [2] them until 1910, when it was observed in Komodo National Park.

[1]
A) NO CHANGE
B) Their
C) Its
D) It's

[2]
A) NO CHANGE
B) researchers
C) those people
D) it

10. There are around 300 octopus species, all of which can change colors, squirt poison, and exert a force greater than their own body weight. In fact, [1] they're part of an elite group of marine creatures with remarkably large brains. Scientists have found that octopuses can not only navigate their way through mazes, but they can also solve problems quickly and remember [2] that.

[1]
A) NO CHANGE
B) their
C) its
D) it's

[2]
A) NO CHANGE
B) the solutions.
C) those.
D) this.

Cumulative Review: All Punctuation and Transitions (answers p. 228)

1. At the age of six Judith Jamison towered over her classmates. **1** Jamisons parents, who wanted to complement their daughter's exceptional height with **2** grace, and they enrolled her in a classical ballet class at the Judimar School of Dance, where she studied throughout her childhood. Jamison decided on a career in dance only after three semesters of coursework in psychology at Fisk University, and she completed her education at the Philadelphia Dance **3** Academy in 1964, she was spotted by choreographer Agnes de Mille, who invited her to appear in a performance with the American Ballet Theater. Jamison moved to New York the following **4** year, eventually joining the Alvin Ailey American Dance Theater.

1

A) NO CHANGE
B) Jamisons parent's
C) Jamison's parents'
D) Jamison's parents

2

A) NO CHANGE
B) grace, enrolling
C) grace – enrolled
D) grace, enrolled

3

A) NO CHANGE
B) Academy. In 1964, she
C) Academy, in 1964, she
D) Academy in 1964 she

4

A) NO CHANGE
B) year, but she eventually joined
C) year; and eventually joined
D) year, she eventually joined

2. When a person breaks a bone, it eventually knits itself back together. **1** Microbiologist, Henk Jonkers, a researcher at Delft University of Technology in the Netherlands, wondered why buildings couldn't do the same thing. Inspired by the human body, Jonkers created self-healing concrete. Concrete is filled with capsules of limestone-producing bacteria along with calcium lactate. When the concrete cracks, air and moisture prompt the bacteria to consume the calcium **2** lactate, they convert it to calcite, an ingredient in limestone. The cracks are sealed, and the concrete is stabilized.

1

A) NO CHANGE
B) Microbiologist Henk Jonkers,
C) Microbiologist Henk Jonkers
D) Microbiologist Henk Jonkers –

2

A) NO CHANGE
B) lactate, they convert the it to calcite –
C) lactate and convert it to calcite,
D) lactate, and this being converted to calcite,

150

This innovation could solve a longstanding problem with **3** concrete; the worlds most common construction material. Concrete often develops micro-cracks during the construction process. These tiny cracks don't immediately affect the building's structural integrity, but they can lead to leakage problems that can corrode the **4** concrete's steel reinforcements, ultimately causing a collapse. With the self-healing technology, cracks can be sealed immediately, preventing future leaks and costly long-term damage. The bacteria can lie dormant for up to two **5** centuries. Far longer than the lifespan of most buildings constructed today.

3. Perhaps the ocean organism most vulnerable to temperature change is coral. There is evidence that reefs will bleach – that is, eject algae that play a key role in maintaining their **1** ecosystems, at even a slight persistent increase in temperature. Bleaching slows coral growth, makes it susceptible to disease, and can lead to large-scale reef destruction. Other organisms affected by temperature change include **2** krill, it is a very important link at the base of the food chain. Research has shown that krill reproduce in significantly smaller numbers when ocean temperatures rise. The resulting decrease in the krill population can have a cascading effect by disrupting the life cycle of krill **3** eaters such as: penguins and seals, which in turn causes food shortages for predators higher up on the food chain.

3
A) NO CHANGE
B) concrete the worlds'
C) concrete – the world's
D) concrete, the world's

4
A) NO CHANGE
B) concretes steel reinforcement's,
C) concretes steel reinforcements,
D) concrete's steel reinforcements;

5
A) NO CHANGE
B) centuries: far longer
C) centuries; far longer
D) centuries far longer,

1
A) NO CHANGE
B) ecosystems at even
C) ecosystems – at even
D) ecosystems; at even

2
A) NO CHANGE
B) krill, a very important link
C) krill, being a very important link
D) krill, and this is a very important link

3
A) NO CHANGE
B) eaters; such as penguins and seals,
C) eaters – such as penguins and seals
D) eaters, such as penguins and seals,

4. We inhabit a world of bridges. For thousands of **1** years, people, who needed to cross bodies of water, have been finding ingenious ways to do so. From the 3,000 year-old Arkadiko bridge in Greece to the brand-new 26.4 mile structure connecting the Chinese port city of Quindao to **2** there suburbs, bridges are everywhere. The simplest type of bridge can be created by dragging a log over a creek, but the construction of modern bridges typically requires years of **3** education today architects, engineers, and artists may spend a decade or more working together to design a single structure.

1

A) NO CHANGE
B) years, people who needed to cross bodies of water,
C) years, people who needed to cross bodies of water
D) years; people who needed to cross bodies of water

2

A) NO CHANGE
B) they're
C) it's
D) its

3

A) NO CHANGE
B) education. Today,
C) education today,
D) education today

5. In the world of airliners, bigger means better. The dawn of the jet age in the 1950s brought in the likes of the **1** Boeing 707; an aircraft capable of carrying more passengers more quickly than any propeller-driven design. Since that time, airliners have grown larger and larger. The sight of an Airbus A380 can still create great excitement. The **2** enormous, double-decker plane can seat over 800 people. While the Airbus 380 is the largest passenger-carrying aircraft ever **3** built; it is dwarfed by another design that may someday take to the skies. With three decks for passengers, the AWWA Sky Whale looks like a cross between a tropical fish and a space shuttle from a science fiction movie.

1

A) NO CHANGE
B) Boeing 707, and it was an aircraft capable
C) Boeing 707, an aircraft capable
D) Boeing 707, an aircraft being capable

2

A) NO CHANGE
B) enormous, double-decker, plane
C) enormous double-decker, plane
D) enormous double-decker plane –

3

A) NO CHANGE
B) built, it is dwarfed
C) built, but it is dwarfed
D) built, it is dwarfed,

6. Optical illusions reveal the human mind's tendency to make assumptions about the world – and what we believe **1** ones sees is often not the truth. For thousands of years, curious minds have questioned why our eyes are so easily fooled by simple drawings. Illusions, **2** scientists have found, can reveal everything from how we process time and space to our experience of consciousness. For example, if a person watching a waterfall shifts his or her gaze to a group of rocks on the side, the rocks appear to move in the opposite direction from the flow of water. **3** However, this effect is known as the waterfall illusion. Tracking the flow of the water seems to "tire" some of the brain's neurons. When the person's gaze moves to the rocks, other neurons **4** overcompensate. They cause the illusion of movement in the other direction.

1

A) NO CHANGE
B) you see
C) he or she sees
D) we are seeing

2

A) NO CHANGE
B) scientists have found –
C) scientists have found;
D) scientists have found

3

A) NO CHANGE
B) For example, this effect
C) Therefore, this experience is known as
D) This effect is known as

4

What is the most effective way of combining the sentences at the underlined portion?

A) overcompensate, this causes
B) overcompensate and causing
C) overcompensate by causing
D) overcompensate, but they cause

7. It seems strange that water is such a scarce resource when the Earth is covered in more than 300 million trillion gallons of **1** them. From oceans to lakes to rivers, water is seemingly everywhere. Unfortunately, though, only about one-half of one percent of water is drinkable. 98 percent of the remaining water is salt water, and 1.5 percent remains locked up in icecaps and glaciers. As advancing technology continues to reduce costs and freshwater continues to grow scarcer and more **2** expensive; more cities are looking to seawater conversion as a way to meet the need for drinking water.

1

A) NO CHANGE
B) that.
C) this stuff.
D) it.

2

A) NO CHANGE
B) expensive. More cities
C) expensive, but more cities
D) expensive, more cities

8. When I used to think of the Middle Ages, I would **1** imagine knights, lords and ladies, jousting competitions, and bloody battles, all taking place in or around a castle. I always assumed that castles were nothing more than large **2** dwellings, that provided a scenic background, for the real action. Then, however, I spent last summer researching castles for a local historical society and discovered that they had many important functions.

As I learned, medieval castles served a primarily military purpose – **3** that is, they housed armies and acted as garrisons that controlled a particular territory. Furthermore, castles were key staging points for conquests and defenses of territories. Many castles, particularly those that were part of fortified **4** towns, which sheltered the surrounding villagers in times of war and siege.

The designs and constructions of these castles varied greatly. **5** Because some were architectural masterpieces, others were crude and utilitarian. It was not until the end of the Middle Ages that castles lost their military function, either becoming homes for the nobility or being abandoned altogether.

1

A) NO CHANGE
B) imagine: knights; lords and ladies; jousting competitions, and
C) imagine: knights, lords and ladies, jousting competitions and
D) imagine knights, lords and ladies, jousting competitions, and,

2

A) NO CHANGE
B) dwellings, that provided a scenic background
C) dwellings that provided a scenic background,
D) dwellings that provided a scenic background

3

A) NO CHANGE
B) however,
C) furthermore,
D) likewise,

4

A) NO CHANGE
B) towns, and sheltered
C) towns, sheltered
D) towns – sheltered

5

A) NO CHANGE
B) While
C) However
D) DELETE the underlined word

9. Machines are often blamed for stealing people's jobs. **1** Moreover, some machines actually create work. Technology can boost productivity, increasing the demand for labor. It can also streamline complex tasks, opening the door for less skilled workers. American inventor Eli Whitney invented machines that did both.

Whitney's most famous invention, the cotton gin, was patented in 1794. The **2** word, "gin," is short for "engine," and the cotton gin revolutionized cotton production by automating its processing. The device consisted of a set of wheels containing metal hooks. As the wheels turned, the hooks caught bits of cotton, pulling them through a screen that kept out seeds. **3** A wire brush periodically swept the cotton off the blade. This brush prevented the machine from jamming.

Inland cotton **4** farmers, who could only cultivate "green seed" cotton – found the gin especially useful. This type of cotton was so labor-intensive that it required 10 hours of hand labor to produce a single unit of cotton. One Whitney cotton gin could do a full **5** days' work of several men in an hour.

1
A) NO CHANGE
B) In reality
C) Likewise
D) As such

2
A) NO CHANGE
B) The word "gin"
C) The word "gin,"
D) The word, "gin"

3
What is the most effective way of combining the sentences at the underlined portion?

A) A wire brush periodically swept the cotton off the blade and prevented the machine from jamming.
B) A wire brush periodically swept the cotton off the blade, it prevented the machine from jamming.
C) A wire brush periodically swept the cotton off the blade; however, this prevented the machine from jamming.
D) A wire brush, which periodically swept the cotton off the blade, and prevented the machine from jamming.

4
A) NO CHANGE
B) farmers who
C) farmers – who
D) farmers; who

5
A) NO CHANGE
B) day's work
C) days work,
D) days' work,

155

10. Every clinical drug trial conducted today randomly assigns patients to one of two **1** groups: members of the first group receive a real drug, while members of the second receive an inactive pill or substance known as a placebo. Some placebos contain **2** sugar, others consist of distilled water or saline solution. Patients are not told which one they are taking, and that information is hidden from researchers as well. Remarkably, the patients taking the inactive drug tend to show some **3** improvement, a result known as the placebo effect.

Alongside the benefits, however, people taking placebos often report **4** puzzling side effects: nausea, headaches, or pain – that are unlikely to come from an inert tablet. The problem is that people in a clinical trial are given exactly the same health warnings, whether they are taking the real drug or the placebo. **5** For example, the expectation of symptoms can produce physical effects in some placebo takers.

1

A) NO CHANGE
B) groups members
C) two
D) towns, sheltered

2

A) NO CHANGE
B) sugar, so others
C) sugar, however, others
D) sugar; others

3

A) NO CHANGE
B) improvement, and such findings are
C) improvement, but this explanation is
D) improvement, this is

4

A) NO CHANGE
B) puzzling side effects – nausea,
C) puzzling side effects; nausea,
D) puzzling side effects, nausea,

5

A) NO CHANGE
B) Although
C) Somehow
D) In fact

14. Verbs: Agreement and Tense

There are two types of verb questions:

1. Subject-verb agreement
2. Verb tense

Although some questions may test both of these concepts, it is important to understand that they are distinct.

- **Agreement** answers the question **"singular or plural?"** Verbs must agree with their subjects: singular subjects must take singular verbs, and plural subjects must take plural verbs.

- **Tense** answers the question **"when?"** It indicates past, present, or future.

Let's consider the following sentence:

> **The feathers** of the black-backed woodpecker **has** evolved to blend in with charred trees so that they are invisible to predators lurking in the forest.

This sentence contains a **disagreement between the subject and the verb** because the subject (*feathers*) is plural and the verb (*has*) is singular. The singular noun *woodpecker*, which appears immediately before the verb, is part of the prepositional phrase *of the black-backed woodpecker* and has no effect on the number of the verb. In order to correct the sentence, it is necessary to use the plural verb *have* rather than the singular verb *has*.

When many students encounter this type of sentence, however, their first instinct is to change the **tense** of the verb and use the simple past, *had*. While this change does make the sentence grammatically acceptable, there is no compelling reason for the sentence to be rewritten in another tense. More importantly, the correction does not truly address the actual problem with the sentence: the subject and the verb disagree.

But, you might wonder, why does that matter if *had* fixes the sentence anyway? Why bother learning all that grammar if you can get the question right without worrying about any of it?

Well, because you could very well see a question that looks like this:

The works of artist Alan Chin has included elements inspired by both the California gold rush and the transcontinental railroad.

A) NO CHANGE
B) includes
C) have included
D) having included

Whether or not you realize it, you're being forced to deal with the actual error. If you can't hear there's a problem and don't have the grammatical tools to figure it out, you're out of luck. You can probably recognize that D) is awkward and breaks the "-ING is bad" rule, but otherwise…you're reduced to guesswork.

Subject-verb agreement errors aren't usually easy to hear, so when they occur in the original version of a passage, many students will quickly glance through the answer choices before picking NO CHANGE and moving on without a second thought. This is not what you want to do.

If you cannot identify the error immediately, the key to dealing with these question is to work backwards, using the answer choices to determine what the question is testing.

If you find yourself lost on a question involving verbs, you can follow these steps:

1) Look at the answer choices.

If you examine the answer choices to the question on the previous page, you can see that A) and B) contain singular verbs, *has*, *includes*, and C) contains a plural verb, *have*. (You can assume that D) is incorrect because it contains an *–ing* word, which is likely to create a fragment.)

When some answer choices contain singular verbs while other answer choices contain plural verbs, the question is testing subject-verb agreement.

2) Identify the subject and determine whether it is singular or plural.

Remember that **the noun right before a verb usually won't be the subject**. If it were, the question would be too easy, and it wouldn't be on the test in the first place!

When an underlined verb is located close to the beginning of a sentence, the subject is typically right at the beginning of the sentence. So back up and look at the first words of the sentence: *The works*. That's your subject. *Works* ends in *–s*, so it's plural.

Alternately, if you really don't want to worry about grammar, you can think about it logically. What "has included elements inspired by both the California gold rush and the transcontinental railroad?" It can only be *the works* of artist Alan Chin. A *person* can't contain elements inspired by both the California gold rush and the transcontinental railroad.

3) Find the verb that agrees with the subject

Since *works* is plural, a plural verb is required. Only C) contains a plural verb (*have*), so C) is correct.

Notice that although B) contains a verb in one tense (*includes*), while the verbs in A) and C) contain verbs in a different tense (*has/have included*), you do not need to worry about tense at all in order to answer the question correctly. The only thing that matters is subject-verb agreement. The fact that different answers contain different tenses is simply a distraction technique designed to make questions look more complicated than they actually are.

Subject-Verb Agreement

Questions testing subject-verb agreement are virtually guaranteed to appear on the SAT, and learning to recognize the various ways in which disagreements are structured is an easy way to boost your score.

These questions ask about verbs in the third person singular (*she/he/it/one*) and third person plural (*they*) forms.

The most important thing to remember about the singular vs. plural forms of a verb is as follows:

- Singular verbs end in –*s* (e.g. it makes)

- Plural verbs do <u>not</u> end in –*s* (e.g. they make)

Note that this is the **opposite of nouns**, which take an –*s* in the plural and no –*s* in the singular. For example, *the book* is singular and *the books* is plural; however, *he speaks* is singular and *they speak* is plural.

	Correct	**Incorrect**
Singular Subject:	The artist paint**s**.	The artist paint.
Plural Subject:	The artists paint.	The artists paint**s**.
Compound Subject (two nouns joined by *and*)	The artist and her helper paint.	The artist and her assistant paints.

To be and *to have* are two of the most common verbs in the English language. Because they are irregular, it is important that you be able to recognize their singular and plural forms.

		To be	**To have**
Present:	**singular**	is	has
	plural	are	have
Past:	**singular**	was	had
	plural	were	had

Unfortunately, questions testing subject-verb agreement are unlikely to make disagreements too obvious. As a result, subjects and verbs are unlikely to appear next to one another. There are, however, a number of fairly predictable ways in which disagreements can potentially be structured.

A. Subject – Non-Essential Clause – Verb

In this structure, a non-essential clause is simply inserted between the subject and the verb to distract from the fact that the subject is singular and the verb is plural or vice-versa. When the information between the commas is crossed out, the disagreement between is revealed. For example:

Incorrect: <u>Green tea</u> with mint, which is a popular drink in many Middle-Eastern countries, **are** said to have many health benefits.

Cross out: <u>Green tea</u> with mint, ~~which is a popular drink throughout many middle-eastern countries,~~ **are** said to have many health benefits.

Correct: <u>Green tea</u> with mint, which is a popular drink in many Middle-Eastern countries, **is** said to have many health benefits.

It is important that you pick up your pencil and physically draw a line through the non-essential clause. Do not simply draw a line in your imagination. Sooner or later your eye will most likely look past an error that you could have easily caught, and you will lose points unnecessarily.

Occasionally, however, the disagreement will occur **within** the non-essential clause:

Incorrect: <u>Green tea</u> with mint, **which are** a popular drink in many Middle-Eastern countries, is said to have many health benefits.

Correct: <u>Green tea</u> with mint, **which is** a popular drink in many Middle-Eastern countries, is said to have many health benefits.

Essential Clause with "That"

Sometimes the disagreement will involve a clause beginning with *that*. As is true for disagreements involving non-essential clauses, the disagreement can be placed around the clause or within it.

Incorrect: **A drink** <u>that is popular in many Middle Eastern countries</u> **are** green tea with mint, said to have many health benefits.

Correct: **A drink** <u>that is popular in many Middle Eastern countries</u> **is** green tea with mint, said to have many health benefits.

Incorrect: The black widow spider has **striking red hourglass markings** <u>that **makes** it one of the most recognizable spiders in the United States.</u>

Correct: The black widow spider has **striking red hourglass markings** <u>that **make** it one of the most recognizable spiders in the United States.</u>

B. Subject – Prepositional Phrase – Verb

As discussed earlier, a prepositional phrase is a phrase that begins with a preposition (e.g. *in the box*, *under the table*, *over the hill*). Prepositional phrases are frequently inserted between subjects and verbs to distract from disagreements.

If you don't see an error the first time you read a sentence, take your pencil and **cross out** all prepositional phrases. Then check for subject-verb agreement. The last word of a prepositional phrase will always be the last word right before the verb, so be careful not to cross out verbs when getting rid of prepositional phrases.

In the sentences below, the subject is underlined, the prepositional phrase is italicized, and the verb is in bold.

Incorrect:	The patent *for the first mechanical pencils* **were** granted to Sampson Morgan and John Hawkins in England during the early nineteenth century.
Cross out:	The patent *~~for the first mechanical pencils~~* **were** granted to Sampson Morgan and John Hawkins in England during the early nineteenth century.
Correct:	The patent *for the first mechanical pencils* **was** granted to Sampson Morgan and John Hawkins in England during the early nineteenth century.

The above sentence contains a classic trick. The subject (*patent*) is singular and requires a singular verb (*was*). However, the prepositional phrase inserted between the subject and the verb has as its last word a plural noun (*pencils*), which, if you are not paying close attention, can easily appear to be the subject of the plural verb *were*.

Hint: If you see an underlined verb close to the beginning of a sentence, the subject will usually be the first word or couple of words of the sentence.

C. Verb Before Subject

In this structure, the normal word order or **syntax** of a sentence is reversed so that verb is placed before the subject. Sentences testing this structure may **begin with a prepositional phrase**, followed by the verb and then subject.

In the sentences below, the subject is underlined, the prepositional phrase is italicized, and the verb is in bold.

Incorrect:	*Along the Loup Canal in Nebraska* **extends** parks, lakes, and trails owned and operated by the Loup power district.
Correct:	*Along the Loup Canal in Nebraska* **extend** parks, lakes, and trails owned and operated by the Loup power district.

Most often, the preposition will be the first word of the sentence, as in the example sentences above, but sometimes it will be the second.

Incorrect:	Running *along the Loup Canal in Nebraska* **is** parks, lakes, and trails owned and operated by the Loup power district.
Correct:	Running *along the Loup Canal in Nebraska* **are** parks, lakes, and trails owned and operated by the Loup power district.

161

This structure can be confusing because the reversed syntax (or word order) makes the sentence sound odd. It is important to understand, however, that the syntax itself is not what makes the sentence incorrect. It is simply a distraction to keep you from hearing the disagreement between the subject and the verb.

Sometimes a sentence in this form will not contain an agreement error. In such cases you will still need to be able to identify the subject and double-check the agreement in order to confirm that no change is necessary.

It is also important that you determine the subject because you will occasionally encounter errors in which the verb comes before the subject but is not preceded by a prepositional phrase:

Incorrect: Radioactivity is generally not considered harmful when people are exposed to it at low levels for brief periods, but less clear **is** <u>its long-term effects</u>.

Correct: Radioactivity is generally not considered harmful when people are exposed to it at low levels for brief periods, but less clear **are** <u>its long-term effects</u>.

When there is no preposition at the start of the sentence, there are unfortunately no real tip-offs for this error besides the presence of both singular and plural verb forms in the answer choices. The easiest way to identify the subject is simply to ask yourself *what* is "less clear" – the plural noun *long-term effects* is the only option that makes sense, so the sentence requires the plural verb *are*.

D. Compound Subjects

A compound subject simply consists of two nouns – singular or plural – joined by the word *and*. Compound subjects are **always plural** and thus take plural verbs.

While compound subjects are generally quite straightforward in short/simple sentences, they can be easy to overlook in longer ones if you do not read carefully or only pay attention to the noun next to the verb. In addition, mistakes involving compound subjects can be extremely difficult to pick out by ear, so even more so than usual, you should not rely on the way the sentence sounds. For example:

Incorrect: Pigeons make highly effective messengers because their <u>speed and homing ability</u> **allows** them to quickly and reliably reach familiar destinations.

Correct: Pigeons make highly effective messengers because their <u>speed and homing ability</u> **allow** them to quickly and reliably reach familiar destinations.

You should be especially careful to determine the **complete subject** when the verb appears before the subject. Agreement errors in sentences that contain this type of syntax are exceptionally hard to hear, even if they would be fairly obvious when subject-verb order was not inverted.

Incorrect: <u>A park and a lake</u> **runs** along the Loup Canal, a hydroelectric and irrigation canal located in eastern Nebraska.

Inverted: Along the Loup Canal **runs** <u>a park and a lake</u>, both of which are owned and operated by the Loup Power District.

Both versions of the sentence contain the same error, but the second one hides it much more effectively.

E. There is/There are, etc.

There is
There was } go with **singular** nouns
There has been

There are
There were } go with **plural** nouns
There have been

Incorrect: In recent months, there **has been** <u>many questions</u> raised about the handling of the company's finances.

Correct: In recent months, there **have been** <u>many questions</u> raised about the handling of the company's finances.

F. Gerunds = Singular

Gerunds (-ING words) take **singular verbs** when they act as subjects. Don't get distracted by a plural noun before the verb!

Incorrect: <u>Playing</u> parlor games such as charades **were** a popular pastime in the early twentieth century, before the invention of radio and television.

Correct: <u>Playing</u> parlor games such as charades **was** a popular pastime in the early twentieth century, before the invention of radio and television.

G. Collective Nouns = Singular

Collective nouns are **singular nouns** that refer to groups of people. Common examples include *agency*, *institution*, *school*, *committee*, *jury*, *city*, *country*, *company*, *university*, and *team*. While such nouns are sometimes used with plural verbs in informal writing, the SAT only considers **singular verbs** to be correct.

Incorrect: For the past several years, the theater company **have** traveled to various schools throughout the city in order to expose students to classic works.

Correct: For the past several years, the theater company **has** traveled to various schools throughout the city in order to expose students to classic works.

H. That/What/Whether as a subject

All of these words can correctly be used as subjects, although the construction may sound very odd to you. *That* = the fact that; *whether/what* = the question of whether/what.

Correct: <u>That</u> Jane Goodall became the world's foremost expert on chimpanzees **was** hardly a surprise to those who had observed her childhood fascination with animals.

163

I. Indefinite Pronouns

Although questions testing these pronouns are very unlikely to make up a significant portion of the test, it is probable that at least some of them will be tested from time to time. In the past, only the pronouns *one*, *each*, *the number/a number*, and *neither* were tested, but preliminary material released by the College Board included a question testing *any*. Because this question represents a departure from established practice, it is possible that other pronouns will be tested as well.

Singular	Plural	Singular or Plural
One Few Each Every Any None The number What That (= the fact that) Whether (=the question whether)	Others Some Several Many Most All A number	Neither*

When these pronouns are tested, they are likely to be followed by prepositional phrases. Don't get distracted!

Incorrect: When <u>any (one)</u> of the committee members **propose** a new regulation, the committee discusses it thoroughly and then takes a vote.

Correct: When <u>any (one)</u> of the committee members **proposes** a new regulation, the committee discusses it thoroughly and then takes a vote.

*When *(n)either* and *(n)or* are paired with two nouns, the verb must agree with the noun right before the verb.

Incorrect: Neither Amy Tan nor <u>Maxine Hong Kingston</u> **were** raised in a literary family, but both became avid readers while growing up near San Francisco.

Correct: Neither Amy Tan nor <u>Maxine Hong Kingston</u> **was** raised in a literary family, but both became avid readers while growing up near San Francisco.

Note: in the past, the SAT has only paired singular nouns connected by *(n)either…(n)or* with plural verbs.

When *(n)either* is <u>not</u> paired with *(n)or* and is used with two singular nouns, a singular verb should also be used. This is because *neither* is actually short for *neither one*, and *one* is singular.

Incorrect: Both Amy Tan and Maxine Hong Kingston became avid readers while growing up near San Francisco, but neither **were** raised in a literary family.

Correct: Both Amy Tan and Maxine Hong Kingston became avid readers while growing up near San Francisco, but neither **was** raised in a literary family.

Exercise: Subject-Verb Agreement (answers p. 229)

For the following sentences, determine whether the underlined verbs agree with their subjects.

1. Galaxies, far from being randomly scattered throughout the universe, <u>appears</u> to be distributed in a series of bubble-shaped patterns.

_____

2. The expansion of roads and the construction of a chemical plant <u>has</u> resulted in a rapid increase in the number of endangered bird species throughout the region.

_____

3. The works of Chippewa author Louise Erdrich <u>explore</u> complex familial relationships among Native Americans as they reflect on issues of identity and belonging.

_____

4. Any of the participants in the study <u>is</u> permitted to withdraw if side effects from the medication become too severe.

_____

5. Each of the compositions by jazz musician Thelonius Monk <u>seem</u> to evoke a self-enclosed world, one with its own telltale harmonies and rhythms.

_____

6. The presence of mysterious cave paintings in the Mississippi Valley <u>have</u> puzzled archaeologists studying images created by ancient inhabitants of the region.

_____

7. Working in public relations generally <u>involves</u> managing the flow of information between a business or government agency and the general public.

_____

8. In the deepest part of the ocean floor <u>sits</u> the Mariana Trench and the HMRG Deep, the two lowest spots that researchers have ever identified on earth.

_____

9. The founding of _The Chicago Tribune_ by friends James Kelly, John Wheeler and Joseph Forrest <u>was</u> prompted by the desire to create a world-class newspaper in a region lacking in serious journalism.

_____

10. Although Andrew Carnegie and Cornelius Vanderbilt established themselves as two of the most powerful figures in business during the late nineteenth century, neither <u>were</u> born into a wealthy family.

_____

11. The study of foreign languages <u>require</u> considerable effort and time. Having access to the right tools <u>makes</u> a huge difference as well. What constitutes the "right" tools, however, <u>changes</u> based on previous exposure to the language being learned as well as the personal preferences of the student.

_____

_____

_____

12. One of the most commonly consumed foods in the world <u>are</u> the banana. Wrapped in its own convenient packaging, the curved yellow fruit is full of nutrients. A decreased risk of heart disease and a reduction in blood pressure <u>is</u> included among its benefits.

_____

_____

13. Peacocks are large, colorful birds known for their iridescent tails. These tail feathers, also known as coverts, <u>spreads</u> out in a distinctive train and boast colorful "eye" markings. The large train, used in mating rituals and courtship displays, is also arched into a magnificent fan that reaches across the bird's back and <u>touch</u> the ground on either side.

_____

_____

14. Forensic accounting is a type of accounting that deals with criminal activities such as fraud and embezzlement. Detective skills and financial knowledge <u>are</u> required to investigate these crimes. Forensic accountants often work with law enforcement officers and attorneys; they can also serve as expert witnesses. A number of public scandals <u>has</u> recently led to new federal legislation creating increased demand for forensic accountants.

_____

_____

15. Though its use has been widely banned in the United States, lead paint, which was formerly used in both domestic and industrial environments, <u>has</u> left potentially dangerous materials in many buildings.

_____

Verb Tense

Correct answers to tense questions are primarily **based on context**. Two or three verbs may be grammatically correct when a sentence is read independently, but only one answer will be correct when it is considered in context. **Unless there is a clear reason for a verb to change tense, a verb should be parallel to the other verbs in sentence or paragraph.** As a result, you will often need to **read the surrounding sentences** in order to obtain enough information to answer verb tense questions.

For example:

> The tomato **is** consumed in many different ways, including raw, as an ingredient in many dishes and sauces, and in drinks. Botanically a fruit, it was considered a vegetable for culinary purposes. It **belongs** to the nightshade family, and its plants typically **grow** from three to ten feet high.

1

A) NO CHANGE
B) had been
C) would be
D) is

Out of context, the sentence is fine. If you looked at it in isolation, you would have no way of knowing whether there was a problem. B), C), and D) are all grammatically acceptable as well (although more complicated tenses such as *would be* and *had been* are less likely to appear as correct answers). We must therefore consider the verbs in the surrounding sentences: *is, belongs, grow*. All of those verbs are in the **present tense**, so the underlined verb must be in the present as well. Only *is* works, so D) is correct.

While the answers to many tense questions will require you to keep the tense of a particular verb consistent with the tense of the surrounding verbs, the correct answer may sometimes depend on other factors.

A. Present Progressive

Present progressive = *is/are* + -ING, e.g. *she is throwing, they are reading, it is growing*

This tense is used to emphasize that an action is happening right at the moment, and it is **considered parallel to another verb in the present tense**.

For example:

> Every year, I help my family grow vegetables in the garden in back of our house. We plant tomatoes every spring and are attempting to sell this year's crop at a local farmers market.

1

A) NO CHANGE
B) will have attempted
C) attempting
D) would attempt

Let's start by looking at the other verbs in the sentence: *help* and *plant*. Both are in the present tense, so the underlined verb must be in the present too. When you look at the answers, you might be confused because you're expecting an answer in the regular old present (*attempt*). If you know that *attempt = are attempting*, however, you can safely pick A).

B. Present Perfect

Present perfect = *has/have* + past participle, e.g. *has walked, has gone, have thrown*

- For regular verbs, the past participle is formed by adding *–ed* to the verb. For a list of common irregular past participles, see p. 171.

- Used for actions that **began in the past** and that are **continuing into the present**.

- **Most important** irregular verb = *to be*, which becomes *has been* (sing.) and *have been* (pl.).

The words *for, since, over*, and *during* usually act as **tip-offs** that the present perfect is required. For example:

Incorrect: <u>Since</u> around 500 B.C., people **cultivate/cultivated** tomatoes in Mesoamerica.

Correct: <u>Since</u> around 500 B.C., people **have cultivated** tomatoes in Mesoamerica.

The present perfect is also commonly used to describe an action that occurred very recently.

Correct: Scientists **have reported** that the breakthrough may result in the development of new technologies.

While answers to most verb questions will depend on the surrounding sentences, **questions involving the present perfect are more likely to depend only on the sentences in which they appear.**

For example:

Computer and information specialists collaborate with a variety of workers. They coordinate activities with management executives, equipment suppliers, and all other contractors. Since the 1990s, computer and information systems manager occupations **1** <u>have expanded</u> at a rate faster than the rate which most other occupations have expanded. As technology evolves, more employees will be necessary to guide this process. Those with a Master's degree in business technology and management will be most qualified for these opportunities.

1
A) NO CHANGE
B) had expanded
C) will expand
D) expanded

Although the previous sentences contain verbs in the present tense (*collaborate, coordinate*), and the following sentences contain verbs in the future (*will be*), the tip-off word *since* requires that the underlined verb be in the present perfect. A) is therefore correct.

C. Simple Past

Simple past = verb + *–ed* (e.g. *talked, played, painted*)

- Describes a **finished** action in the past.

- Usually identical to the past participle, e.g. *she has walked* and *she walked*. For a list of common irregular past participles, see p. 171.

- Most important **irregular verb** = *to be*, which becomes *was* (sing.) and *were* (pl.).

Dates and **time periods** are usually tip-offs that the simple past is required.

Correct: Around <u>500 B.C.,</u> the inhabitants of Central America **began** to cultivate the first tomatoes.

Correct: During <u>the Middle Ages</u>, many members of the nobility **lived** in castles.

D. Past Perfect

Past Perfect = *had* + past participle, e.g. *he had gone, it had rung, they had insisted*

- When a sentence describes two finished actions, the past perfect is used to refer only to the **first** action.

The phrase "by the time" is a tip-off that the past perfect is required.

For example:

Martha Graham an American dancer and choreographer, is known as one of the foremost pioneers of modern dance. Building upon the foundation of turn-of-the-century dancer Isadora Duncan, Graham brought this art form to a new level with her introduction of dance techniques that at first horrified and then later won over the American public. **By the time** she retired from the stage in 1970, she **1** <u>gave</u> hundreds of performances and permanently altered the course of dance in the United States.

1

A) NO CHANGE
B) will give
C) would have given
D) had given

The presence of the phrase *by the time* requires the past perfect. You can also think about it this way: logically, Martha Graham must have given hundreds of performances (action #1) before she retired (action #2). D) is therefore correct.

170

Common Irregular Verbs

- Irregular past participles often end in *–en, –own, –ung,* or *–unk.*
- Irregular simple past forms often end in *–ew, –ang,* or *–ank.*

Infinitive	Simple Past	Past Participle
To (a)rise	(A)rose	(A)risen
To (a)waken	(A)woke	(A)woken
To be	Was	Been
To become	Became	Become
To begin	Began	Begun
To blow	Blew	Blown
To break	Broke	Broken
To choose	Chose	Chosen
To do	Did	Done
To draw	Drew	Drawn
To drink	Drank	Drunk
To drive	Drove	Driven
To fly	Flew	Flown
To freeze	Froze	Frozen
To get	Got	Gotten*
To go	Went	Gone
To hide	Hid	Hidden
To give	Gave	Given
To grow	Grew	Grown
To know	Knew	Known
To ride	Rode	Ridden
To ring	Rang	Rung
To run	Ran	Run
To see	Saw	Seen
To sew	Sewed	Sewn
To shrink	Shrank	Shrunk/Shrunken
To sing	Sang	Sung
To sink	Sank	Sunk/Sunken
To speak	Spoke	Spoken
To spring	Sprang	Sprung
To steal	Stole	Stolen
To stink	Stank	Stunk
To swim	Swam	Swum
To take	Took	Taken
To tear	Tore	Torn
To throw	Threw	Thrown
To wear	Wore	Worn
To write	Wrote	Written

---

*Although *got* is used as the past participle of *get* in British English, *gotten* is standard in American English.

E. Formation Errors: Past Participle and Simple Past

i. Simple past replaces past participle

Only the past participle should be used after any form of verb *to have* or *to be*.

Incorrect: Since the first millennium B.C., tomatoes **have grew** in Central and South America.

Correct: Since the first millennium B.C., tomatoes **have grown** in Central and South America.

Incorrect: Today, tomatoes **are grew** in many varieties in greenhouses around the world.

Correct: Today, tomatoes **are grown** in many varieties in greenhouses around the world.

ii. Past participle without "to have" or "to be"

In this error, a sentence will clearly require the past participle but omit the necessary verb before it.

Incorrect: Since around 500 B.C., tomatoes **grown** in Central and South America.

Correct: Since around 500 B.C., tomatoes **have grown** in Central and South America.

Incorrect: Beginning in around 500 B.C. tomatoes **grown** in Central and South America.

Correct: Beginning in around 500 B.C. tomatoes **were grown** in Central and South America.

iii. Past participle replaces simple past

The past participle can **only** be used after a form of *to have* or *to be*; it cannot stand alone. Only the simple past can stand alone. Some ACT questions, however, will incorrectly replace the simple past with the past participle:

Incorrect: Sometime around 500 B.C., the inhabitants of Central and South America **begun** to grow tomatoes.

Correct: Sometime around 500 B.C., the inhabitants of Central and South America **began** to grow tomatoes.

iv. Past participle without "–ed"

Incorrect: The sculpture was **fashion** from clay, wood, and bronze.

Correct: The sculpture was **fashioned** from clay, wood, and bronze.

F. Would vs. Will

Future = *will* + *verb*

The future is used to describe actions that have not yet occurred.

     Correct: Works choreographed by Martha Graham **will continue** to be performed for many years.

Conditional = *would* + *verb*

Would is used to describe **hypothetical** situations: ones that *could* occur but have not *actually* occurred.

     Correct: Many people who think of the tomato as a vegetable **would be** surprised to learn that it is actually a fruit.

Would + verb can also refer to a **recurring action** in the past.

     Correct: Every summer until I went away to college, I **would visit** my grandparents in Peru.

Finally, *would* can be used to refer to an action that, from the perspective of the past, has not yet occurred, even if from today's perspective that action occurred long ago. As a **shortcut**, know that *would*, not *will*, should generally be used in sentences that include a date in the past.

For example:

When Martha Graham began dancing in the **early twentieth century**, no one knew that she **1** will become one of the greatest choreographers of all time. Born in Pennsylvania in 1894, Graham was 14 years old when her family moved to Santa Barbara, California. After seeing the acclaimed dancer Ruth St. Denis perform, she proclaimed that her future profession was "chosen" for her.

1

A) NO CHANGE
B) would become
C) would have become
D) becomes

Because the sentence clearly describes events in the past, *would*, not *will*, should be used. B) is therefore correct.

Would have is used to describe an action that could have happened, but that did not actually occur.

     Correct: If we <u>had remembered</u> to close the windows, the paintings **would have** been saved.

Will have is used to describe an action in the future that will be finished *before* a second action. As is true for the past perfect, the phrase *by the time* is a tip-off that the future perfect is required.

     Correct: <u>By the time</u> the paintings are complete, the artist **will have** spent more than six months working on them.

Combined Exercise: Subject-Verb Agreement and Tense (answers p. 229)

1. Each July, one of the world's largest folk-art festivals **1** bring together artists from every corner of the globe for a vast and colorful international bazaar. For several weeks, more than 200 artists from 60 countries gather to offer handmade masterworks. The festival is located in Santa Fe, a destination rich in culture and history. The work of master artists **2** lines the walls as market-goers are given the opportunity to find one-of-a-kind treasures and meet their creators.

1
A) NO CHANGE
B) bringing
C) brought
D) brings

2
A) NO CHANGE
B) have lined
C) lining
D) line

2. Kite-flying has a long history in Japan: according to legend, the first kites **1** were flying nearly 1,400 years ago. Since that time, kite-flying **2** had remained a delightful tradition. Kites are made from a bamboo framework and layers of *washi* paper – paper made by hand in the traditional style. Colorful narrative illustrations and legendary heroes from Japanese folklore **3** decorates their surfaces. Every region of the country has its own distinct kite design, with more than 130 varieties in all. For this reason, there is no single design that **4** are typical of Japanese kites.

1
A) NO CHANGE
B) flown
C) were flown
D) had flew

2
A) NO CHANGE
B) would have remained
C) will remain
D) has remained

3
A) NO CHANGE
B) decorate
C) decorating
D) has decorated

4
A) NO CHANGE
B) will be
C) is
D) had been

3. In a village at the edge of the rainforest, the skilled and nimble fingers of a old woman **1** bends fabric and straw into graceful baskets. The baskets are the perfect size to hold papayas, but **2** they also held centuries of craft and tribal identity. Basket weaving is one of the most widespread crafts in history: it originated in the Middle East around 7,000 years ago and spread to every continent except Antarctica. The preservation of ancient baskets **3** is difficult, however, because most items are made of natural materials like wood, grass, and vines, which decay rapidly. As a result, much of the history of basket making **4** would be lost. On the other hand, weaving techniques, which are often passed along from generation to generation, **5** has been preserved throughout the centuries and are still being expanded upon today.

1

A) NO CHANGE
B) will bend
C) bend
D) has bent

2

A) NO CHANGE
B) they would also hold
C) they would have also held
D) they are also holding

3

A) NO CHANGE
B) are
C) were
D) being

4

A) NO CHANGE
B) has been
C) will have been
D) would have been

5

A) NO CHANGE
B) have been preserved
C) is preserved
D) preserved

4. As the world's first supersonic passenger jet, the Concorde was regarded as a marvel of engineering. Most jets fly at maximum speeds of about 550 miles per hour, but the Concorde **1** could have gone more than two times as fast – double the speed of sound. During its 27 years of service, the world's fastest commercial aircraft transported passengers across the Atlantic ocean in only two hours.

Although the Concorde was retired in 2003, a plane that is capable of flying halfway around the world in a mere four hours might soon exist. For engineers, eliminating sonic booms **2** have been one of the biggest challenges involved in building the new plane. Airplanes that break the sound barrier are extremely loud, so they must be flying primarily over water. Engineers claim, however, that they have found a way of reducing the amount of noise the planes **3** makes. The solution involves thinner wings and hidden engines. Moreover, lightweight materials and innovative engine technology **4** allow the plane to fly twice as fast as the Concorde.

1
A) NO CHANGE
B) gone
C) will go
D) went

2
A) NO CHANGE
B) were
C) is
D) are

3
A) NO CHANGE
B) have made.
C) making.
D) make.

4
A) NO CHANGE
B) has allowed
C) is allowing
D) allows

5. In North America, cranberries were cultivated by Native Americans long before the first European settlers arrived, but not until the mid-nineteenth century **1** <u>was</u> the first berries marketed and sold. Sometime around 1800, Sir Joseph Banks, a British scientist, used seeds from the United States to harvest cranberries in England, but Banks **2** <u>did not market</u> his crop. Then, in 1816, Henry Hall, a veteran of the Revolutionary war, planted the first-recorded commercial cranberry bog in Dennis, Massachusetts.

By the mid-nineteenth century, the modern cranberry industry was in full swing, and competition among growers **3** <u>were</u> fierce. The business operated on a small scale at first: families and individuals harvested wild cranberries, selling them locally. As the market **4** <u>grows</u> to include larger cities such as Boston and New York, however, farmers competed to unload their surplus cranberries quickly, and what was once a local venture **5** <u>has become</u> a highly profitable business.

1

A) NO CHANGE
B) were
C) is
D) has

2

A) NO CHANGE
B) has not marketed
C) does not market
D) will not market

3

A) NO CHANGE
B) was
C) have been
D) would be

4

A) NO CHANGE
B) has grew
C) grew
D) had grown

5

A) NO CHANGE
B) had became
C) becomes
D) became

6. Ever since scientists discovered that the fingerprints of each person on earth **1** was unique, fingerprinting has played an important role in law enforcement. Modern fingerprinting has come a long way from the time when police officers **2** lift prints from a crime scene and check them manually. Fingerprints are now used in many ways: to prevent forged signatures, confirm job applicants' identities, and provide personalized access to everything from ATMs to computer networks. Today, fingerprinting techniques can not only check millions of criminal records in a few seconds, but they **3** have also matched faces and other identifiable characteristics specific to each perpetrator.

1
A) NO CHANGE
B) is
C) are
D) being

2
A) NO CHANGE
B) have lifted
C) would lift
D) will lift

3
A) NO CHANGE
B) can also match
C) had also matched
D) having also matched

7. When I recently traveled to Colombia to see my extended family, I had the opportunity to visit a variety of fascinating sites. One of my favorite attractions **1** were the National Coffee Theme Park, an amusement park located just south of the town of Montenegro. The park, which can be reached from cable cars, **2** features a global coffee garden, a roller coaster, coffee-based food stalls, and many examples of Colombian folk architecture. It consists of two main areas: by the entrance **3** is the buildings housing the museum and exhibitions, and in the valley beyond is an amusement park with rides and shows. The museum includes exhibits on coffee farming and growing, and the amusement park offers more than 20 rides and attractions. The two areas are linked by a cable car, but it is also possible to walk between the two areas via an ecological trail that **4** pass through a plantation of coffee bushes.

1
A) NO CHANGE
B) was
C) are
D) being

2
A) NO CHANGE
B) feature
C) having featured
D) have featured

3
A) NO CHANGE
B) were
C) was
D) are

4
A) NO CHANGE
B) passes
C) will pass
D) passing

8. The construction of prefabricated houses is based on the assembly-line production model of car production developed by Henry Ford. In the 1920s, Ford's production method for the Model T **1** transforms the automobile from a luxury item into a purchase that was affordable for the average consumer. Today, assembly-line production and bulk buying **2** has driven down the cost and construction time for prefabricated homes. The production process **3** has evolved significantly since the first prefabricated homes were build at the turn of the twentieth century, and houses can now be constructed in only a matter of weeks. Furthermore, a number of additions now **4** allows buyers to customize their homes. Just as satellite radios and heated seats can be added to cars, Jacuzzis and crown molding can be added to prefabricated houses.

1

A) NO CHANGE
B) transformed
C) has transformed
D) will transform

2

A) NO CHANGE
B) have driven down
C) had driven down
D) driving down

3

A) NO CHANGE
B) had evolved
C) will evolve
D) evolved

4

A) NO CHANGE
B) has allowed
C) allow
D) allowing

15. Word Pairs and Comparisons

Word Pairs

There are two main kinds of comparisons: those that indicate **similarity**, and those that indicate **difference**. Both kinds of comparisons can be formed using **word pairs**, listed below. These words must always appear together; they cannot be mixed and matched with each other or paired with other words.

A. As...as

As...as is used to indicate that two people or things are equal.

Incorrect:	Among pioneers of modern dance, Isadora Duncan is **as** renowned a dancer and choreographer **than** Martha Graham.
Correct:	Among pioneers of modern dance, Isadora Duncan is **as** renowned a dancer and choreographer **as** Martha Graham.

B. Not only...but (also)

Saying that something is **not only** x **but (also)** y means that it is x **as well as** y.

Incorrect:	Martha Graham was **not only** a great dancer **and** she was (also) a great choreographer.
Correct:	Martha Graham was **not only** a great dancer **but** she was **also** a great choreographer.

C. More or –ER/less...than

Incorrect:	Measuring 25 feet, a python named Medusa is **longer as** any other snake in the world.
Correct:	Measuring 25 feet, a python named Medusa is **longer than** any other snake in the world.

D. (N)either...(n)or

Incorrect:	In the United States, **neither** Nikolai Tesla **or** James Joule is as famous as Thomas Edison.
Correct:	In the United States, **neither** Nikolai Tesla **nor** James Joule is as famous as Thomas Edison.

Faulty Comparisons

Use *than*, not *then*, to form a comparison.

Incorrect: Measuring 25 feet, a python named Medusa is **longer then** any other snake in the world.

Correct: Measuring 25 feet, a python named Medusa is **longer than** any other snake in the world.

Always compare **people to people and things to things**.

Singular Faulty Comparison

Incorrect: Throughout the 1950s, the music of composer Charles Ives was far less popular among audiences in the United States than John Philip Sousa.

In the above sentence, music (thing) is being compared to John Philip Sousa (person). In order to make the sentence correct, music must be compared to music. There are several ways to fix this sentence:

Correct: Throughout the 1950s, Charles Ives' music was far less popular among audiences in the United States than **John Philip Sousa's music**.

Correct: Throughout the 1950s, Charles Ives' music was far less popular among audiences in the United States than **the music of John Philip Sousa**.

A singular noun can also be replaced with the phrase *that of*.

Correct: Throughout the 1950s, Charles Ives' **music** was far less popular among audiences in the United States than **that of** John Philip Sousa. (*That = the music*)

Plural Faulty Comparison

Plural faulty comparisons can also be fixed either with nouns or with the phrase *those of*.

Incorrect: Although birds are not generally known for their intelligence, recent findings have established that parrots often possess **skills** similar to **human toddlers**.

Correct: Although birds are not generally known for their intelligence, recent findings have established that parrots often possess **skills** similar to **the skills of** human toddlers.

Correct: Although birds are not generally known for their intelligence, recent findings have established that parrots often possess **skills** similar to **those of** human toddlers. (*Those* = the skills)

Alternately, *that of* may be incorrectly used to refer to a plural noun, and *those of* may be incorrectly used to refer to a singular noun.

Incorrect: Although birds are not generally known for their intelligence, recent findings have established that parrots often possess skills similar to human toddlers.

Incorrect: Although birds are not generally known for their intelligence, recent findings have established that parrots often possess **skills** similar to **that of** human toddlers.

Correct: Although birds are not generally known for their intelligence, recent findings have established that parrots often possess **skills** similar to **those of** human toddlers.

When two things are compared, they must be the same type of thing. Otherwise, a faulty comparison is created.

Incorrect: Unlike a train, the length of a tram is usually limited to one or two cars, which may run either on train tracks or directly on the street.

Even though both *train* and *length* are things, they are not equivalent. We can either compare a train to a train or a length to a length, but we cannot compare a train to a length.

Correct: Unlike **the length of** a train, the length of a tram is usually limited to one or two cars, which may run either on train tracks or directly on the street.

Correct: Unlike **that of** a train, the length of a tram is usually limited to one or two cars, which may run either on train tracks or directly on the street.

Exercise: Word Pairs and Comparisons (answers p. 229)

1. Exploration and discovery have been a part of American history since the fifteenth century, and no expedition was as influential in shaping the United States **1** as Meriwether Lewis and William Clark. In 1803, they set out to find an all-water route to the Pacific Ocean. The purchase of the Louisiana Territory that year had opened vast lands for settlement. Under orders from President Thomas Jefferson, Lewis, Clark and their group of woodsmen, hunters, and translators not only blazed a trail into the wilderness **2** and they spent three years making their way across the continent.

1

A) NO CHANGE
B) than Meriwether Lewis and William Clark.
C) than the expedition led by Meriwether Lewis and William Clark.
D) as the expedition led by Meriwether Lewis and William Clark.

2

A) NO CHANGE
B) and spending
C) and they spent
D) but they also spent

2. Meteoroids are the smallest members of the solar system, ranging from large chunks of rock and metal to miniscule fragments no larger **1** then a grain of sand. Whenever a meteoroid plows into the Earth's atmosphere, it creates a meteor, a very brief flash of light in the sky. Millions of meteors occur in the Earth's atmosphere daily. Just as many meteoroids appear in the atmosphere during daylight **2** as appear at night; however, meteors are usually observed after dark, when faint objects can more easily be identified. The light produced by a meteor may come in a variety of shades, depending on the chemical composition of the meteoroid and the speed of its movement through the atmosphere.

1

A) NO CHANGE
B) than
C) as
D) from

2

A) NO CHANGE
B) as appearing
C) than appear
D) than would appear

3. Julia Child might have been one of the more prominent American chefs of the twentieth century, but **1** her reliance on recipes was greater than almost any other cook of her caliber. Child was famous for the exceptional amount of detail she put into her versions of her recipes as she perfected them for publication. For example, her recipe for white sandwich bread was one of her simplest recipes, but she revised it repeatedly throughout her long career; neither her friends **2** or her fellow cooks could persuade her to be satisfied. The recipe was first published in *Mastering the Art of French Cooking*, but that was just the beginning. Not only did Child re-publish a slightly different version less than a decade later **3** and in 2000 it also appeared in one of her last books, *Julia's Kitchen Wisdom*.

1
A) NO CHANGE
B) her reliance on recipes was more than
C) she relied on recipes more than did
D) she relied on recipes more then

2
A) NO CHANGE
B) nor
C) and
D) but

3
A) NO CHANGE
B) and in 2000 it also appeared
C) also appearing in 2000
D) but it also appeared in 2000

4. When steel magnate Andrew Carnegie purchased the land for his New York City house in 1898, he purposely bought property as far north **1** as possible. The relatively spacious grounds were large enough for a terrace as well as a private garden – one of the few in Manhattan. Completed in 1901, the house had features more modern **2** than any other house in New York City. It was also the first private residence in the United States to be built on a steel frame and one of the first in New York to have a passenger elevator. Furthermore, the house contained not only a central heating system **3** plus an early form of air conditioning. In the basement, a miniature railroad car transported coal to an immense pair of boilers.

1
A) NO CHANGE
B) than
C) then
D) DELETE the underlined word.

2
A) NO CHANGE
B) then any other house in New York City
C) as that of any other house in New York City
D) than those of any other house in New York City

3
A) NO CHANGE
B) as
C) but also
D) in addition to

5. During World War II, a gasoline shortage forced many drivers to install power generators that converted wood into gas, a process known as gasification. The generators were clunky, but there was no alternative: motorists could either use them **1** and give up driving altogether. The generators were quickly forgotten once fossil fuels became ready available, but over 50 years later, gasification was rediscovered 6,000 miles away as a potential source of alternative power. All Power Labs, a California-based company, has slowly begun resurrecting this **2** more then century-old technology. In five years, the company has sold hundreds of generators known as the "Power Pallet." Each pallet is approximately as large **3** as the size of a refrigerator and can produce clean fuel for about fifteen percent of the usual cost. For countries with less resources, the pallets open up a whole new world of possibilities.

1

A) NO CHANGE
B) or
C) with
D) also

2

A) NO CHANGE
B) more than
C) more as
D) more

3

A) NO CHANGE
B) than the size of a refrigerator
C) than a refrigerator
D) as a refrigerator

16. Parallel Structure

Simply put, parallel structure refers to the fact that writing should be kept consistent. **If a construction is used in one part of a sentence or paragraph, it should be used in the other parts as well.** Keeping constructions parallel makes writing clearer and easier for readers to understand.

In any given list of three or more items, each item should appear in the same format, e.g. noun, noun, and/or noun; gerund, gerund, and/or gerund; verb, verb, and/or verb. Any deviation is incorrect.

For example:

> **Changes** in wind circulation, **runoff** from sewage, and to accumulate chemical fertilizers can lead to the creation of ocean waters low in oxygen and inhospitable to marine life.

> 1
>
> A) NO CHANGE
> B) they accumulate chemical fertilizers
> C) accumulating chemical fertilizers
> D) accumulation of chemical fertilizers

The underlined portion of the sentence uses an infinitive (*to accumulate*) to begin the third item in the list, whereas the other items in the list begin with nouns (*changes, runoff*). A noun is required, so D) is correct.

If an entire list is underlined, **you can simplify the question by focusing on the beginning** of each item.

For example:

> 1 **Changes** in wind circulation, **runoff** from sewage, and **they accumulate** chemical fertilizers can lead to the creation of ocean waters low in oxygen and inhospitable to marine life.

> 1
>
> A) NO CHANGE
> B) **Changing** wind circulation, **runoff** from sewage, and **accumulating** chemical fertilizers
> C) **Changing** wind circulation, **having** runoff from sewage, and **to accumulate** chemical fertilizers
> D) **Changes** in wind circulation patterns, **runoff** from sewage, and **accumulation** of chemical fertilizers

Once again, D) is the only answer that contains three nouns. The other options contain various combinations of nouns, verbs, and gerunds (-ING words).

Another type of parallel structure questions will involve only two items joined by a conjunction (*and*, *or*, *but*). While these questions are fairly straightforward, you must take the entire sentence into account because **the answer is likely to depend on information in the non-underlined portion of the sentence**.

For example:

Because they have a highly developed sense of vision, most lizards are able **to use** clear body language and **1** changing their colors in order to communicate.

1

A) NO CHANGE
B) they change
C) will change
D) change

The word *and* pairs the underlined item with the non-underlined item, so the two must match. Note that the repeated *to* is optional. The correct answer could read *to change* or *change*, as is the case here. (D) is thus correct.

Some two-item parallel structure questions may also ask you to work with phrases rather than single words. Consider the following sentence:

Incorrect: The time devoted to books by publishing companies has been reduced by financial constraints **and** the emphasis on marketing considerations has increased.

We know that the constructions on either side of the word *and* must match. So that means we must look at the specific construction of those two pieces of information.

What has the time devoted to books by publishing companies been reduced by?

1)   financial constraints

2)   the emphasis marketing considerations has increased.

When we examine the two sides, we see that their constructions do not match.

- The first side contains a noun.

- The second side contains an entire independent clause. Furthermore, both items must be able to follow the phrase "reduced by," and you cannot say *The time devoted to books by publishing companies has been reduced by the emphasis on marketing considerations has increased.*

To make the two sides parallel, we must eliminate the independent clause and replace it with a noun phrase.

Correct: The time devoted to books by publishing companies has been reduced by both **financial constraints** and **an increased emphasis** on marketing considerations.

Since you can say, *The time devoted to books by publishing companies has been reduced by…an increased emphasis on marketing considerations*, this version is grammatically correct.

Important: two-part questions may also double as word-pair questions. If you can spot the word pair, you can often eliminate several answers immediately.

For example:

> As one of the greatest American dancers and choreographers of the twentieth century, Martha Graham was praised **not only** for the brilliance of her technique **1** **and** in the vividness and intensity of her movements.

1
A) NO CHANGE
B) and also with
C) but also for
D) but also to

If you read from the beginning of the sentence, you'll see the first half of a word pair – *not only*. *Not only* must be paired with *but also*, so A) and B) can be eliminated. Since the preposition *for* is used after *not only*, it must be used after *but also*. So C) is correct.

Although it's a bit more complicated, you can also think of the solution this way: the verb *praised* must be followed by *for*. That verb "applies" to two things: 1) *the brilliance of her technique*, and 2) *the vividness and intensity of her movements*. As a result, the preposition *for* must be used for both.

The preposition before the second noun can also be omitted. That means you could see something like this:

> As one of the greatest American dancers and choreographers of the twentieth century, Martha Graham was praised not only **for** the brilliance of her technique but also **1** **in** the vividness and intensity of her movements.

1
A) NO CHANGE
B) with
C) to
D) DELETE the underlined word.

Because the preposition is optional, the answer is again D). You will not be asked to choose between a version with the preposition and a version without.

Likewise, consider the following:

> As one of the greatest American dancers and choreographers of the twentieth century, Martha Graham was praised not only for the brilliance of her technique but also for the vividness and intensity of her movements. Critics were dazzled and **1** audiences amazed.

1
A) NO CHANGE
B) audiences being amazed.
C) audiences would be amazed.
D) audiences are amazed.

Many people think that the original version is incorrect because the verb *were* should be repeated before the second adjective (*amazed*). In reality, the repetition is optional. It is correct to say both *Critics were dazzled and audiences were amazed*, AND *Critics were dazzled and audiences amazed*.

While you will never be asked to choose between the two constructions, you may be given only the first option (no repeated verb) as an answer choice, and you must be able to recognize that it is acceptable. In the above question, all of the other options seriously disrupt the parallel structure and create unnecessary tense switches.

Parallel Structure with Multiple Sentences

So far we've looked at parallel structure within a single sentence. The SAT, however, may also test your ability to recognize and preserve/create parallel structure when more than one sentence is involved. Although these questions may initially seem very complicated, they can actually be relatively simple to answer – that is, if you know what information to focus on.

For example:

> An actor stands on the stage and delivers a monologue as an audience hangs onto his every word. A singer performs a ballad as listeners fall silent. **1** As a group of spectators watch in awe, dancers glide across the stage.

1

Which choice best maintains the sentence pattern already established in the paragraph?

A) NO CHANGE
B) Watched by a group of spectators, dancers glide across the stage.
C) Gliding across the stage, dancers are watched by a group of spectators.
D) Dancers glide gracefully across the stage as spectators watch in awe.

Remember that the question is asking us to look at the pattern *already established in the paragraph*. That means we're going to look at the preceding sentences before we consider the underlined sentence. We can't do anything until we know what we're looking for.

Let's start by considering just the beginning of the first two sentences:

- Sentence #1: An actor...

- Sentence #2: A singer...

Each of those sentences begins with a noun. That means the third sentence must start with a noun as well. Only D) places a noun right at the beginning of the sentence, so it must be correct.

You can also think of it this way: the first two sentences have the basic structure "Noun...as...noun" (*An actor stands...as an audience, A singer performs...as listeners*). The third sentence must therefore contain that structure, in that order. The original version flips the order so that *as* comes first. B) and C) can both be eliminated because they do not even contain the word *as*. That leaves D), which correctly contains the structure *Noun...as noun*.

189

Exercise: Parallel Structure (answers p. 230)

1. Spiders are predators. In the insect world, they're fearsome animals – the tiny equivalent of wolves, lions, **1** or acting like sharks. Spiders use a wide range of strategies to capture prey, including trapping it in sticky webs, lassoing it with sticky bolas, and **2** to mimic other insects in order to avoid detection. Trap door spiders dig holes, **3** covering them up with doors made of spider silk and lying in wait for passing prey.

1

A) NO CHANGE
B) or they act like sharks.
C) or sharks.
D) or as sharks.

2

A) NO CHANGE
B) they mimic
C) mimicking
D) mimic

3

A) NO CHANGE
B) covering them up with doors made of spider silk, and to lie
C) cover them up with doors made of spider silk, and then they lie
D) to cover them up with doors made of spider silk, and lying

2. Copy editors review documents for errors in grammar, punctuation, and **1** how words are spelled. They suggest revisions, such as changing words and **2** to rearrange sentences and paragraphs to improve clarity or accuracy. They also may carry out research, **3** confirming sources for writers, and verify facts, dates, and statistics. Finally, they may arrange page layouts of articles, photographs, and advertisements.

1

A) NO CHANGE
B) spelling
C) the ways words are spelled
D) how you spell words

2

A) NO CHANGE
B) rearranging
C) rearrange
D) will rearrange

3

A) NO CHANGE
B) to confirm
C) they confirm
D) confirm

190

3. Whether it's with a sympathetic tilt of the head or **1** an excited sweep of the tail, dogs often seem to be saying they can sense exactly what we're feeling. Scientists have long been uncertain whether dogs can read human emotions, but evidence is growing that canines can accurately "read" what people feel. In fact, a recent study found that dogs are able to distinguish between expressions that indicate happiness **2** and those in which anger is indicated.

1

A) NO CHANGE
B) sweeping their tails excitedly
C) their tails sweeping excitedly
D) they sweep their tails excitedly

2

A) NO CHANGE
B) and those in which anger is indicated for.
C) and ones that indicate anger.
D) with ones where anger is indicated.

4. First there was the frostquake. Then there was the firenado. **1** Thundersnow is what there is now. Thundersnow is essentially the same as a thunderstorm; the only difference is that snow falls instead of rain **2** falling. It occurs when the layer of air closest to the ground is cold enough to create snow **3** but being warmer than the air above it. When thundersnow occurs at night, lightning appears brighter because it is reflected against the snowflakes.

1

Which of the following best preserves the sentence pattern already established in the paragraph?

A) NO CHANGE
B) At the present time, thundersnow exists.
C) Thundersnow is here now.
D) Now there's thundersnow.

2

A) NO CHANGE
B) that falls
C) it falls
D) DELETE the underlined word (ending the sentence with a period)

3

A) NO CHANGE
B) and also warmer
C) but it is warmer
D) but warmer

5. Architects design buildings. Civil engineers build bridges. **1** Without structural engineers, everything could twist and shake apart. Their know-how is vital to mastering green construction's novel materials and innovative practices, whether used to harness the force of the wind or **2** capturing the power that the waves have. Green structures excite us by emphasizing particular goals – such as eliminating carbon emissions – and accomplishing them via potentially beautiful forms. Green structural engineers formulate new architectural questions and determine new criteria for evaluating the answers.

6. First popularized in Japan, Haiku is a form of poetry that has become appreciated around the world. Haiku poets are challenged to convey a vivid message in only 17 syllables. In Japan these poems are valued for their simplicity, openness, and **1** being light. Haiku poems can describe anything, but they are seldom complicated or **2** people have difficulty understanding them. Each Haiku must contain a *kigo*, a season word that indicates what season of the year the Haiku is set. For example, blossoms would indicate spring, snow would give the idea of winter, and **3** summertime would be suggested by mosquitoes. The seasonal word isn't always obvious, though. Sometimes it is necessary to consider the theme of the poem to find it.

1

Which of the following best preserves the sentence pattern already established in the paragraph?

A) NO CHANGE
B) Structural engineers keep everything from twisting and shaking apart.
C) Twisting and shaking apart is what structural engineers keep from happening.
D) Everything is kept from twisting and shaking apart by structural engineers

2

A) NO CHANGE
B) capture the waves' power.
C) capturing the power of the waves.
D) capture the power that the waves possess.

1

A) NO CHANGE
B) sense of lightness.
C) having lightness.
D) they are light.

2

A) NO CHANGE
B) cause difficulties in understanding.
C) to understand them is difficult.
D) difficult to understand.

3

A) NO CHANGE
B) a suggestion of summertime is given by mosquitoes.
C) mosquitoes would suggest summertime.
D) summertime is suggested by mosquitoes.

7. Crop circles. Alien abductions. **1** A person travels through time. These are just some of the paranormal phenomena that people have believed in but that were later found to be hoaxes. Some of the largest hoaxes in history started out as one small lie, but they continued to grow because people believed them. Great hoaxes require great numbers of gullible people willing to suspend disbelief and **2** accept outlandish explanations in the face of the inexplicable.

8. For centuries, there have been reports of strange bright lights in the sky just before, during, or **1** after an earthquake. When an earthquake hit New Zealand in 1888, for example, spectators claimed to see "luminous appearances" and **2** feeling "an extraordinary glow." Over the years, however, descriptions have varied widely: the lights have been described as flaring white streaks, floating orbs, **3** and flames that flicker. Sometimes the lights appeared for just a few seconds, but other times they hovered in the sky for minutes or **4** even hours at a time.

1

Which of the following best preserves the sentence pattern already established in the paragraph?

A) NO CHANGE
B) Traveling through time.
C) Time travel.
D) To travel through time.

2

A) NO CHANGE
B) accepting
C) they accept
D) will accept

1

A) NO CHANGE
B) occurring after
C) they occur after
D) DELETE the underlined word

2

A) NO CHANGE
B) feel
C) would feel
D) have felt

3

A) NO CHANGE
B) and flames flicker.
C) and flames that flicker.
D) and flickering flames.

4

A) NO CHANGE
B) even in hours
C) even with hours
D) even on hours

9. Throughout World War II, the United States government rationed foods such sugar, milk, coffee, meat and **1** consuming canned goods. Labor and transportation shortages made it hard to harvest and **2** moving fruits and vegetables to market, so individual citizens were encouraged to grow their own fruits and vegetables in "victory gardens." Millions of gardens in all shapes and sizes produced abundant food to support the war effort. Gardens were planted not only in backyards and empty lots **3** as well as in window boxes. Neighbors pooled their resources, planting different kinds of foods and forming cooperatives. While the gardens themselves are now gone, posters, seed packets, photos, and **4** reading newspaper articles still remain to tell us the story of victory gardens.

1
A) NO CHANGE
B) to consume canned goods.
C) with the consumption of canned goods.
D) canned goods.

2
A) NO CHANGE
B) move
C) they moved
D) having moved

3
A) NO CHANGE
B) and for
C) but also in
D) but also to

4
A) NO CHANGE
B) to read
C) read newspapers
D) DELETE the underlined word.

10. Maria Montessori (1870 – 1952) was an Italian physician and **1** she worked as an educator. She is known for both the philosophy of education that bears her name **2** and for her writings on scientific pedagogy. Today, her educational methods are used in schools throughout the world. Montessori did not set out to be a teacher, however, only **3** she became a scientist. At the age of sixteen, she enrolled at the Leonardo da Vinci Technical Institute, where she did well in the sciences and especially mathematics. She initially intended to study engineering but eventually **4** to settle on medicine.

1

A) NO CHANGE
B) as an educator.
C) to be an educator.
D) educator.

2

A) NO CHANGE
B) as well as from
C) and also through
D) and to

3

A) NO CHANGE
B) becoming
C) to become
D) she would become

4

A) NO CHANGE
B) will settle on
C) settled on
D) settling for

17. Dangling and Misplaced Modifiers

Modifiers should be placed as close as possible to the nouns, pronouns, or phrases they modify. When modifiers are separated from the words or phrases they modify, the result is often unclear and sometimes completely absurd. **Although these errors will be presented in the context of passages, they will involve only the sentences in which they appear; you will not generally need to consider the surrounding information.**

There are two major types of modifier errors:

1) Dangling Modifiers

2) Misplaced Modifiers

Dangling Modifiers

Sentences that include dangling modifiers are characterized by an introductory clause that describes the subject but does not name it. This clause is always set off from the rest of the sentence by a comma.

Whenever a sentence contains such an introductory clause, the subject must appear immediately after the comma. If the subject does not appear there, the modifier is dangling, and the sentence is incorrect.

> Incorrect: **Stretching** from one end of the city to the other, the efficiency of the <u>tram system</u> often surprises both tourists and city residents.

The first thing we can note about the above sentence is that it contains an introductory clause with an –ING word (*Stretching from one end of the city to the other*) that does not name the subject – it does not tell us *what* stretches from one end of the city to the other.

We must therefore ask ourselves what stretches from one end of the city to the other. When we look at the rest of the sentence, it is clear that this description can only refer to the tram system.

The words *the tram system* do not appear immediately after the comma, so the modifier is dangling. In order to fix the sentence, we must place *the tram system*, the subject, immediately after the comma.

> Correct: **Stretching** from one end of the city to the other, <u>the tram system</u> often surprises both tourists and city residents with its efficiency.

Not every dangling modifier will begin with an –ING word, however.

> Incorrect: An elementary school teacher from Arkansas, increased funding and support
>   for public libraries were what Bessie Boehm Moore advocated for.

Who was the elementary school teacher for Arkansas? Bessie Boehm Moore, not *increased funding and support.* So *Bessie Boehm Moore* must be placed immediately after the comma.

> Correct: An elementary school teacher from Arkansas, **Bessie Boehm Moore**
>   advocated for increased funding and support for public libraries.

Watch out for the possessive version of the subject placed immediately after the introductory clause. In general, any possessive noun placed immediately after an introductory clause will be incorrect.

> Incorrect: An elementary school teacher from Arkansas, **Bessie Boehm Moore's goal**
>   was to achieve increased funding and support for public libraries.

Who is the elementary school teacher from Arkansas? *Bessie Boehm Moore,* not her *goal.*

> Correct: An elementary school teacher from Arkansas, **Bessie Boehm Moore** had the
>   goal of achieving increased funding and support for public libraries.

It is, however, acceptable to begin the main clause with a modifier describing the subject because that description is considered part of the complete subject.

> Correct: A native of Arkansas, **elementary school teacher Bessie Boehm Moore** had the goal
>   of achieving increased funding and support for public libraries.

Important: When fixing dangling modifiers, focus on identifying who or what the introductory clause refers to (the subject). The correct answer is the option that places that word/phrase right after the introductory clause. In some cases, you may be able to identify the correct answer based on a single word.

For example:

Born Freda Josephine McDonald in a small Missouri town, **1** the majority of Josephine Baker's career was spent performing throughout Europe. In the 1920s, Baker took Paris by storm. Her jaw-dropping performances – including one in a costume of 16 bananas strung onto a skirt – made her a celebrity. By 1927, she was one of the most photographed women in the world.

1
A) NO CHANGE
B) Josephine Baker's career ~~was mostly spent performing throughout Europe~~
C) Josephine Baker ~~spent the majority of her career performing throughout Europe~~
D) throughout ~~Europe was where Josephine Baker spent the majority of her career performing~~

A) and D) can eliminated immediately because Josephine Baker's name does not appear immediately after the comma. Careful with B). *Josephine Baker* is not the subject, but rather *Josephine Baker's career.* That leaves C).

Misplaced Modifiers

Misplaced modifiers can occur anywhere in a sentence. They also involve modifiers separated from the words/phrases they are intended to modify and often result in unintentionally ridiculous statements.

Incorrect: Claude McKay was one of the most important poets of the Harlem Renaissance that moved to New York City after studying agronomy in Kansas.

This sentence implies that the Harlem Renaissance moved to New York City when it was obviously Claude McKay who did so. To correct the sentence, we must make it clear that McKay moved to New York City. Any rearrangement of the sentence that accomplishes that goal is acceptable.

Correct: One of the most important poets of the Harlem Renaissance, Claude McKay moved to New York after studying agronomy in Kansas.

Correct: Claude McKay was one of the most important poets of the Harlem Renaissance; he moved to New York City after studying agronomy in Kansas.

Important: Be careful with *which*. It must refer to the noun that comes right before it. If it does not, a misplaced modifier is created. For example, the first version of the sentence below implies that the contemporary environmental movement caused the decline in bird populations, when pesticides were clearly the culprit.

Incorrect: Marine biologist Rachel Carson's book *Silent Spring* revealed the dangers of pesticides and set off the contemporary environmental movement, which had caused a decline in bird populations.

Correct: The contemporary environmental movement was set off when marine biologist Rachel Carson's book *Silent Spring* revealed the dangers of pesticides, which had caused a sharp decline in bird populations.

Now let's look at a test-style example:

Pigeons have long played an important role as messengers, as a result of their homing ability, speed, and altitude. **1** During the Franco-Prussian War in 1871, the French military used pigeons to transport messages to Paris, a time when the city was surrounded by Prussian troops.

1

A) NO CHANGE
B) During the Franco-Prussian War in 1871, pigeons were used by the French military to transport messages to Paris,
C) Pigeons were used to transport messages to Paris during the Franco-Prussian War in 1871,
D) In 1871, during the Franco-Prussian War, the French military using pigeons to transport messages to Paris,

Questions like this can be very tricky because the information you need to answer them is not in the underlined phrase but rather placed afterwards. Because the words *a time* appear after the comma, the information immediately before the comma must refer to that time. It is therefore only necessary to look at the **end** of each answer. Only C) ends with a time (1871), so it is the only possibility.

Exercise: Dangling and Misplaced Modifiers (answers p. 230)

1. Born in Italy in 1853, Maria Spelterini emigrated to the United States as a young woman and quickly became known for her breathtaking stunts. In 1876, the 23-year-old Spelterini became the only woman ever to cross the Niagara Gorge **1** <u>over a period of 18 days on a tightrope.</u> On July 12, she made her first attempt while wearing peach baskets strapped to her feet. Balancing on a two and a quarter inch wire, **2** <u>she crossed the Falls just north of the lower suspension bridge.</u> According to spectators, she appeared to exert no more effort than she would have during a stroll in the park. On July 19, **3** <u>the second crossing occurred while blindfolded</u>; three days later, she crossed with her ankles and wrists bound; and on July 26, she crossed for the fourth and last time. **4** <u>Never again performing at Niagara, the story of her life remains a mystery.</u>

1

A) NO CHANGE
B) on a tightrope, accomplishing that feat over a period of 18 days.
C) over a period of 18 days, she did this on a tightrope.
D) on a tightrope and, furthermore, doing this on a tightrope.

2

A) NO CHANGE
B) just north of the lower suspension bridge is where her crossing took place.
C) her crossing took place just north of the lower suspension bridge.
D) and crossing just north of the lower suspension bridge.

3

A) NO CHANGE
B) the second crossing occurred blindfolded
C) Spelterini performed the second crossing while blindfolded
D) the second crossing occurred in a blindfold

4

A) NO CHANGE
B) She never performed at Niagara again, her life story remains a mystery.
C) Never again performing at Niagara, the story of her life, therefore, is a mystery.
D) She never again performed at Niagara, and the story of her life remains a mystery.

199

2.   When President James Polk officially confirmed **1** the discovery by James Marshall of gold at Sutter's Mill in Coloma, California in 1848, hopeful prospectors immediately began planning for the trip out west. Beginning their journey in spring of 1849, **2** these prospectors took an overland route, known as "forty-niners," that was risky and mostly unknown. Some forty-niners traveled alone, but most formed companies that enabled **3** them with other miners to share expenses and supplies during the long journey. Seagoing travelers went south to Panama by boat. After disembarking, **4** a several-day mule ride to the Pacific coast was begun. When they finally arrived, they boarded a ship bound for San Francisco.

1

A) NO CHANGE
B) the discovering by James Marshall of gold at Sutter's Mill
C) James Marshall's discovery of gold at Sutter's Mill
D) the discovery at Sutter's Mill by James Marshall of gold

2

A) NO CHANGE
B) these prospectors, known as "forty-niners," took an overland route
C) an overland route was taken by these prospectors, known as "forty-niners"
D) these prospectors, known as "forty-niners," taking an overland route

3

A) NO CHANGE
B) them to share expenses with supplies and other miners
C) the sharing of expenses with other miners and supplies
D) them to share expenses and supplies with other miners

4

A) NO CHANGE
B) a several-day mule ride to the Pacific coast was begun by them.
C) they began a several-day mule ride to the Pacific coast.
D) the beginning of a several-day mule ride to the Pacific coast.

3. For decades, plastic bags have been a favorite
1 around the world of store owners because of their low
cost: two cents per bag, in contrast to five cents for a paper
bag. **2** Used widely since the 1970s, environmentalists
now estimate nearly a trillion plastic bags are produced
worldwide each year. The problems that these bags cause
are well known. Unable to break down in landfills,
3 the bags harm the animals that consume them. They
also contain toxic dyes that contaminate water and soil. As
a result, an increasing number of cities are banning their
use.

1

A) NO CHANGE
B) around the world because of the low cost of
   store owners
C) of store owner around the world, this is
   because of their low cost
D) of store owners around the world because of
   their low cost

2

A) NO CHANGE
B) The bags have been used widely since the
   1970s, and environmentalists now
   estimate that nearly a trillion plastic bags
C) Having been used widely since the 1970s,
   environmentalists now estimate nearly a
   trillion plastic bags
D) The bags, which have been widely used
   since the 1970s, but environmentalists
   estimate nearly a trillion plastic bags

3

A) NO CHANGE
B) animals are harmed when they consume the
   bags.
C) animals are harmed by consuming them.
D) harm is caused to animals that consume
   them.

4. Bioluminescence is light **1** produced within a living organism that is created by a chemical reaction. Most bioluminescent organisms are found in the ocean, although a few – including fireflies and certain fungi – are found on land. **2** Dwelling almost exclusively in saltwater habitats, some form of bioluminescence is produced by approximately 90% of deep-sea creatures, including fish, bacteria, and jellies.

1

A) NO CHANGE
B) created by a chemical reaction and produced within a living organism.
C) produced within a living organism, it is created by a chemical reaction.
D) produced within a living organism, which is created by a chemical reaction.

2

A) NO CHANGE
B) They dwell almost exclusively within saltwater habitats
C) Saltwater habitats being dwelled in almost exclusively by them,
D) Bioluminescent organisms dwell almost exclusively in saltwater habitats, and

5. Guerilla films are typically made by independent producers who lack the budget to obtain permits, rent locations, and build expensive sets. Consisting mostly of scenes shot in real time, **1** small casts and simple props typically characterize these films. In the past, guerilla films were often poorly made; however, their quality has improved significantly in recent years. While it was once difficult for filmmakers to obtain the necessary equipment, **2** professional quality digital cameras are now widely available to filmmakers that are inexpensive. Furthermore, digital editing technologies allow filmmakers to edit their work from virtually anywhere, eliminating the need for specialized editing studios and technicians.

1

A) NO CHANGE
B) small casts and simple props typically characterizing these films.
C) these films are typically characterized by small casts and simple props.
D) and small casts as well as simple props typically characterize these films.

2

A) NO CHANGE
B) professional quality digital cameras are now widely available to filmmakers, and these are inexpensive.
C) now, professional quality digital cameras are widely available to filmmakers that are inexpensive.
D) inexpensive professional quality digital cameras are now widely available to filmmakers.

18. Relative Pronouns: Who(se), Whom, Which, That, Where & When

As is true for other pronouns such as *it* and *she*, some of the pronouns discussed in this chapter can refer to people only; others can refer to things only; and still others can refer to both people and things.

People	Things	People & Things
Who Whom	Which	Whose That

Which vs. That

To review: both *which* and *that* refer to things; however, *which* follows a comma and sets off a non-essential clause, whereas *that* does not follow a comma and sets off an essential clause.

Incorrect: Farm **animals which** were introduced to the Galapagos Islands by early settlers, have been responsible for the destruction of many native species.

Correct: Farm **animals, which** were introduced to the Galapagos Islands by early settlers, have been responsible for the destruction of many native species.

Incorrect: Farm **animals, that** were introduced to the Galapagos Islands by early settlers have been responsible for the destruction of many native species.

Correct: Farm **animals that** were introduced to the Galapagos Islands by early settlers have been responsible for the destruction of many native species.

Who(m) vs. Which

Use *who* or *whom*, not *which*, when referring to people.

Incorrect: King Henry VIII was a British monarch **which** ruled England during the Tudor period and was known for his many wives.

Correct: King Henry VIII was a British monarch **who** ruled England during the Tudor period and was known for his many wives.

Whose

Whose is the possessive form of both *who* and *which*. Although it looks similar to *who*, *whose* can be used to refer to either people or things.

Correct: Maria Fernanda Cardoso is an artist **whose** installations have appeared in museums in the United States, Great Britain, Colombia, and Australia.

Correct: Mount Hosmer is an "upside down mountain" **whose** oldest rock formations are found near the top of the mountain and **whose** youngest rock formations are found near the bottom.

Who vs. Whom

There are two primary things to know about *who* and *whom*:*

1) *Who* is used before a verb.

2) *Whom* is used after a preposition.

A verb should never come right after *whom*. If it does, *who* should be used instead.

Incorrect: One of the first screen writers to include details such as stage directions in her work was June Mathis, **whom** <u>helped</u> make film into an art form.

Correct: One of the first screen writers to include details such as stage directions in her work was June Mathis, **who** <u>helped</u> make film into an art form.

Whom should, however, be used after a preposition. To reiterate, the most common prepositions include *of, from, for, to, by, with, in, on,* and *about*.

Incorrect: Plans for the Biltmore Estate were created by Frederick Law Olmsted, the urban planner <u>by</u> **who** New York City's Central Park was also designed.

Correct: Plans for the Biltmore Estate were created by Frederick Law Olmsted, the urban planner <u>by</u> **whom** New York City's Central Park was also designed.

Where, When, and "Preposition + Which"

Where refers to places (physical locations) only. It should not be used to refer to stories or times/time periods, even though this usage is common in everyday speech.

When refers to times and events only.

Preposition + which (e.g. *in which*, *during which*, *to which*) can be used instead of *where* or *when*. Although this construction may sound odd to you, it is perfectly acceptable.

Incorrect:	The Middle Ages was a period **where** many farmers were bound to the land they worked.
Correct:	The Middle Ages was a period **when/in which** many farmers were bound to the land they worked.
Incorrect:	*Life of Pi*, written by Yann Martel, is a novel **where** the protagonist survives on a raft in the ocean for nearly a year, accompanied only by a tiger.
Correct:	*Life of Pi*, written by Yann Martel, is a novel **in which** the protagonist survives on a raft in the ocean for nearly a year, accompanied only by a tiger.

Which, however, should not be used without the preposition.

Incorrect:	New York is a city **which** many people travel by subway rather than by car.
Correct:	New York is a city **in which** many people travel by subway rather than by car.
Correct:	New York is a city **where** many people travel by subway rather than by car.

When either *where/when* or *preposition + which* is correct, you will not be asked to choose between them.

Whereby

Whereby means "by which" or "at which." Although this word may sound very awkward to you, it may appear necessarily in a correct answer.

Correct:	Desalination is a process whereby salt and other minerals are removed from water in order to produce a liquid that is suitable for human consumption.

*For a more in-depth discussion of *who vs. whom*, see Appendix D on p. 252.

Exercise: Relative Pronouns (answers p. 230)

1. The tale of Hansel and Gretel, the story of two young children **1** whom stumble across a cottage made of gingerbread, played an important role in the history of sweets. It was published in 1812, a time where many bakers already knew how to create elaborate structures from other types of candy. Inspired by the tale, they began to form their gingerbread into houses. Soon, gingerbread construction was elevated to an art form **2** whose popularity quickly spread through Europe and the United States.

1

A) NO CHANGE
B) which stumble
C) who stumble
D) and stumble

2

A) NO CHANGE
B) who's popularity
C) its popularity
D) and popularity

2. Shortly after I moved from Chicago to Lincoln, Nebraska, I attended the eighty-fifth birthday party of a woman **1** whom was among the city's original settlers. The **2** room, that was decorated with banners and balloons, also held family photographs – crisp new snapshots of grandchildren and great-grandchildren, wedding photos from the 1950s, and worn black-and-white portraits of ancestors whose stoic expressions and sturdy, upright figures seemed to embody the harshness of life in an unforgiving new environment.

These people were immortalized in the works of Willa Cather, **3** whom depicted them in novels such as *My Antonia* and *O Pioneers!* Cather, an **4** author which lived in Nebraska during the late nineteenth century, chronicled the lives and hardships of the settlers, preserving their struggles for generations to come.

1

A) NO CHANGE
B) who was
C) which was
D) she was

2

A) NO CHANGE
B) room that,
C) room, which
D) room, it

3

A) NO CHANGE
B) who
C) which
D) she

4

A) NO CHANGE
B) author, which
C) author who
D) author, that

206

3. More than 85% of mammals sleep for short periods throughout the day. Humans, in contrast, divide their days into two distinct periods: one **1** where they sleep and one for wakefulness. Although this division is considered normal in the United States, it is not clear that this is humans' natural sleep pattern. Young children and elderly people are two **2** groups, that often nap, and napping is an important aspect of many cultures.

While naps do not necessarily make up for inadequate or poor quality nighttime sleep, a short nap **3** where a person simply closes his or her eyes for a few minutes can help to improve mood, alertness and concentration. Although people **4** who sleep in the middle of the day are often perceived as lazy, they're actually a very accomplished group. Famous nappers include Winston Churchill, John F. Kennedy, Napoleon, Albert Einstein, and Thomas Edison, all **5** of whom are known to have valued their afternoon naps.

1
A) NO CHANGE
B) in which they sleep
C) for which they sleep
D) for sleep

2
A) NO CHANGE
B) groups, which often nap
C) groups that, often nap
D) groups that often nap,

3
A) NO CHANGE
B) whereby
C) from which
D) that

4
A) NO CHANGE
B) whom sleep
C) which sleep
D) that sleep,

5
A) NO CHANGE
B) of them
C) of which
D) of these

4. Since the early 2000s, thousands of honey bees have disappeared without a trace, and no one knows just why. The phenomenon, known as Colony Collapse Disorder (CCD), has occurred many times, but this time it has become a global epidemic. David Hackenberg, a Pennsylvania beekeeper, was one of the first people **1** whom called attention to the problem.

1
A) NO CHANGE
B) which call
C) who will call
D) to call

It was in 2006 that Hackenberg realized something was amiss. For years, he had lent his bees to farmers, **2** whom used them to pollinate their crops. In 2006, he delivered 400 bee colonies to a Florida farm, but when he went to collect them, the bees were nowhere to be found. In the end, he lost about two-third of his hives. Although Hackenberg was distraught at first, he now considers himself lucky: some beekeepers **3** whom were less fortunate lost 90% of their bees. Now, scientists are curious to figure out just what is making so many bees disappear in places **4** where they were once found in abundance. The causes of CCD and the reasons for its increasing occurrence remain unclear, but many possibilities have been proposed: pesticides, infections, genetics, loss of habitat, radiation from electronic devices – or a combination of all these factors.

2
A) NO CHANGE
B) which used
C) who used
D) these farmers used

3
A) NO CHANGE
B) who were
C) which were
D) being

4
A) NO CHANGE
B) that
C) when
D) DELETE the underlined word.

5. Having played a central role in helping the United States win its independence from Great Britain, George Washington quickly became a celebrity. Not surprisingly, he acquired many admirers, one **1** of them was Patience Wright. Wright, a sculptor, was known for her remarkably realistic **2** portraits, that were made out of tinted wax. She had always amused herself and her children by molding faces out of putty, dough, and wax, but thanks to a neighbor who encouraged her, she turned her hobby into a full-time occupation.

Wright loved her work, and those **3** whom watched her sculpt often commented on the energy that she brought to the process. In an era where photographs did not exist, skilled portraitists were held in high regard. Despite her

1
A) NO CHANGE
B) of which
C) of whom
D) of these

2
A) NO CHANGE
B) portraits, which
C) portraits in which
D) portraits, they

3
A) NO CHANGE
B) who watched
C) which watched
D) watched

208

lack of formal training, Wright was widely recognized for her talents. By 1770, she had become successful enough to open a waxworks house in New York City. When fire ravaged the New York studio in 1771, however, Wright decided to relocate to London. By that time, she had sculpted many famous figures and had even earned the support of the Queen of England, **4** which admired her work deeply. Still, though, she wasn't satisfied. To sculpt George Washington, a leader **5** to whom so many new Americans owed their deep gratitude, would be the crowning achievement of Wright's career.

4

A) NO CHANGE
B) who admired
C) whom admired
D) and she admired

5

A) NO CHANGE
B) to who
C) to which
D) to him

Practice Test
(answers p. 231)

Questions 1-11 are based on the following passage.

Guy Laliberté's Cirque du Soleil

Guy Laliberté is an accordionist, stilt-walker, and fire-eater. He's also the founder of Cirque du Soleil (French for "Circus of the Sun"), the Canadian circus that has become famous for **[1]** it's spectacular sets and amazing acrobats. While it may be unusual, Laliberte's career choice was hardly **[2]** surprising when he was a child, his parents took him to watch the Ringling Brothers and Barnum & Bailey Circus, an experience that led him to read the biography of its creator, P. T. Barnum.

While still in his teens, Laliberté produced several performing arts events. After leaving college, he entered the world of street **[3]** performance, and he would play the harmonica and accordion on the streets of Quebec. He then **[4]** hitched up with a troupe that included fire-breathers, jugglers, and acrobats who traveled around the country from show to show. Later, he returned to Quebec, where he found a steady job at a hydroelectric dam. Soon after his employment began, **[5]** however, the dam's employees went on strike. Laliberté took the opportunity to return to his life as a street performer.

[1]
A) NO CHANGE
B) its
C) their
D) they're

[2]
A) NO CHANGE
B) surprising, when he was a child
C) surprising. When he was a child
D) surprising, when he was a child,

[3]
A) NO CHANGE
B) performance; and played
C) performance, he played
D) performance, playing

[4]
A) NO CHANGE
B) became involved
C) hung around
D) established relations

[5]
A) NO CHANGE
B) moreover
C) consequently
D) in fact

211

In 1984, Laliberté co-founded Cirque du Soleil with entrepreneur Gilles Ste-Croix and several other colleagues. The name, which Laliberté came up with while on vacation in [6] Hawaii, and reflects his idea that "the sun stands for energy and youth." He wanted the circus to embody those words. Cirque du Soleil was [7] initially set up as a one-year project at first; however, the show proved so popular with audiences that its run was [8] elongated indefinitely and new locations were proposed. Throughout the expansion process, Laliberté participated in the creation of each new show. The circus, which is active on five continents, now employs over 4,000 people from over 40 countries. It has been seen by over 90 million people worldwide and [9] has remained unique because it does not include animals in its acts.

[6]

A) NO CHANGE
B) Hawaii and reflects
C) Hawaii; reflecting
D) Hawaii, reflects

[7]

A) NO CHANGE
B) initially set up as a one-year project for the first time
C) initially set up as a one-year project
D) initially set up as a one-year project originally

[8]

A) NO CHANGE
B) extended
C) multiplied
D) magnified

[9]

Which choice provides the most relevant detail?

A) NO CHANGE
B) has an annual revenue of over $800 million.
C) is popular with adults as well as children.
D) features exceptionally skilled performers.

Laliberte has also used his success to give back to his community – and the world. On October 29, 2007, Laliberté announced the official launch of the One Drop Foundation, an organization that fights poverty by giving people access to water. Inspired by the experience of Cirque du Soleil and its international program for street children, Cirque du Monde, the foundation **10** makes use of theater, music, dance, and the visual arts to promote education, community involvement, and public awareness of water issues in developing countries on six continents. Its projects are also intended to ensure food security and promote equality for women. **11** Convinced that a comprehensive, planetary approach is required to pursue its mission, One Drop puts water at the heart of public debate and international agendas.

10

A) NO CHANGE
B) makes use of theater; music, dance, and
C) makes use of: theater, music, dance, and
D) makes use of theater, music, dance and –

11

The writer wants a concluding sentence that reinforces one of the main ideas of the essay. Which choice best accomplishes this goal?

A) NO CHANGE
B) The program's technical component is aimed at promoting responsible water management and preservation principles.
C) In addition to founding the One Drop Foundation, Laliberté is also a championship poker player who has won several titles.
D) Laliberté is convinced that with a little creativity, people can come together and accomplish remarkable things.

Questions 12-22 are based on the following passage and supplementary material.

Building in Pieces

Inside a warehouse in Brooklyn, New York, steel beams and flat metal sheeting rest on top of a workbench. Lying next to them is a diagram indicating where every beam and metal screw belongs. Each of these components **12** have been carefully checked off – the pieces are all in place and ready to be assembled. The metal might not look like much yet, but it is on its way to becoming part of the **13** world's tallest modular residence. Soon, workers will configure the beams into walls, turning them into scaffolding for rooms. The rooms will then be linked together to form apartments.

14 Modular buildings differ from mobile homes in two important ways. The modules themselves are six-sided boxes consisting of a floor, a ceiling, and four walls. They are constructed in a remote facility and then delivered to their site of use. Since the modules have to be transported on the backs of flat-bed trucks over highways, they are generally no longer than the truck and no wider than 16 feet.

12

A) NO CHANGE
B) has been
C) were
D) being

13

A) NO CHANGE
B) world's tallest, modular, residence.
C) worlds tallest, modular residence.
D) world's tallest modular, residence.

14

Which choice most effectively establishes the main topic of the paragraph?

A) NO CHANGE
B) Most city-dwellers live in apartments rather than free-standing houses.
C) Modular buildings – also known as prefabricated buildings – are buildings that consist of multiple sections called modules.
D) While apartments usually have less space than houses, they have benefits as well.

214

Modular buildings can function not only as temporary structures such as construction camps **15** and as long-term ones such as apartment buildings. In the past, they were primarily used in remote areas where more traditional construction was impossible. **16** Today, however, they are increasingly used in cities with rapidly expanding populations. Additional homes and apartments are urgently needed to house the new inhabitants, and modular construction can deliver quickly. In fact, it takes **17** slightly longer to install a traditional home than it takes to install a modular one.

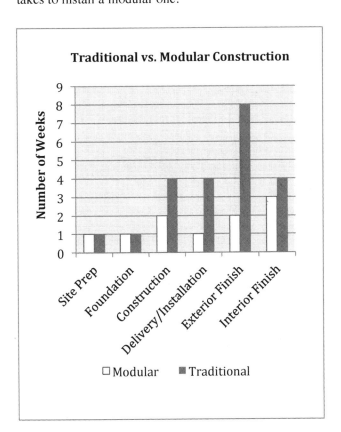

Traditional vs. Modular Construction

□ Modular   ■ Traditional

15

A) NO CHANGE
B) and for
C) but also as
D) but also for

16

At this point in the essay, the writer is considering adding the following sentence.

> In 2010, for instance, modular accommodation pods were used to house researchers during an Antarctic expedition.

Should this sentence be added?

A) Yes, because it provides an example of a situation in which traditional buildings could not be constructed.
B) Yes, because modular construction can be used for both temporary and permanent housing.
C) No, because it is irrelevant to the discussion of construction in cities.
D) No, because modular housing is no longer used in remote locations.

17

Which choice offers an accurate interpretation of data presented in the chart?

A) NO CHANGE
B) just as long to install a traditional home as
C) slightly less time to install a traditional home than
D) significantly longer to install a traditional home than

[1] Modules are usually constructed on an indoor assembly line. [2] During the first stage, the walls are attached to the floor. [3] As a finishing touch, shingles and siding are added. [4] Construction of the modules can take as little as ten days, but more often several months are needed. [5]After the walls are firmly in place, drywall ceiling is sprayed on in a booth, and the roof is attached. [6] **18** During the whole process, building inspectors are required to supervise the construction and ensure that the company adheres to all building codes throughout the entire process. **19**

When the modules are complete, they are transported to the building site. **20** Using a crane, they are set onto the building's foundation by workers where they are joined together. The process can take anywhere from several hours to several days. Workers can place the modules side-by-side or **21** being stacked high like blocks, allowing for a wide variety of configurations and styles in the building layout. The interior finishing process takes just **22** three weeks – a small fraction of the time necessary to finish the interior of a traditional building. After the finishing process is complete, the module is finally ready for its first tenants to move in.

18
A) NO CHANGE
B) Throughout the duration of this process,
C) While this process occurs,
D) DELETE the underlined portion (adjusting the punctuation accordingly)

19

To make the paragraph most logical, sentence 5 should be placed

A) where it is now.
B) after sentence 2.
C) after sentence 3.
D) after sentence 6.

20

A) NO CHANGE
B) They are set by workers, onto the building's foundation, and a crane is used
C) Workers use a crane to set them on the building's foundation,
D) Workers set them on the building's foundation by crane and

21

A) NO CHANGE
B) stack them
C) to stack them
D) they stack them

22

Which choice offers an accurate interpretation of data presented in the chart?

A) NO CHANGE
B) two weeks – far less time than is
C) one week – just half of the time
D) three weeks – slightly less time than is

Questions 23-33 are based on the following passage.

An Author at Last

– 1 –

Throughout my childhood, writing was one of my favorite hobbies. I **23** spend hours dictating my stories to my parents and then, when I got older, writing them down myself. When I got to college, though, I approached my major pragmatically and decided to study engineering. Still, I **24** sheltered hopes of one day publishing a novel.

– 2 –

Although my job at a biotechnology company was tiring, I couldn't shake the need to write. Every night, after the rest of my family had gone to sleep, I would turn on my computer and go to work. It wasn't always easy to keep **25** writing sometimes, I sat for hours in front of a blank screen, racking my brain to figure out what should happen next. Eventually, though, my writer's block would dissolve, and seeing **26** them fill up gave me a feeling of great satisfaction. After nearly a year of working this way, I had completed a draft of my book. Now I just needed to publish it. I sent some inquiries to traditional publishing companies, **27** and I anxiously waited for an answer. My book showed promise, they said, but it would be difficult to market and sell because I did not already have an established reputation as an author. Although I was disappointed, I was also determined.

23

A) NO CHANGE
B) have spent
C) would spend
D) will spend

24

A) NO CHANGE
B) upheld
C) fostered
D) harbored

25

A) NO CHANGE
B) writing: sometimes, I sat for hours
C) writing, sometimes I sat for hours –
D) writing sometimes I sat for hours

26

A) NO CHANGE
B) this
C) these
D) the pages

27

Which choice provides the most effective transition to the information that follows?

A) NO CHANGE
B) but I never received a response.
C) but no one offered me a contract.
D) whose names I had found on the Internet.

Using a website that connected freelance workers with individuals and companies seeking help with short-term **28** projects, and I found an editor as well as a cover artist. Although they lived thousands of miles from my home, we were able to communicate directly using video software. They helped me transform my draft into something much more polished and professional. **29** My final manuscript was almost 300 pages long. I simply entered the title and author information, uploaded my manuscript and cover, and created an e-book. I even received a free ISBN number, the identification number that must appear on the cover of every book.

At first, I wasn't sure how I **30** should precede. Then, while doing some research, I stumbled **31** to the world of self-publishing. Originally used by aspiring authors who wanted to print a handful of books for friends and family, the self-publishing industry now allows thousands of writers to distribute their work both electronically and in paper form to readers all over the world. I found a service that seemed to fit my needs and eagerly created an account. **32** One of the most successful self-published books is *Choose Yourself* by James Altucher, which sold over 40,000 copies in a month.

28

A) NO CHANGE
B) projects and found
C) projects; I found
D) projects, I found

29

Which choice most effectively sets up the information that follows while reinforcing a main theme of the essay?

A) NO CHANGE
B) In the end, I met three or four times with each of them.
C) I couldn't believe how easy the actual publishing process was.
D) I found them pleasant and easy to work with.

30

A) NO CHANGE
B) will precede.
C) should proceed.
D) will proceed.

31

A) NO CHANGE
B) upon
C) through
D) at

32

The writer is considering deleting the underlined sentence. Should the writer make this change?

A) Yes, because it is inconsistent with the focus on the writer's personal self-publishing experience.
B) Yes, because the passage does not mention how many copies the writer wanted to sell.
C) No, because it explains what constitutes success for a self-published book.
D) No, because most self-published books sell fewer copies than traditional books.

While my book didn't immediately shoot to the top of the best-seller list, I am happy to report that it has been downloaded several hundred times. I've even gotten a couple of fan letters: one from North Carolina, and the other all the way from England! Now, I'm hard at work on my second book. I just need to think of a title. **33**

Think about the previous passage as a whole as you answer question 33.

33

To make the passage most logical, paragraph 4 should be placed

A) where it is now.
B) before paragraph 1.
C) before paragraph 2.
D) before paragraph 3.

Questions 34-44 are based on the following passage and supplementary material.

It's Only a Dream

Whether you're flying above the pyramids like a bird, taking a final exam for a class you took two years ago, or [34] explore a pirate ship at the bottom of the ocean, dreaming can be a truly bizarre experience. Scientists have been studying dreams for decades, but they continue to lack answers to fundamental questions about how and why dreaming occurs. [35] For example, they do not know whether dreams actually have a physiological, biological or psychological function. Still, those questions have not stopped them from speculating. [36]

34

A) NO CHANGE
B) to explore
C) you explore
D) exploring

35

A) NO CHANGE
B) Therefore,
C) However,
D) Consequently,

36

The writer is considering adding the following sentence.

> Dream interpretation dates back to 3000-4000 B.C., when the Sumerians documented dreams on clay tablets.

Should the sentence be added?

A) Yes, because it explains the origins of some modern theories about dream.
B) Yes, because it establishes that people have attempted to understand dreams for thousands of years.
C) No, because it is inconsistent with the paragraph's focus on the scientific aspect of dreaming.
D) No, because the Sumerians did not speculate about why dreams occur.

[37] Researchers have determined that there are five stages of sleep. During the day, the brain must work hard to form connections in order to achieve certain goals. When [38] posed with a challenging math problem, for instance, your brain must focus intently on that single task. The same goes for simple tasks such as kicking or throwing a ball. During sleep, however, [39] the brain is far less active than the daytime, so the day's emotions bubble to the surface. If something is weighing heavily on your mind during the day, chances are you might dream about it – either specifically or through obvious imagery. A person who is worried about giving a speech in front of an audience may turn into a mouse squeaking in front of a crowd of giants. [40]

[37]

Which choice most effectively introduces the main topic of the paragraph?

A) NO CHANGE
B) One popular theory is that dreams reflect emotions.
C) Slow sleep waves occur predominantly during the first half of the night.
D) Before the early 1950s, scientists believed that the brain was inactive during sleep.

[38]

A) NO CHANGE
B) enticed
C) confronted
D) encountered

[39]

A) NO CHANGE
B) the brain is far less active than it is during the daytime
C) the brain is far less active then during the daytime
D) the brain is far less active than the daytime is

[40]

Which choice gives a second supporting example that is most similar to the example already in the sentence?

A) A swimmer could become a fish darting through the water.
B) Someone concerned about meeting an important deadline might be running after a train that's pulling away.
C) Violin players must develop impressive coordination in order to manipulate a bow and strings.
D) A scientist might come up with an new theory during the night.

Some researchers also believe that dreams help the brain sort through the millions of pieces of information it encounters each day, allowing it to decide what to retain and **41** what should be forgotten by it. Some of this information consists of simple sensory details, such as the color of a shirt, while others are far more complex, such as a presentation for history class. During REM sleep, when most dreaming occurs, **42** brain activity spikes sharply, rising almost to waking levels. The more learning occurs during waking hours, the more active the brain becomes during REM sleep. One recent dream study compared the dream activity of a group studying a foreign language to a group not studying a foreign language. The foreign language group showed a spike in brain activity during REM **43** sleep; suggesting that dreaming helped the students assimilate and retain new information.

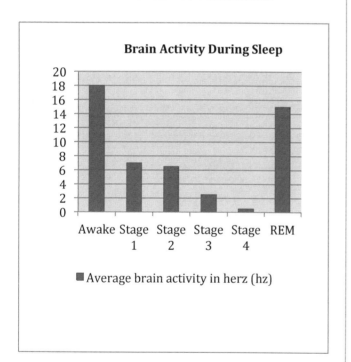

Brain Activity During Sleep

41

A) NO CHANGE
B) what it should forget.
C) what is being forgotten.
D) what to forget.

42

Which choice offers an accurate interpretation of data presented in the chart?

A) NO CHANGE
B) spikes sharply but is still far below
C) increases slightly, rising to almost
D) decreases dramatically, falling to below

43

A) NO CHANGE
B) sleep and suggesting
C) sleep, this suggests
D) sleep, suggesting that

It is also possible that dreams don't serve any function at all – of course, they're the result of random neurons firing in a way that doesn't occur when people are awake. According to this view, dreams are essentially a byproduct of the brain winding down for the night.

A) NO CHANGE
B) that is,
C) at the same time,
D) in contrast,

Answer Key

Preliminary Exercise, p. 12

1. Pronoun
2. Verb
3. Preposition
4. Verb
5. Conjunction
6. Verb
7. Adverb
8. Verb
9. Adjective
10. Verb
11. Preposition
12. Adjective
13. Verb
14. Noun
15. Pronoun
16. Preposition
17. Adverb
18. Verb
19. Verb
20. Conjunction
21. Adjective
22. Preposition
23. Noun
24. Verb
25. Preposition

Adding, Deleting and Revising, p. 24

1.1 D
1.2 A

2.1 A
2.2 C

3.1 A
3.2 C

4.1 C
4.2 B

5.1 B
5.2 A
5.3 C

6.1 C

7.1 D
7.2 A

8.1 C
8.2 B

Sentence Order, p. 30

1. D
2. B
3. D
4. A
5. B

Infographics, p. 45

1. A
2. B
3. B
4. C
5. D

Shorter is Better, p. 52

1.1 D
1.2 D
1.3 A
1.4 A

2.1 D
2.2 C
2.3 D

3.1 D
3.2 D
3.3. A
3.4 A

4.1 B
4.2 C
4.3 D

5.1 B
5.2 A
5.3 D
5.4 D

Diction, Idioms, and Register, p. 64

1.1 C
1.2 D

2.1 D
2.2 A
2.3 B

3.1 D
3.2 A
3.3 C
3.4 C
3.5 B

4.1 A
4.2 B

5.1 B
5.2 A
5.3 C
5.4 C

Is it a Sentence? p. 67

1. Sentence

2. Sentence

3. Fragment

4. Fragment

5. Sentence

6. Sentence

7. Sentence

8. Sentence

9. Sentence

10. Fragment

11. Fragment

12. Sentence

13. Sentence

14. Fragment

15. Fragment

16. Sentence

17. Sentence

18. Sentence

Sentences and Fragments, p. 79

1. Since 2009, physicists **have** been intrigued by possible evidence of dark matter in the center of the Milky Way galaxy.

2. Sentence

3. When they catch sight of their prey, ~~and~~ peregrine falcons drop into a steep, swift dive at more than 200 miles an hour.

4. After publishing her acclaimed novel *The God of Small Things*, author Arundhati Roy **turned** her attention to writing works of non-fiction and working as a political activist.

5. Each spring, students ~~who~~ gather from around the world for the FIRST Robotics Competition, an experience that can change lives.

6. The forestry industry has met and **is** continuing to meet the growing change required to stay competitive within a rapidly transforming economy.

7. Sentence

8. Findings from one recent study about meteorites **suggest** that water has been present on Earth since the planet was formed.

9. Usually structured differently from auto-biographies, ~~but~~ memoirs follow the development of an author's personality rather than the writing of his or her works.

10. Chicago's metropolitan area, sometimes called Chicagoland, ~~which~~ is home to 9.5 million people and is the third-largest in the United States.

11. Sentence

12. Sentence

13. The Great Lakes **are/were** a major highway for transportation, migration, and trade as well as home to a large number of aquatic species.

14. Sentence

15. Cities around the world once maintained extensive cable car systems, most of **which** have been replaced by more modern forms of transportation.

Periods, Semicolons, and Commas + FANBOYS, p. 87

1.1 B

2.1 D

3.1 C

4.1 C

5.1 D

6.1 B

7.1 C
7.2 D

8.1 B
8.2 D

9.1 D
9.2 C

Transition Exercise I, p. 100

1. Contrast, B

2. Cause-and-effect, B

3. Continue, C

4. Contrast, A

5. Contrast, D

6. Contrast, A

7. Cause-and-effect, A

8. Contrast, B

9. Cause-and-effect, C

10. Continue/cause-and-effect, B

Transition Exercise II, p. 103

1.1 C

2.1 D

3.1 A

4.1 D

5.1 B

6.1 D
6.2 C
6.3 C

7.1 B
7.2 A

8.1 A
8.2 C

9.1 A
9.2 B

10.1 D
10.2 A

Identifying Non-Essential Words and Phrases, p. 111

1. The cesium fountain atomic clock, **the most precise form of timekeeper available,** is expected to become inaccurate by less than a single second over the next 50 million years.

2. Frank Gehry's buildings, **often cited as being among the most important works of contemporary architecture,** have become popular tourist attractions in many cities.

3. The most common types of coral, **which are usually found in clear, shallow waters,** require sunlight in order to grow.

4. Used in some martial arts, the Red Belt, **one of several colored belts intended to denote a practitioner's skill level and rank,** originated in Japan and Korea.

5. The Iditarod dog sled race, **an annual event in Alaska,** commemorates the dogsled teams that delivered a life-saving serum during the 1925 diphtheria epidemic.

6. New Zealand, **one of the last lands to be settled by humans,** developed distinctive animal and plant life during its long isolation.

7. Forensic biology, **the application of biology to law enforcement,** has been used to identify illegal products from endangered species and investigate bird collisions with wind turbines.

8. Human computers, **who once performed basic numerical analysis for laboratories,** were behind the
calculations for everything from the first accurate prediction of the return of Halley's Comet to the success of the Manhattan Project.

9. Simone Fortini, **a choreographer born in Italy but a resident of the United States since a young age,** rapidly became known for a style of dancing based on improvisation and everyday movements.

10. The Rochester International Jazz Festival, **which takes place in June of each year,** typically attracts more than 100,000 fans from across the United States.

11. The unusually large size of the komodo dragon, **the largest species of lizard,** has been attributed to its ancient ancestor, the immense varanid lizard.

12. Illegal logging in forests, **once nearly responsible for destroying the monarch butterfly's winter habitat,** has declined in recent years, but the species is still threatened.

13. Fashioned from Russian folk tales, <u>Swan Lake</u>**, one of the most popular ballets,** tells the story of Odette, a princess turned into a swan by an evil sorcerer's curse.

Non-Essential and Essential Clauses, p. 119

1.1 C

2.1 B

3.1 D
3.2 C

4.1 C
4.2 D

5.1 A
5.2 A
5.3 B

6.1 A
6.2 C

7.1 D
7.2 C

8.1 A
8.2 C

9.1 B
9.2 B
9.3 C
9.4 D

227

Colons and Dashes, p. 131

1.1 B
1.2 A

2.1 C
2.2 B

3.1 C
3.2 C

4.1 A
4.2 D
4.3 C

5.1 B
5.2 C
5.3 D

Apostrophes with Nouns and Pronouns, p. 138

1. its
2. whose
3. their attempts
4. Correct (their), echoes that identify its
5. their, correct (its)
6. whose, correct (scientists')
7. its traffics jams, city's
8. their
9. Correct (whose), their
10. you're
11. whose, correct (its)
12. its
13. year's, there

Pronoun/Noun Agreement and Apostrophes, p. 147

1.1 D

2.1 C

3.1 B

4.1 B
4.2 A

5.1 C
5.2 B

6.1 C

7.1 A
7.2 D
7.3 B

8.1 B
8.2 D

9.1 C
9.2 B

10.1 A
10.2 B

Cumulative Review: All Punctuation and Transitions, p. 150

1.1 D
1.2 D
1.3 B
1.4 A

2.1 B
2.2 C
2.3 D
2.4 A
2.5 B

3.1 C
3.2 B
3.3 D

4.1 C
4.2 D
4.3 B

5.1 C
5.2 A
5.3 B

6.1 D
6.2 A
6.3 D
6.4 C

7.1 D
7.2 D

8.1 A
8.2 D
8.3 A
8.4 C
8.5 B

9.1 B
9.2 B
9.3 A
9.4 C
9.5 B

10.1 A
10.2 D
10.3 A
10.4 B
10.5 C

Subject-Verb Agreement, p. 165

1. appear
2. have
3. explore
4. Correct
5. seems
6. has
7. Correct
8. sit
9. Correct
10. was
11. requires, correct (makes), correct (changes)
12. is, are
13. spread, touches
14. Correct (are), have
15. Correct

Subject-Verb Agreement and Tense, p. 174

1.1 D
1.2 A

2.1 C
2.2 D
2.3 B
2.4 C

3.1 C
3.2 D
3.3. A

3.4 B
3.5 B

4.1 D
4.2 C
4.3 D
4.4 A

5.1 B
5.2 A
5.3 B
5.4 C
5.5 D

6.1 C
6.2 C
6.3 B

7.1 B
7.2 A
7.3 D
7.4 B

8.1 B
8.2 B
8.3 A
8.4 C

Word Pairs and Comparisons, p. 183

1.1 D
1.2 D

2.1 B
2.2 A

3.1 C
3.2 B
3.3 D

4.1 A
4.2 D
4.3 C

5.1 B
5.2 B
5.3 D

Parallel Structure, p. 196

1.1 C
1.2 C
1.3 A

2.1 B
2.2 B
2.3 D

3.1 A
3.2 C

4.1 D
4.2 D
4.3 D

5.1 B
5.2 C

6.1 B
6.2 D
6.3 C

7.1 C
7.2 A

8.1 A
8.2 B
8.3 D
8.4 A

9.1 D
9.2 B
9.3 C
9.4 D

10.1 D
10.2 A
10.3 C
10.4 C

Misplaced and Dangling Modifiers, p. 199

1.1 B
1.2 A
1.3 C
1.4 D

2.1 C
2.2 B
2.3 D
2.4 C

3.1 D
3.2 B
3.3 A

4.1 B
4.2 D

5.1 C
5.2 D

Relative Pronouns, 206

1.1 C
1.2 A

2.1 B
2.2 C
2.3 B
2.4 C

3.1 D
3.2 D
3.3 B
3.4 A
3.5 A

4.1 D
4.2 C
4.3 B
4.4 A

5.1 C
5.2 B
5.3 B
5.4 B
5.5 A

Practice Test, p. 211

1. B: Apostrophes, Pronoun Agreement

The underlined pronoun refers to the singular noun *circus*, eliminating both C) and D). *The circus has become famous for it is spectacular sets* is clearly wrong, eliminating A). B) correctly uses the possessive *its*.

2. C: Combining and Separating Sentences

If you read this sentence carefully from beginning to end, you should notice that there are actually two sentences. Although the original version places the phrase *when he was a child* at the end of the first sentence, it actually belongs to the beginning of the second sentence. A) creates a run-on, and both B) and D) create comma splices. C) correctly places a period between the two sentences.

3. D: Parallel Structure, Semicolon, Comma Splice

A) contains an unnecessary tense switch that makes the sentence awkward; B) incorrectly places a semicolon before the FANBOYS conjunction *and*; C) creates a comma splice (tip-off is "comma + he"); and D) eliminates both the comma splice and tense shift problems by joining the two clauses with the participle *playing*.

4. B: Register

Hitched up and *hung around* are both too casual, and *established relations* is too formal, eliminating A), C), and D). *Became involved* correctly maintains the moderately serious tone of the passage.

5. A: Transition

This transition occurs in the middle of the sentence, so you need to back up and consider the relationship between this sentence and the previous sentence. The previous sentences indicates that Laliberté left street performing for a steady job in Quebec, and this sentence tells us that the workers at his new job went on strike (implying that Laliberté couldn't work). Those are opposite ideas,

so a contradictor is required. Only *however* matches that criterion, so A) is correct.

6. D: Sentence vs. Fragment, Non-Essential Clause

The easiest way to answer this question is to recognize that the sentence contains a non-essential clause: "The name, which Laliberté came up with while on vacation in Hawaii, and reflects his idea that the sun stands for energy and youth." (Note that you cannot recognize this unless you back up and read the sentence from the beginning.) When the non-essential clause is removed, you are left with nonsense: "The name…and reflects his idea that the sun stands for energy and youth." The simplest way to turn that statement back into a sentence is to remove the word *and*, which makes D) the answer.

7. C: Shorter is Better, Redundancy

Initially, *at first*, and *originally* are all synonyms so the use of more than one of them in the same sentence is redundant. C) is the only answer to use only one.

8. B: Diction, Idiom

Idiomatic usage requires that *extended* be used to refer to a performance that is adding additional shows. Although the other words have similar meanings, they are not colloquial in this context.

9. B: Add/Delete/Change

Before you can figure out which answer provides the most relevant detail, you need to figure out what the surrounding sentences are about. What do we learn from them? That the circus has been a huge success all over the world. In B), the number $800 million is pretty clearly consistent with that idea. A) and D) refer to distinctive aspects of Cirque du Soleil, but they are not directly related to its success. C) is vaguely related to the idea of success, but the fact that Cirque du Soleil is popular with both adults and children does not explicitly convey the idea of its enormous success.

231

10. A: Colon, Comma with List

The information before the list cannot be a standalone sentence, so no colon should be used after *of*, and commas should be placed between the items of the list. That makes A) correct. B) can be eliminated because commas and semicolons should not be mixed to separate items in a list. (Although semicolons can technically be used to separate long items in a list, this usage is unlikely to appear on the SAT; for the purposes of the test, they should only be used to separate two sentences.) C) can be eliminated because the information before the colon is not a standalone sentence; the fact that it is followed by a list is irrelevant. And D) can be eliminated because there is simply no reason to place a dash (or any punctuation) between *and* and the last item of the list.

11. D: Add/Delete/Change

In order to answer this question, you need to know the main idea of the passage. If you had to put it in your own words, you could say something like "Guy Laliberté is an amazing guy." The answer that comes generally closest to that idea is D), which is also consistent with the discussion of Laliberté's charity in the last paragraph. Notice that this is the only answer that contains a more general idea – all of the other answers contain specific information, primarily related to the One Drop Foundation.

12. B: Subject-verb agreement

Each is singular and requires a singular verb. *Has* is the only singular option; *have* and *were* are both plural (the inclusion of different tenses is a decoy to distract from the real problem). In D), the gerund *being* creates a fragment.

13. A: Commas and adjectives, Apostrophes

Although all those commas might make your head spin, this question is actually easier than it appears if you know what to focus on. The first thing to notice is that the word *world* appears both with and without the apostrophe. *Worlds* is plural, and there's only one world, so C) can be eliminated immediately. Next: since a comma should never be

placed between an adjective and the noun it modifies, and B) and D) place a comma between *modular* and *residence*, both answers can be eliminated, leaving A). You can also think of *modular residence* as a single unit that is in turn modified by *tallest*. Again, since no comma is required between adjectives and the nouns they modify, no comma should be used here.

14. C: Add/Delete/Change

Start by ignoring the first sentence and just reading the rest of the paragraph. What is the paragraph about? Modules. So the correct answer must introduce the topic of modules. C) is the only option that fulfills that requirement, so it is correct.

15. C: Word Pair, Parallel Structure

Work backwards from the answer. The fact that two of them include the phrase *but also* immediately suggests that you need to read the entire sentence to check for *not only*. It appears, so *but also* is required. That means you can eliminate A) and B). Now look at the word after *not only*. It's *as*, so the word after *but also* must be *as* too. That makes C) the answer.

16. A: Add/Delete/Change

When you are asked whether a sentence should be added, start by checking the previous sentence or couple of sentences. The sentence to be inserted must follow logically. What does the previous sentence indicate? That modular buildings used to be built primarily in areas where traditional buildings couldn't be built. What does the sentence in question describe? The use of modular buildings in Antarctica. Logically, that's a remote place where traditional construction would be impossible. This sentence provides an example of the idea in the previous sentence, so it is relevant, and the answer is A).

17. D: Infographic

Start by looking at the full sentence for context. It discusses the length of time necessary to *install* traditional homes vs. modular ones, so you want to focus on the delivery/installation portion of the graph. The white bar (modular) indicates one week, and the gray bar (traditional) indicates four weeks. So it takes about four times as long to install a traditional home. That is "significantly" longer, making D) correct.

18. D: Shorter is Better, Redundancy

Remember that whenever you have a DELETE option, you should check it first. In this case, the underlined phrase has the same meaning as *throughout the entire process*, so it is unnecessary to have both in the sentence.

19. B: Sentence Order

What is sentence 5 about? What happens after the walls are in place. So logically, the previous sentence must have something to do with putting the walls in place. If you scan the paragraph for the word *walls*, you'll see that it appears in sentence 2. Logically, sentence 5 fits after that. That is confirmed by the phrase *As a finishing touch* in sentence 3 – the paragraph must mention the addition of the roof (sentence 5) before it talks about finishing. So B) is correct.

20. C: Dangling Modifier

Let's start with A). Who is using the crane? The workers. But *workers* does not appear immediately after the comma, so the sentence contains a dangling modifier. On its own, B) is awkward and incorrectly places a comma before a preposition (*onto*), but it also creates a nonsense construction when plugged back into the sentence. D) makes sense on its own but creates a fragment when plugged in. C) makes sense both independently and when it is plugged in – *where* correctly refers back to *foundation*.

21. B: Parallel Structure

The word *or* indicates that the underlined word must be parallel to *place* ("Workers can place or stack them…"). Only B) contains that construction.

22. D: Infographic

All of the answer choices contain two parts, so you want to deal with them one piece at a time. The first part of each answer refers to weeks, so start there. Looking at the "Interior Finish" section of the graph, you can see that the time for modular buildings is three weeks. Based on that information, you can eliminate B) and C). Now you can deal with the other half of the answer. Just looking at the graph, you can see that the bar for modular construction is almost as high as it is for traditional construction, so interior finishing for modular construction takes only a *little* less time than that for traditional construction. That corresponds to D).

23. C: Tense

All of the verbs in the sentence itself and the surrounding sentences are in the past tense (*was, got, approached*), so the underlined verb must be in the past as well. Remember that *would + verb* is grammatically equivalent to the regular old past, so *would spend* is the same as *spent*. That makes D) correct. In B), *have spent* should only be used for an actual that is still continuing, and the passage is in the past. In A), *spend* is in the present, and in C), *will spend* is in the future.

24. D: Diction/Idiom

To "harbor" hopes means to hold onto hope. It is a fixed idiomatic phrase, and *harbor* cannot be replaced by another verb.

25. B: Combining and Separating Sentences

The construction "comma + I" in the original version should be an immediate tipoff that you're probably dealing with a comma splice and that A) is incorrect. In fact, if you back up and read the entire sentence from the beginning, you should notice that there are two full sentences, not one. That means the correct answer is going to require a full stop somewhere. A comma can never be used to divide two sentences, so that immediately eliminates A), C), and D). Although you might be expecting a semicolon or a period here, this question throws in a twist. In this case, the colon is used as the grammatical equivalent of a semicolon. A colon is appropriate here because the second sentence explains what the writer means by *it wasn't easy*. Note that although *sometimes* appears to make sense at the end of the first sentence, it also works as the beginning of the second sentence.

26. D: Pronoun Agreement, Missing Antecedent

The original version does not specify what *them* refers to. The only logical possibility would be *the screen*, which is singular and requires a singular pronoun. Although *this* is singular, B) is incorrect because *this* should not be used without a noun immediately afterward – it's simply too ambiguous and awkward. C) is incorrect because like *this*, *these* should be followed by a noun. D) is correct because it correctly supplies the noun, eliminating the ambiguity.

27. C: Add/Delete/Change

This question indicates that the correct answer must supply a transition to the information that follows, so you need to focus on that information before you worry about the answer itself. What do we learn from the rest of the paragraph? That the publishing companies all said no. C) is the only answer consistent with that idea. The fact that all of the other answers make sense in context of the first half of the sentence is irrelevant.

28. D: Sentence vs. Fragment

Semicolon = comma + and. If both appear as answers, both must be wrong since no question can have more than one right answer. That eliminates A) and C). B) creates a fragment when plugged into the sentence because it eliminates the subject, *I*. D) correctly places a comma between a dependent clause (*Using a website that connected freelance workers with individuals and companies seeking help with short-term projects*) and an independent clause (*I found an editor as well as a cover artist*).

29. C: Add/Delete/Change

The question throws a lot of information at you, so start by focusing on the most concrete part. You're essentially being asked to provide a transition to the information that follows, so look at that information. What does it indicate? That creating a book was a simple process. The only answer that corresponds to that idea is C), which is correct.

30. C: Diction, Tense

All four answers are very similar, and all are broken into two components (verb, vocabulary), so you want to do your best to deal with them one at a time. If you're not sure about *precede vs. proceed*, worry about the tense issue first. The general rule is that you shouldn't combine past (*wasn't*) and future (*will*) in the same sentence, so you can eliminate B) and D). Now the second part. *Precede* means "come before," whereas *proceed* means "go ahead." If you're not sure, you can make an educated guess by using roots: *pre* means "before," so you can assume that *precede* is related to that idea. There's nothing in the passage to indicate that the writer is discussing something that "came before," so A) can be eliminated, leaving C).

31. B: Idiom/Preposition

The correct idiomatic phrase is "stumble upon." Any other preposition is incorrect.

32. A: Add/Delete/Change

What is the paragraph about? The writer's discovery of self-publishing and personal experience with it (note the repeated use of the word *I*). What is the sentence in question about? James Altucher's success with *his* book. So it's off topic. That makes A) correct. (NB: whenever you see an off-topic answer, pay it special attention. The primary reason that any sentence shouldn't be added or should be deleted is that it's off topic.)

33. D: Paragraph Order

Focus on the beginning of paragraph 4, which must follow logically from the end of the paragraph that comes before it. The statement *At first, I wasn't sure how I should proceed* and the subsequent discussion of the writer's discovery of self-publishing tells us that it does not belong where it is. Paragraph 3 describes the steps the writer took to actually self-publish the book, and logically, the writer must have taken those steps *after* learning about self-publishing. The beginning of paragraph 4 fits with the end of paragraph 2 – the writer did not know how to proceed after being rejected by traditional publishing companies. So paragraph 4 belongs after paragraph 2, i.e. before paragraph 3, making the answer D).

34. D: Parallel Structure

All of the items in a list must be in the same format. The non-underlined items in the list both begin with –ING words (*flying*, *taking*), so the underlined word must be an –ING word as well.

35. A: Transition

Start by eliminating B) and D). *Therefore* and *consequently* have the same meaning, so neither can be correct. Now you need to figure out whether you need a continuer or a contradictor, so back up and consider the previous sentence. What does it tell us? That scientists lack answers to fundamental questions about dreaming. What does the sentence in question tell us? That scientists *don't know* how dreams originate. So the two sentences express similar ideas, making A) correct.

36. C: Add/Delete/Change

What is the paragraph about? It basically introduces the topic of dreaming and discusses the fact that dreams are still pretty mysterious. What is the sentence in question about? The origins of dream *interpretation*, which the rest of the paragraph says nothing about. So the sentence is off topic and should not be added, making C) correct.

37. B: Add/Delete/Change

This question asks you about the main topic of the paragraph, so you need to establish that piece of information before you answer the question. What is the paragraph about? That the brain is active during the day but less so at night, allowing emotions to express themselves in dreams. That idea is most consistent with B). Notice that you need to read the entire paragraph to figure that out; if you only read the first couple of sentence after the topic sentence, you won't have enough information to answer the question. The word *however* halfway through the paragraph is a big clue that important information will follow.

38. C: Diction, Idiom

The original version is incorrect because *posed* is a synonym for "asked." A question can only be "posed" to or by someone (e.g. "The teacher posed a difficult question) – a person cannot be "posed" with a question. The correct idiom is *confronted with a question*, making C) correct.

39. B: Faulty Comparison, Diction

A) and D) incorrectly compare the brain's activity to the daytime, when brain activity should be compared to brain activity. C) incorrectly uses *then*, not *than*, to make the comparison. B) correctly makes the comparison, using the pronoun *it* to replace the noun *brain*.

40. B: Add/Change/Delete

In order to figure out which second example would be most consistent with the first example, you need to know what the first example is all about. For the fullest explanation, back up two sentences to get the point that the examples must support: when people are worried about something, they tend to dream about it. The correct answer must simply describe a negative situation that expresses itself in a dream. The word *concerned* in B) is the only negative word in all the answer choices, suggesting that it is correct. Logically, being concerned about missing an *important* deadline would be stressful. All of the other answers are neutral or positive.

41. D: Parallel Structure, Shorter is Better

The word *and* indicates that the underlined portion of the phrase must match the non-underlined portion (*what to retain*). What + infinitive = what + infinitive. The only answer that contains the correct construction (*what to forget*) is D).

42. A: Infographic

Start by looking at the whole sentence for context. It's talking about what occurs during REM sleep, so start by considering that part of the graph. What does the REM section show? A bar that is much higher than any stage other than the "awake" stage. That is most consistent with A). The first half of B) is correct, but the second half is wrong – REM levels of activity are almost as high as "awake" levels, not far below them. C) is incorrect because the bar increases dramatically, not "slightly." And D) is incorrect because the REM bar increases.

43. D: Sentence vs. Fragment, Comma Splice

The original version incorrectly places a semicolon between a dependent and an independent clause, and a semicolon should only be placed between two independent clauses. B) creates a fragment when plugged back into the sentence; C) creates a comma splice; and D) is correct because it uses a comma to separate an independent clause (*The foreign language group showed a spike in brain activity during REM sleep*) and a dependent clause (*suggesting that dreaming helped the students assimilate and retain new information*).

44. B: Transition

Start by crossing out the transition and considering the two statements side by side. The first statement proposes a theory (dreams don't serve a function), and the second statement expands on it by explaining how it works. So the purpose of the second statement is to clarify or further explain the first. The transition that serves that purpose is *that is*, which is used to introduce an explanation. *Of course* is incorrect because the second statement is not obvious from the first, eliminating A). C) does not make sense because neurons do not fire

randomly *at the same time* dreams don't serve a purpose – that transition is used to describe two actions that occur simultaneously, and this sentence does not describe two *actions*. And D) is incorrect because the second statement continues the idea of the first statement, and *in contrast* is used to indicate a contradiction.

Index of College Board/Khan Academy Writing Questions

Questions by Category

Add/Delete/Revise

Sentence Order

Infographic

Shorter is Better

Diction, Idioms, Register

Additional Comma Uses/Misuses

Test 2	33	Comma with preposition
Test 2	27	Comma with "that"
Test 1	4	Comma with list
Test 4	22	Colon

Colons

Test 1	4	Comma, Semicolon
Test 1	16	Semicolon
Test 1	26	List
Test 1	32	List
Test 4	22	
Test 4	29	Semicolon, Dash

Dashes

Test 3	35	Non-essential clause
Test 4	29	Colon, Semicolon
Test 4	35	Non-essential clause

Parallel Structure

Test 1	8	
Test 2	6	
Test 3	1	
Test 3	19	Word pair
Test 4	6	
Test 4	9	
Test 4	24	Word pair

Pronoun and Noun Agreement

Test 1	13	"This" without noun
Test 1	44	
Test 2	5	Missing antecedent
Test 3	12	
Test 3	15	Subject-verb agreement
Test 4	7	Missing antecedent
Test 2	30	Missing antecedent
Test 4	40	Noun agreement

Subject-Verb Agreement

Test 1	40
Test 3	5
Test 3	15
Test 3	36
Test 4	19
Test 4	28

Tense

Test 1	18	
Test 3	28	
Test 3	38	Parallel structure
Test 4	6	Parallel structure
Test 4	34	

Faulty Comparisons

Test 2	32	Register
Test 4	12	

Dangling/Misplaced Modifiers

Test 1	24	Dangling
Test 2	21	Misplaced
Test 4	43	Dangling

Relative Pronouns

Test 1	30	Who vs. whom
Test 2	39	Who vs. whom
Test 2	34	Whereby
Test 3	27	Who vs. which

Appendices A-D

The previous chapters in this book are based on a combination of the redesigned SAT Writing Test specifications, sample questions, and practice PSAT and SATs released by the College Board/Khan Academy. Because the content of the redesigned exam may continue to evolve even after the first administration of the new SAT in March 2016, I am including material detailing concepts that have not yet been included on any of the released material but that have traditionally been featured prominently on both the SAT and the ACT. It is not impossible that some of the concepts in Appendices A-C will eventually find their way onto the exam (the use of "who vs. whom" covered in Appendix D is extremely unlikely to be included), and you may want to spend a few minutes familiarizing yourself with them.

Appendix A: Adjectives and Adverbs

Adjectives modify nouns and pronouns.

If you have difficulty recognizing nouns, you can use this **shortcut**: a noun is a word that can follow *a* or *the*. For example, *idea* is a noun because you can say *the idea*, but *create* is not a noun because you cannot say *the create*.

Correct:	Ken Nakamura is known for designing **simulated** <u>cities</u>.
Correct:	Martha Graham was among the **greatest** <u>choreographers</u> of the twentieth century.
Correct:	<u>It</u> was very **challenging**.

Adverbs usually modify verbs. They can also modify adjectives or other adverbs.

They are normally formed by adding *–ly* to the adjective. When an adjective ends in *–y*, then *-ily* is added. watch out for these adjectives (e.g. *busy*, *noisy*, *hungry*). If you don't read carefully, you can mistake them for adverbs.

Adjective	**Adverb**
Quick	Quickly
Noisy	Noisily

In the sentences below, the adverb is in bold, and the word it modifies is underlined.

Adverb modifies verb:	Jonas Salk <u>worked</u> **diligently** on a cure for polio for many years.
Adverb modifies adjective:	Martha Graham was a **highly** <u>influential</u> choreographer.
Adverb modifies adverb:	The crocodile moved **astonishingly** <u>quickly</u> through the water.

An adjective **cannot** be used to modify a verb:

Incorrect:	When the curtain rose, the dancer began to <u>move</u> **graceful** across the stage.
Correct:	When the curtain rose, the dancer began to <u>move</u> **gracefully** across the stage.

Likewise, an adverb **cannot** be used to modify a noun.

Incorrect:	When the curtain rose, the **gracefully** <u>dancer</u> began to move across the stage.
Correct:	When the curtain rose, the **graceful** <u>dancer</u> began to move across the stage.

Adjectives and adverbs should appear next to the nouns that they modify. Adjectives are placed **before** the noun, while adverbs can be placed **before or after**. If adjectives and adverbs are placed elsewhere in the sentence, the sentence may not make sense.

Incorrect: The wooden fish is a <u>percussion instrument</u> used **traditional** throughout China, Japan, and Korea.

Because *traditional* is an adjective, it must be placed before a noun. *Throughout* is a preposition, so the sentence cannot be correct. In order to correct it, we must place it before the noun it would most logically modify.

Correct: The wooden fish is a **traditional** <u>percussion instrument</u> used throughout China, Japan, and Korea.

Let's look at an example with an adverb:

Incorrect: The wooden fish is a percussion instrument <u>used</u> throughout **traditionally** China, Japan, and Korea.

Since *traditionally* is an adverb, it should appear either before or after a verb. *Throughout* is a preposition, and *China* is a noun, so the placement is incorrect. We must therefore place the adverb next to the verb it would most logically modify:

Correct: The wooden fish is a percussion instrument **traditionally** <u>used</u> throughout China, Japan, and Korea.

Correct: The wooden fish is a percussion instrument <u>used</u> **traditionally** throughout China, Japan, and Korea.

Appendix B: Comparatives and Superlatives

Comparative = *–ER* or *MORE + ADJECTIVE*. It is used to compare **two** things.

Incorrect: Between the black leopard and the snow leopard, the black leopard possesses the more effective camouflage while the snow leopard has the **most striking** tail.

Correct: Between the black leopard and the snow leopard, the black leopard possesses the more effective camouflage while the snow leopard has the **more striking** tail.

Superlative = *–EST* or *MOST + ADJECTIVE*. It is used to compare **three or more** things.

Incorrect: London, Paris, and Seattle are all known for their rainy weather, but of the three cities, Paris receives the **higher** amount of rainfall each year.

Correct: London, Paris, and Seattle are all known for their rainy weather, but of the three cities, Paris receives the **highest** amount of rainfall each year.

In the above sentence, the number is specified, but sometimes you will be left to infer that information:

Incorrect: Out of <u>all the American choreographers</u> who were active during the twentieth century, Martha Graham is perhaps the **more famous** one.

Correct: Out of <u>all the American choreographers</u> who were active during the twentieth century, Martha Graham is perhaps the **most famous** one.

Even though the above sentence does not include a number, it can very reasonably inferred that more than three American choreographers were active during the twentieth century.

Forming Comparatives and Superlatives

One-syllable adjectives and two-syllable adjectives ending in *–y* take *–er* (comparative) and *–est* (superlative).

All other adjectives take *more* or *most* (e.g. *interesting, more interesting, most interesting*).

Adjective	Comparative	Superlative
Strong	Stronger	Strongest
Funny	Funnier	Funniest
Interesting	More interesting	Most interesting

Although they are formed differently, *-er* and "more + adjective" or *–est* and "most + adjective" are considered parallel to one another if used in a list (e.g. *newer, more innovative, and more exciting*).

Double Positives and Double Negatives

A comparative or superlative that ends in -ER or –EST should never take *more* or *most* as well. When this occurs, a **double positive** is formed. Double positives are always incorrect.

Comparative

Incorrect: Roald Amundsen and four members of his expedition arrived at the South Pole five weeks **more earlier** than Robert Falcon Scott and his team.

Correct: Roald Amundsen and four members of his expedition arrived at the South Pole five weeks **earlier** than Robert Falcon Scott and his team.

Superlative

Incorrect: When traveling over large distances, many people choose to go by airplane because the airplane is the **most fastest** option available.

Correct: When traveling over large distances, many people choose to go by airplane because the airplane is the **fastest** option available.

The words *scarcely* and *hardly* should always be followed by *any*. When *any* is replaced with *no*, a **double negative** is created. Like double positives, double negatives are always incorrect.

Incorrect: Since the invention of commercial flight and high-speed rail in the twentieth century, **hardly no** significant technological change has affected the traveling public.

Correct: Since the invention of commercial flight and high-speed rail in the twentieth century, **hardly any** significant technological change has affected the traveling public.

Comparing Amounts: Can it be Counted?

Fewer and *many* refer to things that are **quantifiable** – things that can be counted.

Less and *much* refer to things that are **not quantifiable** – things that cannot be counted.

As a **shortcut**, you can also think of it this way: singular nouns should generally be used with *less* and *much*, while plural nouns should generally be used with *fewer* and *many*.

Fewer vs. Less

| Incorrect: | Because Antarctica is characterized by extreme temperatures and harsh living conditions, it supports **less** <u>animal species</u> than any other continent does. |
| Correct: | Because Antarctica is characterized by extreme temperatures and harsh living conditions, it supports **fewer** <u>animal species</u> than any other continent does. |

Since *animal species* is plural and can be counted, *fewer* should be used.

| Incorrect: | Because Antarctica is characterized by extreme temperatures and harsh living conditions, it supports **fewer** <u>animal life</u> than any other continent does. |
| Correct | Because Antarctica is characterized by extreme temperatures and harsh living conditions, it supports **less** <u>animal life</u> than any other continent does. |

Since *animal life* is singular and cannot be counted, *less* should be used.

Many vs. Much

| Incorrect: | Despite blazing heat and constant threats from predators, **much** <u>types of animals</u> inhabit the African savannah. |
| Correct: | Despite blazing heat and constant threats from predators, **many** <u>types of animals</u> inhabit the African savannah. |

Since *types of animals* is plural and can be counted, *many* should be used.

| Incorrect: | With over 1,100 animal species of mammals and over 2,600 species of bird, Africa is home to **many** more <u>animal life</u> than any other continent. |
| Correct | With over 1,100 animal species of mammals and over 2,600 species of bird, Africa is home to **much** more <u>animal life</u> than any other continent. |

Again, since *animal life* is singular and cannot be counted, *much* should be used.

Appendix C: Pronoun Case

Case refers to whether a pronoun is used as a **subject** or an **object**.

Nouns that act as subjects can be replaced by **subject pronouns**:

	Singular	Plural
1st person	I	We
2nd person	You	You
3rd person	She/He/It/One	They

If we replace the subjects in the following sentences with subject pronouns, they become:

1. **Hernán Cortés** was the first explorer to bring the tomato to Europe.
    → **He** was the first explorer to bring the tomato to Europe.

2. **Members of the Spanish Court** were intensely suspicious of the small yellow fruit.
    → **They** were intensely suspicious of the small yellow fruit.

3. Tramping through the woods, **Jane and I** could hear birds singing and leaves crackling.
    → Tramping through the woods, **we** could hear birds singing and leaves crackling.

Nouns that act as objects can be replaced by **object pronouns**:

	Singular	Plural
1st person	Me	Us
2nd person	You	You
3rd person	Her/Him/It/One	Them

If we replace the objects in the following sentences with object pronouns, they become:

1. Members of the Spanish Court greeted Hernán Cortés with surprise.
    → Members of the Spanish courted greeted **him** with surprise.

2. Architect Ken Nakamura is known for designing simulated **"cities."**
    → Architect Ken Nakamura is known for designing **them**.

3. Later on that day, Jane's dog sat with **Jane and me** in the garden.
    → Later on that day, Jane's dog sat with **us** in the garden.

When you look at the charts on the previous page, notice that some pronouns have the same subject and object forms (e.g. *it, one, you*) while others can only be used as subjects or objects (e.g. *me, she, they*).

In contrast, all proper names (*Hernán Cortés, Jane, Ken Ito*) can be either subjects or objects. So, for example, we can write the following sentence several ways:

Correct: Ann went to the museum with Bob.

Correct: **She** went to the museum with Bob. (*Ann* replaced with subject pronoun)

Correct: Ann went to the museum with **him**. (*Bob* replaced with object pronoun)

What we cannot do, however, is replace a subject pronoun with an object pronoun or vice-versa.

Incorrect: **Her** went to the museum with Bob.

Incorrect: Ann went to the museum with **he**.

Incorrect: **Her** went to the museum with **he**.

When subjects and objects are singular, mistakes are pretty easy to catch by ear. But when subjects and objects are plural, things suddenly get trickier. **The only thing you have to know, however, is that what goes for singular goes for plural. If the singular pronoun is wrong, it's still wrong when paired with a name.**

Correct: Ann and Maria went to the museum with Bob.

Incorrect: **Her** and Maria went to the museum with Bob.

If we cross out the proper name + *and*, the error is apparent.

Cross out: **Her** ~~and Maria~~ went to the museum with Bob.

Since you obviously would not say *Her went to the museum*, you cannot say *Her and Rosita went to the museum* either.

Correct: **She** went to the museum with Bob.

Correct: **She** and Maria/Maria and **she** went to the museum with Bob.

The same thing is true for object pronouns:

Incorrect: Ann went to the museum with **he** and Maria.

Cross out: Ann went to the museum with he **~~and Maria~~**.

Correct: Ann went to the museum with **him**.

Correct: Ann went to the museum with **him** and Maria/Maria and **him**.

You can also use this rule: **an <u>object</u> pronoun must follow a preposition.** In the above example, *with* is a preposition, so it must be followed by the object pronoun *him* rather than the subject pronoun *he*.

If a pronoun is not paired with a proper name, the same strategy applies:

Incorrect: When Jane Austen was young, her father encouraged **she** and her siblings to read from his extensive library.

Cross out: When Jane Austen was young, her father encouraged **she** ~~and her siblings~~ to read from his extensive library.

Correct: When Jane Austen was young, her father encouraged **her** and her siblings to read from his extensive library.

And if there are two pronouns, cross out each one in turn:

Incorrect: Every Chinese New Year, my cousins come to my house to celebrate. My parents give **them and I** tangerines and bright red envelopes filled with money.

Cross out: Every Chinese New Year, my cousins come to my house to celebrate. My parents give **them** ~~and I~~ tangerines and bright red envelopes filled with money.

That's fine, but now you have to check the other side.

Cross out: Every Chinese New Year, my cousins come to my house to celebrate. My parents give ~~**them and**~~ **I** tangerines and bright red envelopes filled with money.

Correct: Every Chinese New Year, my cousins come to my house to celebrate. My parents give **them and me** tangerines and bright red envelopes filled with money.

Appendix D: Who vs. Whom

Who = subject pronoun, used before a verb

Who refers to the subject of a sentence. It can be replaced by the subject pronouns *she/he* or *they*. For example:

Sentence 1:   <u>Martha Graham</u> was a choreographer.

Sentence 2:   **She** revolutionized dance in the twentieth century.

To combine the sentences smoothly, we can use a relative clause set off by the relative pronoun *who*:

Combined: <u>Martha Graham</u> was a choreographer **who** revolutionized dance in the twentieth century.

Why use *who* rather than *whom*? Because *who* refers to back to Martha Graham, and Martha Graham is the subject of the sentence.

One more example:

Sentence 1:   The first African American woman to travel into space was <u>Mae Jemison</u>.

Sentence 2:   **She** trained as a dancer before becoming an astronaut.

Combined: The first African American woman to travel into space was <u>Mae Jemison</u>, **who** trained as a dancer before becoming an astronaut.

Even though *Mae Jemison* does not appear at the beginning of the sentence, she is still the subject of the second clause. We know this because we could also replace her name with the subject pronoun *she* (*she trained as a dancer before becoming an astronaut*). *Who* should therefore be used.

Whom = object pronoun, used before a noun or pronoun

Whom is used when a person is the object of a verb or preposition. It can be replaced by the object pronouns *her/him* or *them*.

As a general rule, *whom* is only tested as the direct object of a <u>preposition</u> (as discussed in Chapter 18), not as the direct object of a <u>verb</u> (as below). If a question contains answer choices that use both *who* and *whom* in this context, there will virtually always be an additional, unrelated factor that makes one or both of the answer choices incorrect.

Sentence 1:   One biologist who struggled for her work to gain acceptance was <u>Lynn Margulis.</u>

Sentence 2:   Members of the scientific community initially regarded **her** as unworthy of their attention.

Combined: One biologist who struggled for her work to gain acceptance was <u>Lynn Margulis</u>, **whom** members of the scientific community initially regarded as unworthy of their attention.

In the example above *whom* is the object of the verb *regarded*. Because Margulis's name could be replaced by the object pronoun *her* (*they regarded <u>her</u> as unworthy of their attention*), *whom* is correct.

ABOUT THE AUTHOR

Erica Meltzer has worked as a tutor, test-prep writer, and blogger since 2007. In addition to *The Ultimate Guide to SAT Grammar*, she is the author of *The Critical Reader*, *The Complete Guide to ACT English*, and *The Complete Guide to ACT Reading*. Her books are used by tutors and tutoring companies both in the United States and around the world. She lives in New York City, and you can visit her online at www.thecriticalreader.com.

Made in the USA
Charleston, SC
11 November 2015